# Understanding Sports Coaching

Every successful sports coach knows that good teaching and social practices are just as important as expertise in sport skills and tactics. Now in a fully revised and updated third edition, *Understanding Sports Coaching* is still the only introduction to theory and practice in sports coaching to fully explore the social, cultural and pedagogical concepts underpinning good coaching practice.

The book examines the complex interplay between coach, athlete, coaching programme and social context, and encourages coaches to develop an open and reflective approach to their own coaching practice. It covers every key aspect of coaching theory and practice, including important and emerging topics, such as:

- athletes' identities;
- athlete learning;
- emotion in coaching;
- coaching ethics;
- professionalization;
- talent identification and development;
- coaching as a (micro)political activity.

*Understanding Sports Coaching* also includes a full range of practical exercises and extended case studies designed to encourage coaches to reflect critically upon their own coaching strategies, their interpersonal skills and upon important issues in contemporary sports coaching. This is an essential textbook for any degree-level course in sports coaching, and for any professional coach looking to develop their coaching expertise.

**Tania Cassidy** is an Associate Professor in the School of Physical Education, Sport and Exercise Sciences at the University of Otago, New Zealand. She also holds an adjunct position at University College Cork, Ireland. Tania's research interests are informed by interpretive and critical perspectives and primarily focus on the pedagogy of sports coaching and coach development. She is on the editorial boards of eight international journals, including *Sports Coaching Review, International Journal of Sports Science and Coaching* and *International Sport Coaching Journal*.

**Robyn L. Jones** is a Professor of Sport and Social Theory at the Cardiff School of Sport, Cardiff Metropolitan University, UK, a Visiting Professor (II) at the Norwegian School of Sport Sciences, Oslo, Norway, and a Visiting Associate Principal Lecturer (Research) at Hartpury College, UK. He has also been a Visiting Professor at the University of Malaysia. He has (co) published in excess of 60 peer reviewed articles and several books on sports coaching and pedagogy; the latter include *Sports Coaching Cultures*, *The Sports Coach as Educator* and *The Sociology of Sports Coaching*. In addition to serving on the editorial board of *Sport, Education and Society*, Robyn is also the General Editor of the Taylor & Francis journal *Sports Coaching Review*.

**Paul Potrac** is a Professor of Sports Coaching at the Department of Sport and Physical Activity, Edge Hill University, UK, and an Honorary Professor at the University of Hull, UK. His research focuses on the political and emotional features of practice in coaching and coach education. He has (co) published several books on sports coaching, including *Sports Coaching Cultures*, the *Routledge Handbook of Sports Coaching*, *Research Methods in Sports Coaching* and *The Sociology of Sports Coaching*. Paul is also an Associate Editor of the Taylor & Francis journal *Sports Coaching Review*.

www.routledge.com/cw/cassidy

# Understanding Sports Coaching

The pedagogical, social and cultural foundations of coaching practice

THIRD EDITION

**Tania Cassidy, Robyn L. Jones and Paul Potrac**

Routledge
Taylor & Francis Group

LONDON AND NEW YORK

First published 2004
by Routledge
2 Park Square, Milton Park, Abingdon, Oxon OX14 4RN

This edition published 2016
by Routledge
2 Park Square, Milton Park, Abingdon, Oxon OX14 4RN

and by Routledge
711 Third Avenue, New York, NY 10017

*Routledge is an imprint of the Taylor & Francis Group, an informa business*

*British Library Cataloguing-in-Publication Data*
A catalogue record for this book is available from the British Library

*Library of Congress Cataloging in Publication Data*
Cassidy, Tania, 1964-
Understanding sports coaching : the pedagogical, social and cultural foundations of coaching practice / Tania Cassidy, Robyn L. Jones and Paul Potrac. -- Third edition.
pages cm
Includes bibliographical references and index.
1. Coaching (Athletics) 2. Coaching (Athletics)--Philosophy. 3. Coaches (Athletics)--Training of. I. Jones, Robyn L. II. Potrac, Paul, 1974- III. Title.
GV711.C34 2016
796.07'7--dc23
2015019471

ISBN: 978-0-415-85746-8 (hbk)
ISBN: 978-0-415-85747-5 (pbk)
ISBN: 978-0-203-79795-2 (ebk)

Typeset in Berling
by Saxon Graphics Ltd, Derby

# Dedication

In memory of Denis Cassidy – a loving and playful father.
And; to T & *S*, as always.

# Contents

# Acknowledgements

Many people have contributed to the ideas presented in this book. We especially acknowledge the thousands of undergraduate students who, over the years, have enrolled in PHSE 101 and PHSE 201. The earlier students were the catalyst for the book, while the latter students have been the 'guinea pigs' for ideas reflected in some of the chapters.

TC: To my family and friends, a very big thank you for your constant love and support. A special thank you to Georgia, Jake, Toby, Zach, Lewis, Greta, Annabella, Rosa and Maurice for your love, making me laugh and giving me reasons to play.

PP: To Susi, Megan and Abigail – as promised!

RJ: For all the students who have, are and will engage with the sociology of coaching.

# Setting the scene

# Introduction

## INTRODUCTION

When the first edition of this book was penned, a case was still being made for coaching to be recognized as a pedagogical and social enterprise. Over ten years later, this perspective is much more widespread and accepted. For example, Kirk (2010), in arguing for coaching to be viewed as a socio-pedagogical practice, reiterated an earlier point made by one of us that coaching at all levels really is about athlete learning (Jones 2006a and b). Drawing on the work of Mauss (1973) who stated that 'there is no technique and no transmission in the absence of tradition' (cited in Kirk 2010: 166), Kirk tied learning to both culture and society. Such a view positions coaching as a social construction, in that all 'techniques of the body' are socially learned. It is a stance supported by Loland (2011), who argued that coaches socialize athletes into the movement schemes of their sport; a process often carried out by instruction and using other 'good' athletes as positive role models. It would make sense, therefore, to view coaching as a social, relational and pedagogical practice; that is, an activity between people within a cultural context. As we have previously argued, this pedagogical aspect can most obviously be seen when working with young athletes, where a degree of mastery or general understanding is needed for meaningful participation to occur. However, it is also evident when working with elite athletes where adjustment to technique or the implementation of novel attacking or defensive strategies is required. Naturally, such a position takes issue with the continuing division of coaching by some into various artificially constructed 'domains' (i.e. 'performance', 'developmental' and 'participation'). Of course, we are not advocating that coaches behave the same way in all contexts. Rather, we question if coaching can be so divided in terms of the given lines of demarcation? For example, if such lines are based on chronological age, where do early specialization sports like swimming and gymnastics fit, where teenagers are regularly Olympic medalists? It also begs the question: once athletes graduate to the performance realm, do they stop developing? (They certainly don't stop participating!) The case made here is that overarching all coaching, whatever the athletic level, is the goal of athlete learning. This was the case put forward by Carl Rogers in his philosophy of education, where the pedagogical principles given were applicable regardless of age or ability of the learner(s) in question (Nelson *et al.* 2012).

In addition to Kirk, others also agree with the notion of coaching as principally to do with athlete learning. For example, Armour (2011) commented when participants are involved in sport-related activities, they become learners with the potential to gain much or little from the experience. Correspondingly, pedagogical developments such as Teaching Games for Understanding (Bunker and Thorpe 1982) and the associated counter-part Game Sense (Australian Sports Commission 1997) have increasingly found their way into the coaching realm (e.g. Light 2004; Harvey *et al.* 2010) in efforts to improve both athletes' and coaches' knowledge. Some scholars have also used educational theorists such as Vygotsky (Potrac & Cassidy 2006), Leont'ev (Jones *et al.* 2010) and Rogers (Nelson *et al.* 2012) to better understand and inform coaching practice. Such theorists, of course, do not view learning as taking place in a social vacuum, but as created in and influenced by cultural forces.

The notion of coaching as a distinctly social practice has also gained substantial credence over the previous decade, with a plethora of scholars producing considerable empirical and positional work in support of it (e.g. Cushion & Jones 2006; Denison 2007; Hemmestad *et al.* 2010; Potrac *et al.* 2013; Purdy & Jones 2011). This was further emphasized in Jones *et al.*'s (2011) recent *Sociology of sports coaching* text, which argued for coaching to be positioned as a relational activity inclusive of such concepts as power, interaction, structure and agency. Indeed, this once peripheral social agenda appears today to have become a leading perspective in the analysis of sports coaching.

Nevertheless, despite increasing recognition of coaching as a social practice, some still remain unconvinced (e.g. Abraham & Collins 2011; North 2013). Such authors advocate (to various degrees) a more reductionist 'modelling' approach to coaching, founded along psychological and 'decision-making' lines. It is a view that presents the coach as operating within a rather 'closed self-centred' circle almost independently of personal historicity and biography, as opposed to being part of a wider social and cultural arrangement (Engström 2000): a standpoint which considers coaching (and related athlete learning) as being relatively untouched – or uncorrupted – by values, interests and politics (Seidman & Alexander 2001). Continuing in the spirit of the earlier editions of this text, we naturally challenge such a position and alternatively see coaching as a socio-pedagogical construction undertaken by actors in context.

## THE AIMS OF THE BOOK

A considerable amount of empirical research (e.g. Jones *et al.* 2004; Potrac 2001; Santos *et al.* 2013; Hauw & Durand 2005) indicates that good coaches can (to varying degrees) evaluate and reflect on what they do in terms of how they coach. They think about, and are aware of, their practice before, during and after the event: reflecting in some depth about plans, actions and consequences. Taking our lead from such findings, and of growing support for the socio-pedagogic nature of coaching (Cassidy 2010; Jones *et al.* 2011; Kirk 2010), we believe that if coaches are to increasingly understand why they are doing what they are doing, inclusive of related limitations and possibilities, it is useful for them to have a grasp of social, cultural and educational concepts. The principal aim of this book is to highlight some of these concepts, and to link them directly to the practice of coaching.

We recognize that good coaches almost certainly already use some educational and sociological concepts in how they coach. However, the adoption of these concepts often occurs implicitly rather than explicitly and, as a consequence, leaves coaches unaware of the assumptions and beliefs that inform their practices. This was a driving issue behind Jones and colleagues related texts '*Sports coach as educator*' (2006a) and '*The sociology of sports coaching*' (2011) where pedagogical and social theories were explicitly presented as relevant possibilities for coaches and coaching. By not questioning or critically engaging with their actions, coaches make it difficult to systematically develop their programmes for the maximal benefit of athletes; they also make it problematic for themselves to fully understand the ethical, moral and political consequences of what they do. Given that coaching does not occur in a cultural void (Jones 2000; Schempp 1998), we also believe that the social and educational values that construct the person of the coach need careful and thoughtful consideration if coaches are to act in enlightened, effective and sensitive ways (Jones 2000). Similarly, recognizing the constraints and possibilities for practice enables coaches to become aware of the suppressed culture of coaching rather than only of its visible, formal face as presented through dominant discourses (i.e. ways of talking about it) (Grace 1998).

We recognize that building a purely theoretical case about the value of sociological and educational concepts for coaching would, in all probability, have a limited impact on practice. Consequently, in an effort to give this book a wider application, we have provided practical exercises and thought provoking questions at the end of each chapter. We hope that the exercises provided will resonate with coaches, as they are grounded in the messy reality of coaching itself. The aim of these exercises is two-fold. First, it is to illustrate how the sociological and educational concepts discussed can be workably integrated into general practice and wider coach education programmes. Secondly, it is to encourage coaches and students of coaching to personally reflect on, and engage with, the technical, moral, ethical and political issues that occur in their own coaching contexts. In doing so, we hope to make a small contribution to closing the gap between theory and practice.

## WHY IS THE BOOK NEEDED?

The principal rationale for writing this book is to further question some of coaching's taken-for-granted practices. This is done from a sociocultural and pedagogical perspective, thus giving further credence to the view of coaching as a multivariate, interpersonal and dynamic activity. Such a stance implores us to avoid treating coaches as 'cardboard cut-outs' (Sparkes & Templin 1992: 118), and athletes as non-thinking pawns.

Indeed, the last decade has witnessed a growing number of coach educators and academics who are prepared to engage with the sociology of coaching (see Denison 2007; Jones & Armour 2000; Denison 2007; Jones *et al.* 2011; Piggott 2012). Equally, there are a number who have now critically engaged with the pedagogy of coaching (e.g. Armour 2011; Bergmann Drewe 2000; Jones 2006a; Kirk 2010). It is a position which resonates with our interpretation of pedagogy as a problematic process that incorporates the interaction between how one learns, how one teaches, what is being taught (Lusted 1986) and the context in which it is being taught (Cassidy 2000). The key to adopting this view lies in making coaches aware of the social and educational dynamics which have created (and continue to create) their identities and philosophies, and hence, their abilities to perform (Armour & Jones 2000). Developing such an awareness provides coaches with the ability to evaluate information from a range of sources, and the insight, confidence and courage to take responsibility for their decisions.

We contend that a growing number of coaches want to develop athletes who can make decisions and adapt to changing situations on the field or court. Such a stance implicitly supports the view that learning is less the reception of acts and facts, and more a social practice that implies the involvement of the whole person in relation not only to specific activities but also to social communities. In this respect, we agree that 'the study and education of the human is complex' (Zakus & Malloy 1996: 504) requiring sensitivity, subtlety and subjectivity. If coaches want to produce responsible decision-making athletes, then it is useful for them to adopt coaching practices that take account of, and can facilitate, such a socially determined goal. However, this doesn't advocate a collapse into a blanket questioning approach under the rather simplified mantra that coaches should 'make themselves increasingly redundant'. Rather, taking a lead from Sfard's (1998) notions of acquisition and participation, Bruner's idea of scaffolding (e.g. Wood, Bruner & Ross 1976), and Vygotsky's (1978) earlier conceptualization of learning as directed by a 'more capable other', we view the coaching role as being constantly contested and negotiated by relational social actors in context.

What we offer in this book are not 'handy hints' for coaches to neatly dip into when the perceived need arises. On the contrary, we present social and pedagogic notions which themselves should be viewed as pedagogic; in the sense of assisting readers for what is required of them, 'to learn what can only be implied, and never as direct advice' (Flyvbjerg *et al.* 2012: 4). By insisting that we only give readers ideas to think with as opposed to exact and 'correct' practical prescriptions, we hope to privilege the quality of communicative interaction over any preciseness of instruction (Pineau 1994). As in previous work then, the concepts here still need to be thought about hard, with imagination, and not just taken as *a priori* knowledge (Jones *et al.* 2011). The point is to continue to develop a 'quality of mind' in coaches to explore such questions as: do I understand why I act and coach in certain ways? Why do I espouse certain values and ideas and reject others? Can I explore ideas with which I do not normally conform? Am I able to see situations from others' points of view? Are my coaching methods congruent with my principles? And, can I devise alternative pedagogies that may be more educative? (Fernández-Balboa 2000). Those hoping for a list of 'effective' coaching behaviours then, will inevitably be disappointed; a dissatisfaction for which we offer no apology.

The significance of the book also lies partly in response to Knudson and Morrison's (2002) call for a reality-based integrative approach to human movement. It is a position rooted in the belief that a sociocultural pedagogic approach is imperative for understanding such a complex and dynamic activity as coaching, where, invariably, the whole is considerably greater than the sum of the constituent parts. Within this approach, the coach is viewed as a more holistic problem-solver involved in the planning, prioritization, contextualization and orchestration of provision in an ever-changing environment. Adopting such a framework means that our discussion calls on theoretical ideas from disciplines which take account of the problematic human factor as well as real-life sports coaching scenarios, as we seek to develop a more credible view of the coaching process.

## WHO IS THE BOOK FOR?

The book is principally written for sports coaching students, whose numbers are rapidly rising as programmes related to sports science, kinesiology, and physical education, in addition to coaching itself, proliferate in higher education institutions worldwide. It is also aimed at the physical education teacher market, the students of which invariably become involved in coaching school sports teams. For undergraduate students of coaching, it can serve as an introductory text to illustrate the social, cultural and educational nature of their principal subject matter, and how interacting related considerations can inform professional practice. Additionally, for beginning postgraduate students, the book may assist them to make links between theory and practice, and further develop their recognition that coaching can and should be a reflective endeavour. Since many sports science students are also working coaches, the book holds the potential to give such practitioners a greater awareness of the factors that influence their coaching and, where necessary, to consider alternatives.

We believe the book is applicable to coaches at any level; those working with children through to mature international athletes. Indeed, the concepts discussed within it are relevant to any coach who wishes to maximize the sporting experience for his or her charges, whatever the context might be. This is because coaching, as we have previously argued, in whatever guise it is packaged, is essentially a socio-pedagogical enterprise. It is social in that it involves human interaction, and educational in that it extends from learning basic skills to knowing about the minute intricacies of body adjustment and tactical awareness so necessary for success in elite sport (Jones 2006b). Finally, there is a potential market for this book within coach education programmes. It is perhaps here that the text could have the greatest impact as many sports' national governing bodies (NGBs) and those responsible for more generic coach education programmes appear to be increasingly recognizing that at the heart of coaching lies a complex social-learning interface.

## HOW IS THE BOOK ORGANIZED?

The framework of this book is informed by our belief that coaching is fundamentally a social, cultural and pedagogical practice that comprises the interconnections between the teacher, learner, content (Lusted 1986) and context (Cassidy 2000). Although we are aware that the term pedagogy could be taken as including both social and cultural aspects, we decided to keep them somewhat separate to emphasize the importance of each component within the totality of coaching. Consequently, to fully understand (and achieve) high quality coaching (resulting in intended and appropriate athlete learning), we need to take account of coaches' biographies, their socialization and their personal interpretations of practice within respective working environments; a perspective that takes account of social and cultural factors on coaches' delivery and general interactive behaviours. Hence, the book is divided into four principal sections, namely (1) the context; (2) the coach; (3) the athlete(s); and (4) knowledge. Each section contains a number of chapters relevant to it, while each chapter concludes with an exercise or set of questions that encourage readers to critically reflect upon their own and others' coaching.

Preceding the aforementioned sections, we present this Introduction (Chapter 1) and a chapter on reflection (Chapter 2) to 'set the scene'. The general purpose here is two-fold. First, it is to clarify the purpose of the book, and to provide some insight into how our thoughts and considerations have evolved since the publication of the last edition. Second, by following this with a developed chapter on reflection and reflective practice, the goal is to assist a more critical reading of the text as a whole; an encouragement for readers to become increasingly reflexive practitioners, particularly in terms of the concepts presented within it. The ensuing Section One explores the context of coaching in relation to coaching ethics (Chapter 3), coaching as a (micro)political activity (Chapter 4) and the professionalization of coaching (Chapter 5). Section Two ('the coach') includes an examination of coaching selves (Chapter 6) and the coach as a pedagogical performer (Chapter 7). Section Three ('the athletes') contains discussions on athlete learning (Chapter 8), 'developing' athletes (Chapter 9), talent identification and development (Chapter 10) and athlete identities (Chapter 11). Finally, Section Four ('knowledge') explores issues related to content knowledge (Chapter 12), knowledge (re)production and discourse (Chapter 13) and assessing knowledge and ability (Chapter 14). Although the analysis has been presented in a linear format, many of the concepts discussed have cross-chapter relevancy, highlighting the inter-disciplinary nature of the subject matter. At relevant points, to assist in making the interconnections between the coach, athlete(s), content and context, we will direct readers to complementary discussion in other chapters.

## THE COACH AS PRACTICAL THEORIST

Some years ago, one of us attended a coaches' seminar at a plush hotel venue in the UK. The lead speaker was a well-known coach educator and policy 'guru'. He was to give a short address about a 'future vision' to start proceedings. Although he (thankfully) kept to time, his talk was littered with references to 'mental models', 'meta theory', 'values-driven best practice' and 'cohesive effective lobbying'. When he was done, a coach in the preceding row leant across to a colleague and asked 'what the **** did he just say?' It is certainly a problem that some rhetorically rich 'theories' remain far beyond the reach of those they should benefit, namely the practitioners. But the fault here can be seen as lying on both sides; theoreticians for not making their thoughts and research accessible enough, and coaches for a relative unwillingness to engage with more abstract complex thinking. The irony here, of course, is that coaches experience this complexity every day in their practice; they live it, yet many prefer to cling to a 'how-to hand book', perhaps because it's just easier to follow.

Far from remaining distant, the notions and ideas presented in this book are intended to both inform and guide practice. How can we be so sure? Precisely because most of the work cited and discussed has not only arisen from everyday achievements and actions, but also addresses pressing contemporary coaching issues. In this respect, we adhere to the words of the educator Kurt Lewin who famously proclaimed that 'there is nothing so practical as good theory' (in Sandelands 1990: 235). In doing so, we have also tried to respect Apple's (1999) call that theory needs to be 'connected' to issues and people, and that abstract concepts should be contextualized in practical experiences and perceptions (LeCompte & Preissle 1993). In this way, the text marks an attempt to take theory 'off the table and into the field' (Macdonald *et al.* 2002: 149), allowing for a deeper understanding of coaching and more realistic coach preparation programmes that better mirror the complex reality of practice (Jones *et al.* 2011).

Consequently, this book is not a bid or proposition for more 'coaching consultants' and policy sound bites. Neither does the text foreground the often-heard lament for 'more empirical research' ignoring the considerable amount that has been done. It is a call for coaches (and scholars of coaching), through the ideas presented, to play a more important role in developing perspectives to help themselves. Hence, it does not respect the traditional distinction between academic and practitioner knowledge, but encourages a more direct link between intellectual knowledge and moment-to-moment personal and social action (Reason & Torbert 2001). Following Lewin, we urge readers to approach the ideas given within the book 'with a view to making things happen' (Sandelands 1990: 248). The key here, of course, is having the courage to experiment, which, in turn, is reliant on possessing considerable knowledge of the concept(s) in question.

We locate this discussion here, not to blur but to clarify the difference between theory and practice and, in particular, the value of the former to the latter. Theories can never be translated into practice, because they are not simple 'tools' to be used – like a hammer to hit a nail. In this regard, theories stand a little apart from practice. However, theories are able to bring new observations or insight to light. In this respect, although theoretical notions can rarely be directly practiced, they can often be 'practical', as evident 'when contact with theory calls into mind action which otherwise would have gone unnoticed' (Sandelands 1990: 254). Theory and 'intellectual' concepts then, can often bring out new sensitivities and subsequent ways of practice.

Acknowledging the practical nature of theory requires coaches to become 'practical theorists', increasingly aware of the often-unnoticed constraints on, and opportunities for, action. This should not be such a big step, particularly as the concepts presented in this book have been generated and inspired from the field (e.g. Denison 2010; Jones *et al.*

2004, 2011; Purdy & Jones 2011; and others). Indeed, this continues to be the place where our data and related thinking originates; where our intellectual challenges are grounded. This was an issue recently engaged with by Cassidy (2010) in making the case that 'theories of practice' (more formally developed concepts and notions) in addition to 'practice theories' (knowledge largely developed from experience) can be of great benefit to coaches. This is because they (i.e., theories of practice) are often able to provide a sense-making framework inclusive of a grammar and vocabulary 'for what is observable' (Cassidy 2010: 177). It was a point made earlier by Eisner (1993: viii), who believed theory can 'make coherent what otherwise appear as disparate individual events', whilst being 'the means through which we learn lessons that can apply to situations we have yet to encounter'. This is not to say that the linkages between theory and practice are smooth and seamless. On the contrary, they are almost always riven with dynamic tension (as is coaching itself). We see this tension, however, as a positive, constructive force; a potency which makes the relationship between theory and practice collaborative and synergistic.

The case for the coach as a practical theorist was recently developed by Hemmestad *et al.* (2010), who offered the notion of phronesis (interpreted as 'practical wisdom') to describe coaches' actions. Here, coaching was depicted as the product of context-dependent tacit skills, what the sociologist Bourdieu (1990) famously called a 'feel for the game'. The point here is to generate the ability to recognize the presence and power of social structures and prevailing attitudes that make us act in ways that we do, and the agency available that allows us to act in the ways we want. In addressing the theory-practice gap or relationship then, phronetic thinking demands that we deliberate about (often unrecognized) values, objectives and interests as a precursor for action (Flyvbjerg 2001). Here, Flyvbjerg believed that, as an individual progresses from beginning to advanced skills, behaviour becomes increasingly intuitive and situation-dependent rather than rule-governed; a sentiment that most (if not all) coaches are familiar with.

## COACHING HOLISTICALLY: OR AT LEAST WITH SOCIAL, CULTURAL AND PEDAGOGICAL CONSIDERATIONS IN MIND

Although the value of holistic coaching has been increasingly recognized, this has tended to remain at the level of abstract thought and generalized support (Cassidy 2010). In response, Kretchmar (2010: 445) claimed that 'if we don't understand something, or if we use terminology in ways that confuse more than enlighten, we need to do some homework'. Indeed, for Kretchmar (2010), greater attention needs to be given to definitions, as we shouldn't argue for anything unless we can articulate what the associated key terms mean. In order to avoid such confusion and subsequent criticism, we begin this section by defining what we mean by the term 'holistic coaching'. A dictionary definition of the term 'holistic' equates to a consideration 'of the whole person, including mental and social factors' (*Concise Oxford Dictionary* 1991: 562). Even though this sets us on our way, we would like to be more wide-ranging in asserting that the person is also an emotional, political, spiritual and cultural being. To coach holistically then, is to coach with these considerations in mind. Although this inevitably leads to discussion about appropriate and workable boundaries for the coaching role, we consider that if such factors affect athletic performance and enjoyment then they should warrant consideration within the coaching remit. It is a position which somewhat resonates with that of Lyle (2010: 450), who saw holistic coaching in terms of recognizing 'balance and comprehensiveness in all of the factors impinging on sport performance and the welfare of individual athletes'.

Taking such a holistic approach to coaching, as I'm sure you've recognized, is not literally in line with the stated aim of this book. This is because the text does not take into account the rationalistic thought which has characterized much psychological, physiological and biomechanical writings on coaching. This is not to say we do not support the concept of the need to coach holistically. In fact, we very much believe that coaches should treat each situation, inclusive of its many variables, on its merits, assess it, carefully weigh the options and choose the most appropriate course of action available. To do so, a coach must draw on many knowledge sources and decide, with insight, how to amalgamate and utilize them in what fashion, when and where. Our goal here, however, is to redress the balance a little away from the predominant bio-scientific view of coaching, and to highlight the need to also take account of the personal, emotional, cultural and social identity of the athlete if maximal performances are to be obtained. It is to raise awareness in coaches and students of coaching about factors which need to be considered if the goal of coaching holistically is to be achieved; factors which have remained for too long hidden in the depth of the activity.

Such a position is based on recognizing coaching as intellectual as opposed to technical work, requiring higher order thinking skills to deal with the humanistic, problematic and dynamic nature of the tasks involved. The case is summarized around three principal issues. These include the need for coaches to consider: (1) cultural factors; (2) the development of social competencies; and (3) the pedagogical contextualization of practice, if lasting improvement is to occur. In making the case that Kenyan middle-distance athletes are culturally as opposed to naturally produced, Bale and Sang (1996: 17) stated that 'running can mean different things to different cultures'. They argued that sport participation and achievement should be firmly placed within the context of culture if they are to be properly explained. The same could be said of coaching. Douge and Hastie (1993: 20) agreed that 'effective leadership qualities may be unique to a social fabric', while Schempp's (1998) declaration that 'our social worlds offer no immunity to sports fields or gymnasia' provide further evidence of the belief that knowledge of culture and related social factors should be prime considerations for coaches. For instance, in the context of Aotearoa/New Zealand, a coach expecting a Māori athlete to engage in direct eye-to-eye contact is potentially problematic, since for many Māori, looking an older person in the eye is taken as a sign of disrespect (Durie 1998). Additionally, many Māori are more impressed by the unspoken signals conveyed through subtle gesture, with words, in some situations, being regarded as superfluous and even demeaning (Durie 1998). Within the cultural context then, learning is considered both an individual and a social process, with meanings being constructed both in the mind of the learner and through his or her community of practice (Langley 1997). Consequently, we need to be culturally sensitive; that is, to develop social competencies when coaching, as culture exerts a considerable influence over identities and motivations particularly when it comes to influencing others.

Research continues to suggest that elite coaches, although not often educated to do so, have a tendency to coach contextually (Jones *et al.* 2011). That is, they appear to utilize flexible planning strategies within detailed set routines that permit improvised adaptation to the evolving situation at hand. Such practice is based on the belief that definitive standards cannot be applied outright, as they often conflict with other structural constraints within the coaching situation, and are often witnessed in relation to reacting to athletes' particular needs (Saury & Durand 1998). Consequently, in what clearly can be seen as a more holistic approach, such coaches appear aware of the need to care for athletes' well-being beyond the sporting arena, and of exercising social competencies to ensure the continuance of positive working relationships (Jones *et al.* 2003, 2004). The message here is that coach–athlete relationships need to be carefully nurtured, and be flexible enough to deal with the multiple realities and needs that exist within given processual boundaries if athletes are going to reach their potential, and success is to be achieved. Current practice then suggests that the coach is (or should be) much more than a subject-matter specialist and method applier (Squires 1999). Rather, he or she is a person with multiple dimensions operating within given structural constraints in a dynamic social environment. From this perspective, coaching is fundamentally about making a myriad of connections between subject, method and other people to overcome the many and varied problems faced.

## THE SOCIOCULTURAL NATURE OF PEDAGOGY AND COACHING

During the process of conceptualizing this amended Introduction, we thought it pertinent to further explore and clarify coaching's relationship to pedagogy (and culture). What is not intended here, however, is a revisiting of old ground (e.g. Jones 2006a), where the similarities between teaching and coaching are again emphasized. Neither is the purpose to discuss particular pedagogical 'strategies', styles or techniques which coaches could (in theory) use in practice; a sort of an easy-to-use pedagogical 'tool box' to dip in and out of at will. Rather, it is to present the pedagogical act within coaching (and the subsequent intended learning trajectory) as one inherently influenced by sociocultural factors (Hardman 2008); in that it is a terrain possessing a particular past, which allows a certain, bounded present. Consequently, the interaction evident within coaching is taken as located in, and influenced by, a wider 'social order'. What complicates things a little here, however, is that this shaping process is not one directional. Hence, not only is practice moulded or sculpted by culture, but it also has an active role in moulding culture; that is, people also 'shape the very forces that are active in shaping them' (Daniels 2001: 1). This was the case made recently by Jones *et al.* (2014) in arguing for activity theory as an insightful lens through which to view and better understand sports coaching.

Derived from the work of the Soviet educational psychologists Vygotsky (1978) and Leont'ev (1978), activity theory is a perspective drawn from the idea that all social action, including pedagogy, is mediated, mainly by language, discourse and other cultural means. One cannot, therefore, understand or (effectively) use pedagogical action without recourse to the situation in which it takes place and that situation's foregrounding history. That is, pedagogy, in Vygotsykan terms, is declared as never being politically indifferent (Vygotsky 1997). Rather, it arises, and is fashioned, in particular social circumstances. From such a perspective, learning is also viewed as a collaborative activity devoid of uniform methods, where cultural production and reproduction takes place. It is a view of pedagogy as a rule-bound activity system, built over time, involving mediated action by an experienced 'other', and where power and control influence practice (Hardman 2008). Central to the perspective then, is the belief that athlete learning and, hence, coaching is a 'culturally based social endeavour' (Hardman 2008: 67), where an appreciation of the social, beyond the interactional, needs to be developed and accepted. Indeed, this critique can also be aimed at much coaching research which, to date, has given primacy to individual mediation processes at the expense of socio-institutional and historical factors from which such interactions arise. In short, there is no separate reality that constitutes the coach–athlete relationship.

In developing these ideas further, Daniels (2001: 15) claimed that 'the very idea of mediation carries with it a number of significant implications concerning pedagogic control'. Similarly, as we argue in this book (and have done elsewhere), sometimes context dictates action, while the idea of a coach having total control over any environment is naive in the extreme. This is not to say that coaches (and other pedagogues) are merely cultural dupes. Far from it, as they can legitimately be considered active agents in athletes' development. Rather, it is a view that gives credence to situational effects, and individuals' actions which shape those effects, on that development. In the words of Vygotsky (1978: 28), 'just as a mould gives shape to a substance, words can shape an activity into a structure'. This is why the work of a pedagogue or coach should never be stereotyped or routinized. On the contrary, it should 'always carry a profoundly creative character' (Davydov 1995: 17).

What enables this creativity, are the use of 'tools' and/or 'artefacts', which also are considered culturally bound. Such tools could be material, demonstrative or psychological in nature, but all carry certain meaning and messages, which can be used in the internalization of knowledge. That such meanings are, on the whole, understood by most if not all contextual actors, reminds us again of their historico-cultural character and location. Without an appreciation of such shared understandings, every social act or challenge would have to be negotiated and explained anew. The tools themselves could range from physical items, through to other people, to interpersonal relations. Indeed, as suggested by Jones *et al.* (in press), perhaps the most prevalent tool used in this respect is that of coaches' talk. This is in terms of the concepts discussed or presented to athletes (or other contextual stakeholders), how messages are delivered, and how resultant interactions are structured and re-structured. Indeed, the ideas and notions presented throughout this book can, in many ways, be considered the artefacts through which coaches (can) attempt to develop and improve athletes' knowledge and related performances. This, then, is how they should be read.

## THOUGHTS ON 'GOOD' COACHING

Despite increasing evidence and nuanced arguments alluding to the non-linear contested nature of coaching, many still search for the holy grail of 'what works', the 'silver bullet', which guarantees success. Although the push for effectiveness has been prevalent since the 1970s, its presence in the coaching literature can be traced as far back as the 1950s through Friedrichsen's (1956) analysis of loop films as instructional aids in coaching gymnastics. Since then, grids have been developed to increase the efficiency and value of coaching games (Bean 1976), coaching effectiveness programmes have been designed (Bump 1987), and guides written that have focused on helping coaches to know 'how to' more successfully teach sport skills (Christina & Corcos 1988). This, of course, led to, and was informed by, the systematic observation of 'good' and 'winning' coaches, and to a 'models for' approach. Although this may appear rather 'old ground', the legacy of such thinking firmly remains in the 'competency approach' still currently evident in coach education (e.g. Jones & Allison 2014). Here, it is assumed that coaching practice can be judged as 'good' or 'bad' contingent on the proficient demonstration of certain behaviours. The fallacy of the assumption was recently highlighted by Chesterfield *et al.* (2010), whose coach-certification candidates engaged in a form 'synthetic coaching' to satisfy their examiners' related expectations and successfully obtain the desired qualification. Here, the required demonstration of given competencies was more important than any evidence of (coaching) outcome. Similarly, Piggott (2012: 535) witheringly concluded that where 'courses were governed by prescriptive and rigid rationalities, coaches found them useless'.

As any serious researcher or practitioner knows, the search for the 'best coaching recipe' is a fool's errand. Such a 'one size fits all' just does not exist. However, this does not mean that 'anything goes' within coaching either, as plenty of 'good practice' guidelines certainly exist. In this respect, many of us can consensually identify a good coach when we see one working. Here, notions akin to being innovative, caring, focused, pedagogically-orientated, reflective, responsible and deeply engaged immediately come to mind. However, as opposed to being tightly defined proficiencies, the guidelines under which such practitioners operate and display such attributes are more-than-often considered steering principles; that is, they are used and implemented with perceptive flexibility within given boundaries (which are also, to various extents, permeable) (Jones & Wallace 2005). Of course, many of the ideas and concepts that could act as such principles form the basis of this book.

A further exploration of seemingly 'successful practice' was recently carried out by Jones and colleagues (2012). Believing that the 'what' and 'how' of coaching had been relatively well engaged with, the question of 'who is coaching?' was deemed worthy of consideration. Here, the person of the coach, as much if not more than the methods he or she applies, was deemed a crucial element in what constitutes 'good' or successful coaching. In borrowing from the work of Agne (1998: 166) among others, the case was made that 'children [read athletes] learn by absorbing who you are to them, not memorising what you say'. Indeed, if coaching is enacted by somebody, then it naturally matters who that somebody is. The primary thrust of such work is humanistic in nature, emphasising caring as a key characteristic. According to Agne (1998: 168), such committed caring is more significant in the generation of 'student learning and effective teaching than anything else'. Similarly, Jones, Armour and Potrac (2004) found elite coaches to invest high levels of time and energy into their work, achieving a form of self-actualization, a 'self-in-role', through their actions. This was not seen as merely a matter of being unique (Mead 1952) or a simplistic recourse of being somehow 'true to self'. Rather, it was to do with developing greater sensitivity towards the self in the coaching role, which can result in relationships of considerable trust and respect – crucial components for 'good' coaching.

## POSTSCRIPT

Over a decade ago when we began the project of writing the first edition of this book, we were united in the belief that linking sociological and educational concepts to coaching practice would assist coaches and students of coaching to make some sense of the muddled realities of their work. What we did not foresee was that the practice of writing a consensual text about coaching was just as messy and complicated as coaching itself. The influence of the contextual factors became very evident as we swapped our 'draft' chapters for the first, second and now third editions. Suffice to say, it did not look as if we were singing from the same hymn sheet. Over time, and with the help of each other, the ideas became more harmonious again. The reason we briefly share this experience is to highlight that even with the best of intentions, and a reasonable level of theoretical and practical understanding, collective compromise and consideration, in addition to individual determination are required to realize one's coaching goals.

## REFERENCES

Abraham, A. & Collins, D. (2011). Taking the next step: Ways forward for coaching science. *Quest*, 63: 366–384.

Agne, K.J. (1998). Caring: the way of the master teacher. In R. Lipka & T. Brinthaupt *The Role of Self in Teacher Development*. Albany, NY: State University of New York.

Apple, M. (1999). *Ideology and Curriculum*. New York: Routledge.

Armour, K.M. (2011). Introduction. In K.M. Armour (ed.) *Sport Pedagogy: An Introduction for Teaching and Coaching*. Harlow: Pearson.

Armour, K.M. & Jones, R.L. (2000). The practical heart within: The value of sociology of sport. In R.L. Jones & K.M. Armour (eds.) *The Sociology of Sport: Theory and Practice*. London: Addison Wesley Longman.

Australian Sports Commission (1997). *Game Sense: Developing Thinking Players*. Belconnen: Australian Sports Commission.

Bale, J. & Sang, J. (1996). *Kenyan Running: Movement Culture, Geography and Global Change*. London: Frank Cass.

Bean, D. (1976). Coaching grid: A simple way to increase effectiveness in teaching games. *HPECR Runner*, 14(3): 16–20.

Bergmann Drewe, S. (2000). An examination of the relationship between coaching and teaching. *Quest*, 52: 79–88.

Bourdieu, P. (1990). *The Logic of Practice*. Stanford, CA: Stanford University Press.

Bump, L. (1987). *Coaching Young Athletes*, (video recording). Champaign, IL: Human Kinetics.

Bunker, D. & Thorpe, R. (1982). A model for the teaching of games in the secondary school. *Bulletin of Physical Education*, 10: 9–16.

Cassidy, T. (2000). Investigating the pedagogical process in physical education teacher education, unpublished doctoral dissertation, Deakin University, Australia.

Cassidy, T. (2010). Understanding athlete learning and coaching practice: Utilising practice theories and theories of practice. In J. Lyle & C. Cushion (eds.) *Sports Coaching: Professionalism and Practice*. London: Elsevier.

Chesterfield, G., Potrac, P. & Jones, R.L. (2010). Studentship and impression management: Coaches' experiences of an advanced soccer coach education award. *Sport, Education and Society*, 15(3): 299–314.

Christina, R. & Corcos, D. (1988). *Coaches' Guide to Teaching Sport Skills*. Champaign, IL: Human Kinetics.

Cushion, C. & Jones, R.L. (2006). Power, discourse and symbolic violence in professional youth soccer: The case of Albion F.C. *Sociology of Sport Journal*, 23(2): 142–161.

Daniels, H. (2001). *Vygotsky and Pedagogy*. Routledge: London.

Davydov, V. (1995). The influence of L.S. Vygotsky on education theory, research and practice. *Educational Researcher*, 24, 12–21.

Denison, J. (2007). Social theory for coaches: A Foucauldian reading of one athlete's poor performance. *International Journal of Sports Science & Coaching*, 2: 369–383.

Denison, J. (2010). Messy texts, or the inexplainable performance. Reading bodies' evidence. *International Review of Qualitative Research*, 3(1): 149–160.

Douge, B. & Hastie, P. (1993). Coach effectiveness. *Sport Science Review*, 2: 14–29.

Durie, M. (1998). *Whaiora: Māori Health Development*. Oxford: Oxford University Press.

Eisner, E. (1993). Foreword, in D.J. Flinders & G.E. Mills (eds.) *Theory and Concepts in Qualitative Research*. New York: Teachers College Press.

Engström, Y. (2000). Comment on Blackler *et al.*, activity theory and the social construction of knowledge: A story of four umpires. *Organization*, 7(2): 301–310.

Fernández-Balboa, J-M. (2000). Discrimination: What do we know and what can we do about it. In R.L. Jones & K.M. Armour (eds.) *Sociology of Sport: Theory and Practice*. London: Pearson.

Flyvbjerg, B. (2001). *Making Social Science Matter: Why Social Inquiry Fails and How It Can Succeed Again*. Cambridge: Cambridge University Press.

Flyvbjerg, B., Landman, T. & Schram, S. (2012) Introduction: New directions in social science. In B. Flyvbjerg, T. Landman & S. Schram (eds.) *Real Social Science: Applied Phronesis*. Cambridge: University Press.

Friedrichsen, F. (1956). *Study of the Effectiveness of Loop Films as Instructional Aids in Teaching Gymnastic Stunts*. Eugene, OR: University of Oregon.

Grace, G. (1998). Critical policy scholarship: Reflections on the integrity of knowledge and research. In G. Shacklock & J. Smyth (eds.) *Being Reflexive in Critical Educational and Social Research*. London: Falmer Press.

Hardman, J. (2008). Researching pedagogy: An activity theory approach. *Journal of Education*, 45: 65–95.

Harvey, S., Cushion, C. & Massa-Gonzales, A.M. (2010). Learning a new method: Teaching Games for Understanding in the coaches eyes'. *Physical Education and Sport Pedagogy*, 15(4): 361–382.

Hauw, D. & Durand, M. (2005). How do elite athletes interact with the environment in competition? A situated analysis of trampolinists' activity. *European Review of Applied Psychology* 55 (3): 207–215.

Hemmestad, L.B., Jones, R.L. & Standal, Ø.F. (2010). Phronetic social science: A means of better researching and analysing coaching? *Sport, Education and Society*, 15(4): 447–459.

Jones, R.L. (2000). Toward a sociology of coaching. In R.L. Jones & K.M. Armour (eds.) *The Sociology of Sport: Theory and Practice*. London: Addison Wesley Longman.

Jones, R.L. (ed.) (2006a). *The Sports Coach as Educator: Re-conceptualising Sports Coaching*. London: Routledge.

Jones, R.L. (2006b). How can educational concepts inform sports coaching? In R. Jones (ed.). *The Sports Coach as Educator: Re-conceptualising Sports Coaching*. London: Routledge.

Jones, R.L. & Allison. W. (2014). Candidates' experiences of elite coach education: A longitudinal study ('tracking the journey'). *European Journal of Human Movement*, 33: 110–122.

Jones, R.L. & Armour, K. (2000). *Sociology of Sport: Theory and Practice*. London: Addison Wesley Longman.

Jones, R.L. & Wallace, M. (2005). Another bad day at the training ground: Coping with ambiguity in the coaching context. *Sport, Education and Society*, 10(1): 119–134.

Jones, R.L., Armour, K. & Potrac, P.A. (2003). Constructing expert knowledge: A case study of a top level professional soccer coach. *Sport, Education and Society*, 8(2): 213–229.

Jones, R.L., Armour, K. & Potrac, P. (2004). *Sports Coaching Cultures: From Practice to Theory*. London: Routledge.

Jones, R.L., Bailey, J., Santos, S. & Edwards, C. (2012). Who is coaching? Developing the person of the coach, in D. Day (ed.). *Sports and Coaching: Pasts and Futures*. Crewe: MMU Press.

Jones, R.L., Bowes, I. & Kingston, K. (2010). Complex practice in coaching: Studying the chaotic nature of coach-athlete interactions, in J. Lyle & C. Cushion (eds.) *Sports Coaching: Professionalism and Practice*. London: Elsevier.

Jones, R.L., Edwards, C. & Viotto Filho, I.A.T. (2014). Activity theory, complexity and sports coaching: An epistemology for a discipline. *Sport, Education and Society*. DOI: 10.1080/13573322.2014.895713

Jones, R.L., Potrac, P., Cushion, C. & Ronglan, L.T. (eds.) (2011). *The Sociology of Sports Coaching*. London: Routledge.

Kirk, D. (2010). Towards a socio-pedagogy of sports coaching. In J. Lyle & C. Cushion (eds.) *Sports Coaching: Professionalization and Practice*, London: Elsevier.

Knudson, D. & Morrison, C. (2002). *Qualitative Analysis of Human Movement*, 2nd edn. Champaign, IL: Human Kinetics.

Kretchmar, R.S. (2010). Holism in sports coaching: Beyond humanistic psychology. *International Journal of Sports Science and Coaching*, 5(4): 445–447.

Langley, D. (1997). Exploring student skill learning: A case for investigating the subjective experience, *Quest*, 49: 142–160.

LeCompte, M. & Preissle, J. (1993). *Ethnography and Qualitative Design in Educational Research*. San Diego: Academic Press.

Leont'ev, A. (1978). *Activity, consciousness and personality*. Englewood Cliffs NJ: Prentice-Hall.

Light, R. (2004). Coaches' experiences of Game Sense: Opportunities and challenges. *Physical Education and Sport Pedagogy*, 9(2): 115–131.

Loland, S.L. (2011). The normative aims of coaching: The good coach as an enlightened generalist. In A. Hardman & C. R. Jones (eds.) *The Ethics of Sports Coaching*. London: Routledge.

Lusted, D. (1986). Why Pedagogy? *Screen*, 27(5): 2–14.

Lyle, J. (2010). Holism in sports coaching: Beyond humanistic psychology: A commentary. *International Journal of Sports Science and Coaching*, 5(4): 449–452.

Macdonald, D., Kirk, D., Metzler, M., Nilges, L.M., Schempp, P. & Wright, J. (2002). It's all very well in theory: Theoretical perspectives and their applications in contemporary pedagogical research. *Quest*, 54: 133–156.

Mauss, M. (1973). Techniques of the body. *Economy and Society*, 2: 70–87.

Mead, G.H. (1952). *Mind, Self, and Society.* Chicago: University of Chicago Press.

Nelson, L., Cushion, C., Potrac, P. & Groom, R. (2012). Carl Rogers, learning and educational practice: Critical considerations and applications in sports coaching. *Sport, Education and Society*, 1–19 iFirst Article.

North, J. (2013). Philosophical underpinnings of coaching practice research, *Quest.* 65, 278–299.

Piggott, D. (2012). Coaches' experiences of formal coach education: a critical sociological investigation. *Sport, Education and Society*, 17(4): 535–554.

Pineau, E.L. (1994). Teaching is performance: Reconceptualising a problematic metaphor. *American Educational Research Journal*, 31(1): 3–25.

Potrac, P. (2001). A comparative analysis of the working behaviours of top-level English and Norwegian soccer coaches. Unpublished doctoral thesis. Brunel University, London.

Potrac, P. & Cassidy, T. (2006). The coach as a more capable other. In R. L. Jones (ed.) *The Sports Coach as Educator: Re-conceptualising Sports Coaching*. London: Routledge.

Potrac, P., Jones, R.L., Purdy, L., Nelson, J. & Marshall, P. (2013). Coaches, coaching and emotion: A suggested research agenda. In P. Potrac, W. Gilbert & J. Denison (eds.) *The Routledge Handbook of Sports Coaching*. London: Routledge.

Purdy, L. & Jones, R.L. (2011). Choppy waters: Elite rowers' perceptions of coaching. *Sociology of Sport Journal*, 28(3): 329–346.

Reason, P. & Torbert, W. (2001). The action turn: Toward a transformational social science. *Concepts and Transformation*, 6(1): 1–37.

Sandelands, L.E. (1990). What is so practical about theory? Lewin revisited. *Journal for the Theory of Sport Behavior*, 20(3): 235–262.

Santos, S., Jones, R.L. & Mesquita, I. (2013). Do coaches orchestrate? The working practices of elite Portuguese coaches. *Research Quarterly for Exercise and Sport*, 84(2): 263–272.

Saury, J. & Durand, M. (1998). Practical knowledge in expert coaches: On-site study of coaching in sailing. *Research Quarterly in Exercise and Sport*, 69(3): 254–266.

Schempp, P. (1998). The dynamics of human diversity in sport pedagogy scholarship. *Sociology of Sport On Line*, 1(1): Available at http://physed.otago.ac.nz/sosol/v1i1/v1i1.htm.

Seidman, S. & Alexander, J.C. (2001). Introduction. In S. Seidman and J.C. Alexander (eds.) *New Social Theory Reader,* 2nd edn. Abingdon, Oxon: Routledge.

Sfard, A. (1998). On two metaphors for learning and the dangers of choosing just one. *Educational Researcher*, 27(2): 4–13.

Sparkes, A. & Templin, T. (1992). Life histories and physical education teachers: Exploring the meanings of marginality, in A. Sparkes (ed.) *Research in Physical Education and Sport: Exploring Alternative Visions*. London: Falmer Press.

Squires, G. (1999). *Teaching as a Professional Discipline*. London: Falmer Press.

Vygotsky, L. (1978). *Mind and Society*. Cambridge, MA: MIT Press.

Vygotsky, L. (1997). *Educational Psychology*. Boca Raton, Fla: St Lucie Press (Originally written 1921–1923).

Wood, D.J., Bruner, J.S. & Ross, G. (1976). The role of tutoring in problem solving. *Journal of Child Psychiatry and Psychology*, 17(2): 89–100.

Zakus, D.H. & Malloy, D.C. (1996). A critical evaluation of current pedagogical approaches in human movement studies: A suggested alternative. *Quest*, 48: 501–517.

# Reflection

## INTRODUCTION

For over three decades a focus on reflection, or on becoming a reflective practitioner, has gained popularity in a wide range of contexts. These include education (Smyth 1991), graphic design (Poynor 1994), art (Roberts 2001), engineering (Adams *et al.* 2003), medicine (Middlethon & Aggleton 2001) and coaching (Gilbert & Trudel, 2001; Knowles *et al.* 2001). Practitioners are being encouraged to 'stand back and reflect upon the construction and application of their professional knowledge' (Hardy & Mawer 1999: 2). The surge of interest can largely be attributed to the work of Schön (1983), who discussed reflection in relation to architecture, town planning, engineering and management. Reflection is a term that has been described in multiple ways including: 'turning a subject over in the mind and giving it serious and consecutive consideration' (Dewey 1910: 3), to having 'a capacity for autonomous professional self-development through systematic self-study' (Stenhouse 1975: 144). Although useful in a general sense, there are negative consequences of having multiple interpretations of reflection, particularly in relation to it becoming a popular rallying call. This is because such ambiguity has the potential to lose the concept's core meaning (Smyth 1991), while paradoxically, allowing reflection to be used in 'an unreflected manner' (Bengtsson 1995: 24). The primary purpose of this chapter is to introduce the concept of reflection, and discuss how four interpretations of reflection have been utilized in the sports coaching context. In addition, the chapter also serves as a conceptual framework through which the concepts introduced in this book can be thought about and possibly integrated into personal practice.

When attempting to gain an understanding of the complexities associated with reflection, it is useful to consider Tinning's (1995: 50) point that 'if becoming reflective were simply a rational process, then it would be easy to train … teachers [read coaches] to be reflective'. He argues that becoming reflective is not simple, because the issues on which practitioners are encouraged to reflect often possess 'a large measure of emotion and subjectivity embedded within them' (1995: 50). Additionally, many coaches learn how to coach from being an apprentice to another coach – often one they admire – and base their own practices on those of a mentor. Therefore, it can be challenging to reflect upon, and possibly analyze, taken-for-granted practices that are associated with valued memories that may also have become integral to a sense of self.

Increasingly, there is encouragement for coaches to become reflective practitioners (see Armour 2010; Cropley *et al.* 2012; Denison 2007; Denison & Avner 2011; Gallimore *et al.* 2013; Gearity & Mills 2012; Gilbert & Trudel 2006; Handcock & Cassidy 2014; Jones *et al.* 2011). This is despite, nearly 20 years ago, Crum (1995) raising the question: should being a reflective practitioner become standardized practice; in other words should it become the 'norm'? While he debated this question in the physical education context, the issue has relevancy for sports coaches. According to Crum, the answer depends on the definition held of physical education or, in this case, coaching. If a practitioner holds a 'training-of-the-physical' perception of coaching and believes his or her role is only to improve fitness and adopt a technical/utilitarian approach, then becoming a coach who reflects deeply is not going to be paramount. While some coaches still cling to this view, growing recognition exists that it is useful for coaches to engage in some degree of reflection, even if it is only at the practical level (Handcock & Cassidy 2014). Coaches who recognize their work as being 'a teaching-learning process', that is 'socially constructed and historically situated', see much greater merit in reflecting on practice (Crum 1995: 15). By doing so, coaches can expose their perceptions and beliefs to evaluation, creating a heightened sense of self-awareness. This may, in turn, lead to 'certain openness to new ideas' and potentially improved action (Hellison & Templin 1991: 9).

## WHAT IS REFLECTION?

Over 100 years ago, John Dewey contrasted routine behaviour with reflective thought, defining the latter as the '[a]ctive, persistent, and careful consideration of any belief or supposed form of knowledge in the light of the grounds that support it, and the further conclusions to which it tends' (Dewey 1910: 6). According to Dewey (1966), those who adopt a reflective pose investigate the assumptions that inform their behaviour and accept responsibility for their actions. Dewey (1916) suggested that before an individual can engage in reflective thinking, three personal attributes need to be present: open-mindedness, wholeheartedness and responsibility. Open-mindedness was conceived as 'an active desire to listen to more sides than one ...; to give full attention to alternative possibilities; [and] to recognise the possibility of error even in the beliefs that are dearest to us' (Dewey 1916: 224). Wholeheartedness, meanwhile, as the name suggests, referred to being 'absorbed' and/or 'thoroughly interested' in a particular subject. Finally, responsibility concerned the consequences of actions being fully recognized and accepted, thereby securing integrity in one's beliefs.

These attributes appear relevant to contemporary coaches as evidenced by Wayne Smith's (ex-coach of the All Blacks, the national rugby union team of New Zealand) description of the qualities needed to be a good coach. In his own words:

> the key thing I think is the openness to learning. I think coaches need to look at things on merit and understand that just because they've played the game, they don't know everything about it ... Having a passion to improve is important. Knowing that you are a part of the problem means that you can also be part of the solution.
>
> (Kidman 2001: 43)

Similarly, when Denison and Avner (2011: 209) used a Foucauldian framework to reflect on the concept of 'positive coaching', they suggested that 'for coaches to become a positive force for change, they must engage in an ongoing critical examination of the knowledges and assumptions that inform their problem-solving approaches'.

Despite Dewey's early theorizing, the increased recent interest in reflection can be attributed to the work of Schön (1983, 1987) and Zeichner (1983, 1987). While Dewey's view of reflection focused on 'future action rather than current action' (Eraut 1995: 9), Schön's (1983) interpretation took existing practice into account. Hence, Schön (1983: 50) introduced the notion of reflection-in-action, which described what people do in practice; namely 'thinking about what they are doing, even while doing it'. In other words, Schön (1983) considered reflection-on-action to be integral to reflection-in-action. For example, a big-league baseball pitcher described the process of reflecting-in-action by explaining how in the midst of playing the game, '[You get] a special feel for the ball, a kind of command that lets you repeat the exact same thing you did before that proved successful' (1983: 54). Further, Schön stressed that phrases such as 'keeping your wits about you', 'thinking on your feet' and 'learning by doing' highlight 'not only that we can think about doing, but that we can think about doing something while doing it' (1983: 54).

Schön (1983: 50) identified three general patterns prevalent within reflection-in-action. First, that reflection is often initiated when a practitioner is 'stimulated by surprise'. In the process of dealing with an unexpected phenomenon, an individual reflects on his or her understandings that are implicit in the action, before critiquing, restructuring and embodying the practice in future action. In other words, when something unexpected happens people 'turn thought back on action' (1983: 50) and try to deal with it. The second pattern prevalent in reflection-in-action was what Schön (1983: 268) called a 'reflective conversation with the situation'. What he meant by this was that while an 'inquiry begins with an effort to solve a problem ... [t]he inquirer remains open to the discovery of [new] phenomena' (1983: 268). Here, in attempting to solve a problem, a discovery is often made that is incongruous or incompatible with the efforts to solve that problem. When this happens, the inquirer 'reframes' the problem (1983: 268). Schön argued that a consequence of having such a reflective conversation with the situation is that it enables practitioners to achieve some degree of professional growth by reflecting-in, and -on, practice.

The third pattern inherent in reflection-in-action was what Schön (1983: 62) termed the 'action-present'. He described this as the 'zone of time in which action can still make a difference to the situation' (1983: 62). While all processes of reflection have an 'action-present', Schön conceded that this 'may stretch over minutes, hours, days, or even weeks or months, depending on the pace of activity and the situational boundaries characteristic of the practice' (1983: 62). How the 'action-present' is interpreted will dictate whether a more generic reflection-in-action term is utilized to describe the reflective process, or whether more specific terms such as reflection-on-action (Schön, 1983) or retrospective reflection-on-action (Gilbert & Trudel 2001, 2005, 2006) are used.

While Schön (1983) viewed reflection-on-action to be integral to reflection-in-action, not everyone agrees. Gilbert and Trudel (2001, 2005, 2006), for instance, view them as separate types of reflection with reflection-on-action occurring 'within the action-present, but not in the midst of activity' (Gilbert & Trudel 2001: 30). They contended that when a coach reflects on an issue in between practice sessions, he or she is reflecting on action. Reflection-on-action can also occur before the action; for example, when a coach reflects on what could happen and acts, thereby pre-empting a possible problem arising (Bengtsson 1995). Gilbert and Trudel (2006) also suggested a third type of reflection, which they termed 'retrospective reflection-on-action'. This was described as 'that [which] occurs outside the action-present (e.g. after the season or after a coach's reflection can no longer affect the situation)' (Gilbert & Trudel 2001: 30).

## BECOMING A REFLECTIVE COACH

In the first edition of this text, we had a section entitled 'Why is it useful to become a reflective coach?' That we decided to re-title it to read 'Becoming a reflective coach' is testament to our belief that the coaching community has 'bought into', at least rhetorically, the value of coaches becoming reflective practitioners. While mindful of Gilbert and Trudel's (2006) different types of reflection, in this chapter, we follow the lead of Schön (1983) by using the general term reflection-in-action, which recognizes the three aforementioned reflective patterns. Empirical evidence has highlighted the value of reflection-in-action when aiming to improve coaching practice (for example see Cassidy *et al.* 2006; Cushion *et al.* 2003; Denison, 2007; Gallimore *et al.* 2013; Gilbert & Trudel 2001; Jones *et al.* 2004; Kidman 2001; Knowles *et al.* 2006). When Cushion and colleagues (2010) reviewed the literature on coach learning and development, they noted that reflection was consistently mentioned in conjunction with how to support experimental learning. However, they also noted that 'time and space is required within a learning programme to develop reflective skills, otherwise these are likely to be superficial and uncritical' (2010: ii). Similarly, Cropley and Hanton (2011) went further to suggest that many who embrace the concept of reflective practice, and work within the sports coaching field, have done so without being fully aware of what is required to become a reflective coach.

Reflecting on one's practice is not an easy or quick exercise (see for example Gallimore *et al.* 2013). Indeed, there are many traditions, rituals, and so-called norms associated with coaching culture(s) that act as constraints on an individual's willingness and ability. For example, one's unwillingness to experiment with reflection is associated with a commonly held belief that 'thinking interferes with doing' (Schön 1983: 276). This is founded on many perceptions; one of them being that there is no time to reflect when in the middle of the action, or that it can be 'dangerous to stop and think' (Schön 1983: 278). In a sporting context, for example, it could be physically risky for a scrum half in rugby union to stop and consider all the options when he or she is holding the ball at the back of the scrum. But, as Schön (1983: 278) reminds us, 'not all practice situations are of this sort'. Indeed, it is unlikely that coaches would find themselves in 'dangerous' positions if they chose to stop and think in the middle of a coaching session. Yet, while a coach may not be in any physical danger, Jones *et al.* (2004) pointed out that the 'front' coaches use is crucial to maintain credibility. Therefore, if a coach visibly 'stopped and thought', there is a danger that athletes could interpret the action as indecision or a lack of knowledge, thus putting the coach's standing at risk.

The view that thinking interferes with action is also reflected in the common saying; 'paralysis by analysis'. This is considered to occur when there is a tendency to over-analyze behaviour and consequently lose the 'naturalness' of the action. For example, a golf coach may suggest a player change his or her grip. Here, it is reasonable to expect that the player would feel less comfortable playing a shot until she or he becomes accustomed to the new grip. Also, if a coach incorporated a new pedagogical strategy like providing open-ended scenarios, which require time for deliberation in the middle of a session, it would not be surprising that the amount of physical activity would be reduced. However, coaches and athletes can be taught to think about new information and their respective behaviours in a very short period of time. For example, utilizing the same strategies to assimilate reflection into coaching action, a tennis player can be taught to 'take a moment' after they have seen the outcome of a shot, and integrate subsequent learning into their next shot. Over time, when reflection is incorporated this way, it is likely that performance will be enhanced which may, in turn, assist in the recognition of its merits.

Sometimes thinking does interfere with action, albeit temporarily. Whether or not coaches are prepared to pay this price, and incur 'a temporary loss of spontaneity' (Schön 1983: 280), depends on their willingness to construct a 'high-risk' environment. We contend that, more often than not, the cost is worth the gamble. This is because reflection-in-action is often initiated when performance is unsatisfactory or a problem has been identified. As such, we agree with Schön (1983: 279), who asserted that the question then becomes 'not so much *whether* to reflect, as what *kind* of reflection is most likely to help us get unstuck'. The purpose of the next section is to provide an overview of some of the frameworks used to facilitate reflection whilst recognizing the social conditions in which practice occurs. In particular, we introduce four frameworks, and illustrate how they have been used within sports coaching. It is worth noting that the frameworks described below are not the only ones that have been used to understand the reflective practices of coaches (see Gallimore *et al.* 2013).

# FRAMEWORKS FOR ENCOURAGING REFLECTION

## Three levels of reflection

Zeichner and Liston (1996: 19) were concerned that the reflective process had a potentially 'inward' focus, and thus lacked 'sufficient attention to the social conditions that frame and influence practice'. They, along with Van Manen (1977), believed that one way to encourage consideration of the social context of practice was to think of reflection as occurring on a number of levels. Drawing on the work of sociologists associated with the Frankfurt School, Van Manen (1977) argued for three levels of reflection: (1) technical; (2) practical; and (3) critical. Although he identified differing levels, he did not position one as necessarily better than any other. Rather, he acknowledged that they could occur in conjunction with one another. According to Van Manen (1977) and Zeichner and Liston (1987), a *technical* level of reflection occurs when a pedagogical practitioner (read coach) focuses on achieving set objectives, and on the effective and efficient application of knowledge. Examples of questions a coach could ask at this level include:

- What resources could I utilize to improve the teaching of this task?
- What goals did I achieve in this session?
- What can I do to fix this problem?
- What part of the training could I change so that it finishes on time?
- What can I do to better structure this drill?

Alternatively, a *practical* level of reflection occurs when coaches acknowledge that athletes (as well as themselves) bring assumptions to the coaching environment. It may also occur when a coach views the culture of the sport as being flexible, in addition to recognizing the practical and educational implications of an action (Van Manen 1977, 1995; Zeichner & Liston 1987, 1996). Examples of questions illustrative of a practical level of reflection include:

- How can I structure the session so that it better suits athletes?
- How does my posture(s) and what I am wearing influence the verbal messages I am giving?
- How are my experiences of being coached influencing what I do and my expectations of athlete behaviour?
- How does my behaviour reinforce stereotypes?
- How does the type of feedback I provide influence what athletes learn?
- How do I include a range of learning media to facilitate athletes' learning?

Finally, a *critical* level of reflection occurs when a coach focuses on the political, moral and ethical meaning of knowledge, and the domination of various forms of authority. It occurs when coaches question the worth of knowledge, work towards justice and equality, and problematize the context in which coaching occurs (Van Manen 1977; Zeichner & Liston 1987). Examples of questions a coach could ask illustrative of a critical level of reflection include:

- Whose knowledge, and whose point of view, is represented in the knowledge being (re)produced in the training session?
- Why do I play the best athlete who is coming back from injury and is only 80 per cent fit, when I have a fully fit but less skilled athlete on the bench?
- What do I do about practices that are inequitable or unjust, but are part of the team or club traditions?
- Is there a difference between the type of feedback I give to the more skilled and less skilled members of the team? If so, why?

Many conscientious coaches already ask themselves these sorts of searching questions. The challenge is to answer them rigorously and systematically taking into account multiple contextual pressures and constraints. Examples of the three levels of reflection being used in the sports coaching context are limited, but there are exceptions (see Cassidy *et al.* 2006b; Handcock & Cassidy 2014).

## Action research

Another framework that encourages coaches to have a reflective conversation with the situation is that of action research. Although there is no universal interpretation of action research, Carr and Kemmis, in taking a socially critical slant, described it as:

> a form of *collective* self-reflective enquiry undertaken by participants in social situations in order to improve the rationality and *justice* of their own social or educational practices, as well as their understanding of these practices and the situations in which these practices are carried out.
>
> (in Kemmis & McTaggart 1992: 5 *emphasis added*)

Notwithstanding the variations in interpretations, it is generally agreed that the action research process comprises four phases (planning, acting, observing and reflecting), in addition to the basic spirals of observation, interpretation (including the integration of theory), action and reflection. In this respect, Tsai *et al.* (2004) suggested that the action research process allows for the continuous construction and testing of theoretical explanations in practice, leading to improved understanding and learning. According to Carr and Kemmis (1986), the *plan* must be orientated around some future action and be flexible enough to cope with unforeseen circumstances. The plan should also assist a coach to realize new potential for action. The *action* is a carefully considered, and critically informed, variation of practice, and is acknowledged as a 'platform for the further development of later action' (Kemmis & McTaggart 1992: 12). Action is also considered to be dynamic, 'requiring instant decisions about what is to be done, and the exercise of practical judgement' (1992: 12). The role of *observation* in the action research process is to document the effects of the action, and to provide data upon which to reflect. Not only is the overt action observed, but so are 'the effects of action (intended and unintended), the circumstances of and constraints on action, [and] the way circumstances and constraints limit or channel the planned action and its effects' (1992: 13).

Collective self-enquiry is a characteristic of Kemmis and McTaggart's (1992) interpretation of action research, and it was this interpretation that Cassidy and colleagues used to increase their understanding of how technology was utilized by a software developer to support coaches (Cassidy *et al.* 2006b). While the collective self-enquiry was appropriate and generative in this instance, it is important to recognize that collegiality cannot be forced. Hence, it may be difficult for some potentially reflective coaches to be part of a like-minded group, given that various sport cultures can limit access to such colleagues (Rynne 2008). Collective self-enquiry was also difficult to achieve when an action research pedagogical approach was used in a UK graduate sports coaching programme (Jones *et al.* 2011). Here, issues linked to power and voice increasingly came to the fore as discussion surrounding what and how reflection was to take place occurred.

## Experiential learning model

It has been well documented that a relationship exists between reflection and experiential learning (Moon 2004) (also see Chapter 8 on Learning). Hence, it has been suggested that an ability and willingness to reflect are important attributes for coaches if they are to benefit from experience and other informal learning opportunities (Cushion & Nelson 2013). Gilbert and Trudel (2001) drew on the work of Schön (1983) to develop an explanatory model for how youth coaches reflectively conversed with their own situations. The model has six components: '(1) coaching issues, (2) role frame, (3) issue setting, (4) strategy generation, (5) experimentation, and (6) evaluation' (2001: 22). For Gilbert and Trudel (2001), a reflective conversation is stimulated by what a coach views as a coaching issue and his or her personal role frame. However, the key to the reflection process lay in the consideration given to issue setting, strategy generation, experimentation and evaluation. The conversation is not necessarily a 'one-off'. Rather, it is possible for it to be on a sub-loop, with the above process being continuously revisited (Gilbert & Trudel 2001). This model illustrates the type of reflection Schön (1983) termed reflection-on-action because the reflection takes place after the coaching session has been completed. While the reflective conversation model does not explicitly collaborate with others, Gilbert and Trudel (2001) identified that 'having access to knowledgeable and respected coaching peers' was 'critical to facilitating the reflective process' (11: 32).

Building on earlier work, and recognizing the importance of engaging with knowledgable others, Gilbert and Trudel (2006) suggested that four conditions influence the reflective conversation. These were listed as;

> (1) access to respected and trusted peers, (2) a coach's stage of learning (coaches with more experience are less likely to consult coaching material, instead relying on creative thought and joint construction), (3) issue characteristics (for challenging dilemmas it is more likely that coaches will consult during strategy generation, experimentation and evaluation) and (4) environment, for example, the support provided by the community.
>
> (Gilbert & Trudel 2006: 119–120)

### 'Technologies of the self'

Another framework beginning to be used by coaches to reflect on practice is Foucault's (1985) 'technologies of the self'. Such technologies have been described as 'those intentional and voluntary actions by which men [sic] not only set themselves rules of conduct, but also seek to transform themselves' (1985: 10). Foucault claimed that by utilizing technologies of the self, he was able to 'go back through what I was thinking, to think it differently, and see what I had done from a new vantage point and in a clearer light' (1985: 11). Doing so provided him with a framework to question 'the manner in which one ought to "conduct oneself" – that is, the manner in which one ought to form oneself as an ethical subject acting in reference to the prescriptive elements that make up the [moral] code' (1985: 26).

When discussing the relationship between social theory, reflective practice and personal experience, Denison (2007: 380) suggested that engaging with technologies of the self offers coaches 'a workable framework to know how to change their coaching practices for the better' by enabling them to engage with the social, moral and political dimensions of coaching (see Gearity & Mills 2012; Pringle & Crocket 2013). Not only has Foucault's framework been used by coaches, it has also been used by athletes (Pringle & Hickey 2010) and coach educators (Cassidy 2013) to problematize the moral codes associated with sport. Developing such self-awareness in relation to taken-for-granted practices, holds much promise for coach development. This is not only in relation to 'what is', but in realizing unwritten constraints on practice, 'what could be'.

## CONCLUDING THOUGHTS

Over the past two and a half decades, and thanks largely to the work of Schön (1983), the concept of reflection has become popular in many fields. Nowhere has this been more evident than in sports coaching. Much of the current sports coaching literature thus encourages coaches to become reflective practitioners whilst providing considerable empirical evidence in support of such a position. Yet, some environments are more supportive of practitioners becoming reflective than others. Schön (1983) asserted that reflection was more likely to occur in an environment that prioritizes flexibility, acknowledges that multiple views exist, appreciates the complexity of issues, and is non-hierarchical. In the previous edition of this book, we said that Schön's ideal environment hardly sounds like a typical coaching context. Since then, however, coaching has come to be increasingly realized as a complicated practice possessing many dynamic social and personal elements, thus better aligning with Schön's vision.

As the sports coaching community strives to become recognized as a profession, practices will change and questions will be asked of some traditional customs and sentiments. These may come from those who have graduated with tertiary qualifications in coaching science (or the equivalent), from coaches working in the 'swamp of practice' (Schön 1983) or from a combination of both. The challenge is to ensure that any change is engaged with integrity and an open mind (two of the attributes Dewey identified necessary when adopting a reflective pose) and not 'the modernist desire for certainty and for getting things "right"' (Cassidy & Tinning 2004: 187). While certainty may be desirable for some, aiming for such a state has the potential to close down discussion and experimentation. Once we accept that we cannot 'control social life completely' (Giddens 1990: 153), it becomes easier to experiment and to reflect. Such willingness is needed because 'social practices are constantly examined and reformed in the light of incoming information about those very practices, thus constitutively altering their character' (Giddens 1990: 38).

## END-OF-CHAPTER TASKS

1 Van Manen (1977) argued that reflection could occur on three levels. Drawing on a sports coaching context with which you are familiar:

   a Identify the three levels, then for each level, provide two questions you could ask to facilitate reflection on your coaching practice.
   b Identify and describe some of the factors that could constrain and enable you to become a reflective practitioner.

2 Identify an area of your coaching practice you wish to improve. Design an action research project (incorporating planning, acting, observing and reflecting), making note of what resources would be required to successfully conduct each phase.

3 It has been argued that using 'technologies of the self' can provide opportunities to 'know how to change coaching practices for the better' (Denison 2007: 380). Reflect on how engaging with a social, moral or political dimension of coaching could improve your coaching practice.

## REFERENCES

Adams, R., Turns, J. & Atman, C. (2003). Educating effective engineering designers: the role of reflective practice. *Design Studies*, 24(3): 275–294.

Armour, K. (2010). The learning coach ... the learning approach: Professional development for sports coach professionals. In J. Lyle & C. Cushion (eds.) *Sports Coaching: Professionalisation and Practice*. London: Elsevier.

Bengtsson, J. (1995). What is reflection? On reflection in the teaching profession and teacher education. *Teachers and Teaching: Theory and Practice*, 1(1): 23–32.

Carr, W. & Kemmis, S. (1986). *Becoming Critical: Education, Knowledge and Action Research*, London: Falmer Press.

Cassidy, T. (2013). Holistic sport coaching: A critical essay. In P. Potrac, W. Gilbert & J. Denison (eds.) *Routledge Handbook of Sports Coaching*. London: Routledge.

Cassidy, T. & Tinning, R. (2004). Slippage is not a dirty word: Considering the usefulness of Giddens' notion of knowledgeability in understanding the possibilities for teacher education. *Journal of Teaching Education*, 15(2): 175–188.

Cassidy, T., Potrac, P. & McKenzie, A. (2006a). Evaluating and reflecting upon a coach education initiative: The CoDe of rugby. *The Sports Psychologist*, 20(2): 145–161.

Cassidy, T., Stanley, S. & Bartlett, R (2006b). Reflecting on video feedback as a tool for learning skilled movement. *International Journal of Sports Science and Coaching*, 1(3): 279–288.

Cropley, B. & Hanton, S. (2011). The role of reflective practice in applied sport psychology: Contemporary issues for professional practice. In S. Hanton & S. Mellalieu (eds.) *Professional Practice in Sport Psychology: A Review*. London: Routledge.

Cropley, B., Miles, A. & Peel, J. (2012). *Reflective Practice: Value of Issues, and Developments within Sports Coaching*. London: Sports Coach UK.

Crum, B. (1995). The urgent need for reflective teaching in physical education. In C. Pare (ed.) *Training of Teachers in Reflective Practice of Physical Education*. Trois-Rivieres, Quebec: Université du Quebec a Trois-Rivieres.

Cushion, C. & Nelson, L. (2013). Coach education and learning: Developing the field. In P. Potrac, W. Gilbert & J. Denison (eds.) *Routledge Handbook of Sports Coaching*. London: Routledge.

Cushion, C., Armour, K.M. & Jones, R.L. (2003). Coach education and continuing professional development: Experience and learning to coach. *Quest*, 55: 215–230.

Cushion, C., Nelson, L., Armour, K., Lyle, J., Jones, R., Sandford, R. & O'Callaghan, C. (2010). *Coach Learning and Development: A Review of Literature*. London: Sports Coach UK.

Denison, J. (2007). Social theory for coaches: A Foucauldian reading of one athlete's poor performance. *International Journal of Sport Science and Coaching*, 2(4): 369–383.

Denison, J. & Avner, Z. (2011). Positive coaching: Ethical practices for athlete development. *Quest*, 63(2): 209–227.

Dewey, J. (1910). *How We Think*. Boston: Heath.

Dewey, J. (1916). *Democracy and Education: An Introduction to the Philosophy of Education*. New York: Macmillan.

Dewey, J. (1966). *Selected Educational Writings*. London: Heinemann.

Eraut, M. (1995). Schön shock: A case for reframing reflection-in-action? *Teachers and Teaching: Theory and Practice*, 1(1): 9–22.

Foucault, M. (1985). *The Use of Pleasure. The History of Sexuality: 2*. London: Penguin.

Gallimore, R., Gilbert, W. & Nater, S. (2013). Reflective practice and ongoing learning: A coach's 10-year journey. *Reflective Practice: International and Multidisciplinary Perspectives*, 1–21. Available at http://dx.doi.org/10.1080/14623943.2013.868790.

Gearity, B. & Mills, J (2012). *Sports Coaching Review*, 1(2): 124–134.

Giddens, A. (1990). *The Consequences of Modernity*. Cambridge: Polity Press.

Gilbert, W. & Trudel, P. (2001). Learning to coach through experience: Reflection in model youth sport coaches. *Journal of Teaching in Physical Education*, 21(1): 16–34.

Gilbert, W. & Trudel, P. (2005). Learning to coach through experience: Conditions that influence reflection. *Physical Educator*, 62(1): 32–43.

Gilbert, W. & Trudel, P. (2006). The coach as reflective practitioner. In R.L. Jones (ed.) *The Sports Coach as Educator: Re-conceptualising Sports Coaching*. London: Routledge.

Handcock, P. & Cassidy, T. (2014). Reflective practice for rugby union strength and conditioning coaches. *Strength and Conditioning Journal*, 36 (1): 41–45.

Hardy, C. & Mawer, M. (1999). *Learning and Teaching in Physical Education*. London: Falmer Press.

Hellison, D. & Templin, T. (1991). *A Reflective Approach to Teaching Physical Education*. Champaign, IL: Human Kinetics.

Jones, R., Armour, K.A. & Potrac, P.A. (2004). *Sports Coaching Cultures: From Practice to Theory*. London: Routledge.

Jones, R., Harris, K. & Morgan, K. (2011). Finding a better way to teach coach education: Using an action research framework. *Sport, Education and Society*, 17(3): 313–329.

Kemmis, S. & McTaggart, R. (eds.) (1992). *The Action Research Planner* (3rd edn). Geelong, Australia: Deakin University Press.

Kidman, L. (2001). *Developing Decision Makers: An Empowerment Approach to Coaching*. Christchurch, NZ: Innovative Press.

Knowles, Z., Gilbourne, D., Borrie, A. & Nevill, A. (2001). Developing the reflective sports coach: A study exploring the process of reflective practice with a higher education coaching programme. *Reflective Practice*, 2(2): 185–207.

Knowles, Z., Tyler, G., Gilbourne, D. & Eubank, M. (2006). Reflecting on reflection: Exploring the practice of sports coaching graduates. *Reflective Practice*, 7: 163–179.

Middlethon, A. & Aggleton, P. (2001). Reflection and dialogue for HIV prevention among young gay men. *AIDS Care*, 13(4): 515–526.

Moon, J. (2004). *A Handbook of Reflective and Experiential Learning. Theory and Practice*. London: Routledge.

Poynor, R. (1994). Building bridges between theory and practice. *ID*, 41: 40–42.

Pringle, R. & Crocket, H. (2013). Coaching with Foucault: An examination of applied ethics. In P. Potrac, W. Gilbert & J. Denison (eds.) *Routledge Handbook of Sports Coaching*. London: Routledge.

Pringle, R. & Hickey, C. (2010). Negotiating masculinities via the moral problematisation of sport. *Sociology of Sport Journal*, 27(2): 115–138.

Roberts, C. (2001). China, china. *Ceramic Review*, 189: 40–41.

Rynne, S. (2008). Clarifying the concepts of communities of practice in sport: A commentary. *International Journal of Sports Science and Coaching*, 5(2): 11–14.

Schön, D. (1983). *The Reflective Practitioner: How Professionals Think in Action*. New York: Basic Books.

Schön, D. (1987). *Educating the Reflective Practitioner: Toward a New Design for Teaching and Learning in the Professions*. San Francisco: Jossey-Bass.

Smyth, J. (1991). Problematising teaching through a critical approach to clinical supervision. *Curriculum Inquiry*, 21(3): 321–352.

Stenhouse, L. (1975). *An Introduction to Curriculum Research and Development*. London: Heinemann.

Tinning, R. (1995). We have ways of making you think, or do we? Reflections on training in reflective teaching. In C. Pare. (ed.) *Training of Teachers in Reflective Practice of Physical Education*. Trois-Rivieres, Quebec: Université du Quebec a Trois-Rivieres.

Tsai, S.D., Chung-Yu, P. & Hong-Quei, C. (2004). Shifting the mental model and emerging innovative behaviour: Action research of a quality management system. *Emergence, Complexity & Organisation*, 6(4): 28–39.

Van Manen, M. (1977). Linking ways of knowing with ways of being practical. *Curriculum Inquiry*, 6: 205–228.

Van Manen, M. (1995). On the epistemology of reflective practice. *Teachers and Teaching: Theory and Practice*, 1(1): 33–50.

Zeichner, K. (1983). Alternative paradigms of teacher education. *Journal of Teacher Education*, 34(3): 3–9.

Zeichner, K. (1987). Preparing reflective teachers: An overview of instructional strategies which have been employed in preservice teacher education. *International Journal of Educational Research*, 11(5): 565–575.

Zeichner, K. & Liston, P. (1987). Teaching student teachers to reflect. *Harvard Educational Review*, 1: 23–48.

Zeichner, K. & Liston, P. (1996). *Reflective Teaching: An Introduction*. New Jersey: Lawrence Erlbaum Associates.

# The context of coaching

# Coaching ethics

## INTRODUCTION

The notion that sport builds character has been a popular claim for decades, and rests on the taken-for-granted assumption that there is some sort of internal connection between the practice of sport and the development of moral qualities (Carr 1998). The belief has often led to a culture of non-teaching or coaching in relation to moral values, as it is based on the perception that a coach's task is simply to organize sporting activities for children and athletes who learn ethical behaviours from simply participating in them. Despite the popularity of the notion of sport being a character builder, it has not been the subject of widespread critical examination. Indeed, it has not garnered anything approaching consensus, let alone necessary operational definitions. This is particularly so in relation to what is meant by the term 'character', and how the context and/or the coach is meant to develop it (Sheilds & Bredemeier 1995). This lack of clarity has led to inadequate conceptualization of the professional responsibilities associated with the coaching role in terms of coaches' own moral development and that of athletes (Carr 1998).

Since antiquity, people have debated the constitution of ethics. Hence, it should come as no surprise that dispute and deliberation still exist on the nature of ethics and morals. Nevertheless, before we enter the discussion related to coaching ethics and coaches' moral behaviour in earnest, it is appropriate that we provide some related conceptual definitions, lest there should be similar confusion in the ensuing analysis. Morality has traditionally been associated with the differentiation of intention and action (i.e. the goodness or badness of human behaviour, or with the distinction between right and wrong). Ethics, on the other hand, refers to the series of rules provided to an individual by an external source (e.g. society). In this sense, ethics address questions about morality. The terms are plainly interrelated and, therefore, as has been done elsewhere (Kretchmar 1994), will be used interchangeably in this chapter.

In trying to debunk the myth of the character-building qualities of sport, Carr (1998) contended that involvement in sport is no more morally or ethically educative than any other pursuit or school subject that involves children learning to work cooperatively with others. The important caveat here is that, although it cannot, and should not, be assumed that ethical behaviour will be learnt through mere participation, the sporting environment may well be a place where it can happen. Perhaps the preliminary question to be addressed then, is whether coaches should be regarded as moral educators.

Echoing earlier work situating coaches as, above all, social pedagogues (Jones *et al.* 2004; Jones 2006), and in light of their often influential positions as 'significant others', we believe that coaches should qualify as agents of moral education. This, however, is a consequence of the particular professional role occupied and not because of the peculiar nature of physical activities. The ethical learning context then is one that is created and maintained by the coach, and not by virtue of it being defined as 'sport'. It is a case given recent support by Hardman and colleagues (Hardman *et al.* 2010; Hardman & Jones 2011), who argued that the coach should play a central role in sculpting the 'moral terrain within contemporary sport practices' (Hardman *et al.* 2010: 345). To fashion such an environment, coaches must first recognize that the ethical development of the athletes in their charge is a part of their role, and that, similar to other pedagogic professionals, they are 'employed to teach in a context of wider concerns about how to live and what to value in life' (Carr 1998: 131). They hold important positions (often being in *loco parentis*) with regard to caring for minors; a duty that, like it or not, carries significant ethical obligations and responsibilities. In this respect, a coach's moral responsibilities should extend beyond policing foul play, to the fostering and cultivation of certain virtues, which are directly implicated in the realization of the value of sport.

Having declared our stance that a coach should act as a moral guide, the purpose of this chapter is to explore how his or her subsequent behaviour can be representative of such a person. However, the aim is to go further than to merely document circumstances where ethical dilemmas could typically emerge for coaches, or to direct coaches to 'ready made' moral decisions as manifest in existing codes of conduct. Rather, it is to promote an understanding of the often complex and relative ethical dilemmas in sport, and how to better deal with them. In this respect, it builds on the earlier work of Sheilds and Bredemeier (1995) in seeking to extend current theory by discussing a framework useful for understanding, investigating and promoting ethical action in coaching. What informs our approach here is the need to avoid the individual–social dualism, which has so far over-simplified much of the work into coaches' ethical dilemmas, and to emphasize that social interactions and the cultural contexts in which they occur, affect moral behaviour. Moral dilemmas in coaching, therefore, are often better viewed as 'shades of grey', with a fine line of distinction, itself open to interpretation, existing between ethical and unethical behaviour.

However, this is not to advocate a totally relativist stance, thus abdicating responsibility for trying to live a life founded on good ethics. Indeed, following a discussion on the purpose of an ethical code and selected writings on ethical coaching issues, we introduce the work of scholars who utilize a Foucauldian lens to reflect upon and explore the challenges coaches face to practice in an ethical manner. The work of McNamee (1998, 2011) and Fernandez-Balboa (2000) are then used to provide a framework whereby coaches' ethical decisions are personalized and made accountable. Here, the case is made for a 'virtues' as opposed to a 'rules-based' approach, in order to secure lasting change in the moral climate within which coaching occurs (McNamee 1998, 2011). This places the onus firmly on coaches to carefully consider courses of action and their consequences in relation to ethical behaviour.

## ETHICAL CODES AND ETHICAL ISSUES IN COACHING

Sport is often thought to mirror society and its prevailing value trends. Additionally, because of its popularity, it is often considered a primary medium through which many young people come to learn about the core values of their culture. Having the potential to convey social values however, also encompasses the possibilities of transmitting undesirable as well as desirable ones (Sheilds & Bredemeier 1995). Consequently, some critics have claimed that sport impedes, as opposed to develops, 'good' character, and point to the many reports of unethical behaviour related to violence, parental brawls, aggressive nationalism, sexism, racism, homophobia and the illegal use of performance-enhancing drugs as evidence (Reddiford 1998). Such actions result from both adopting values that are counter to the norm, and of following desired social values too closely. This latter tendency has been termed 'positive deviance', which distorts ideals and leads to twisted value priorities where the ends are seen as justifying the means. Indeed, recent questions about the morality of sport have largely arisen from such deviance, as witnessed by a harsh competitive ethic driven by huge extrinsic rewards. It is a concern about the emphasis placed on the prize more than the process, which tends to blur 'our vision of the human and humane potential of sport' (Sheilds & Bredemeier 1995: 2). According to Kretchmar (1994), it is through such a distorted focus that we develop 'moral calluses' which, in turn, keep us from engaging with ethical questions of right and wrong at any meaningful level.

Ethical issues then, are very much a contemporary concern for coaches, with considerable attention having been given over recent years to appropriate and inappropriate coaching behaviour. This has been generated by a seemingly endless array of athletes failing drug tests, allied to some high-profile sexual harassment cases and allegations of child abuse (Fasting & Brackenridge 2009; Lyle 2002). Such abuses were starkly highlighted by the recent Pennsylvania State University scandal in the US, where a former defensive football coach was found guilty of sexually abusing boys over a 15-year period. Not only did this tragedy cover the obvious sexual wrongdoing, but also the intersecting vectors of institutional violence, media coverage of the event and its aftermath (Giardina & Denzin 2012), an institution's mission drift to market values (Giroux & Giroux 2012), and a general abuse of power. On a more localized level, the range of ethical issues likely to concern coaches was categorized by Lyle (2002) into interpersonal relationships, power differentials, social role (failure to maintain) and inappropriate goal setting. Although we recognize the limitations of such discrete classifications, because most coach–athlete relationships are characterized by differences in age, experience, knowledge and gender, as well as close physical contact, psychological dependency and emotional intensity, they are a potentially fruitful context within which unethical behaviour can occur. The resulting tension is heightened in elite sport, where both coaches and athletes constantly stretch the boundaries of permissible action in order to maximize performance. In many ways, this is hardly surprising as they are actively encouraged to do so by a performance-driven culture which values the development of an 'edge' over opponents.

As a consequence of the potential to break the rules, and in response to those who have done so, many sport-specific and generic ethical codes of conduct have been established. For example, in 1979, Martens and Seefeldt proclaimed the Bill of Rights for Young Athletes, while in 1992, the Council of Europe created the European Sports Charter, both of which arose from unease regarding issues of over-competitiveness in youth sport. These were followed, in 1998, by the Brighton Declaration on Women and Sport in response to concerns over gender equity, and in 1996 by the National Coaching Foundation's wide-ranging guide to ethical practice (Kidd & Donnelly 2000). Their value has been justified by the premise that by giving an outline of what is permissible and what is not, they demonstrate to everyone concerned what behaviours can be expected from coaches and other related personnel (Lyle 2002).

Such codes are considered to be 'issues-led' with general concerns related to cheating, drug taking and child abuse dominating the agenda. In doing so, they have historically focused on apparently inappropriate behaviour. Thus, such codes remind us of the social rules by which we should live, of what 'ought to be', by emphasizing what we should not do. Similarly, the rationales for writing such codes have been couched in negative terms; for example, 'to avoid arbitrariness', 'to highlight impermissible conduct', 'to impose clarity and simplicity in a confusing world', 'to set out standards and criteria by illustrating the need for them' and 'to provide a framework for resolving conflict' by confirming what is not allowable (McNamee 1998). It is a common-sense view of morality, expressed as a set of rules, which are designed to stop people from acting unfairly in the pursuit of their own interests to the detriment of others.

## FOUCAULT, ETHICS AND COACHING

In contrast to the given codes of conduct discussed above, recent work has utilized the writings and thoughts of Michel Foucault to examine concepts associated with ethical coaching. Foucault's (1992) conception of morality or the 'moral code' referred to a set of behavioural rules promoted by various regulatory agencies; that is, those values and behaviours endorsed and maintained by powerful social structures and interests. Foucault's moral code then, was grounded in a cultural relativism; that is, how we come to think of ourselves 'is the result of various (historical) discourses and practices' (Denison & Avner 2011:214). In doing so, he acknowledged that morals do not exist in a social or political vacuum. Within such a conceptualization, however, Foucault believed that ethical behaviour did not necessarily mean compliance with such rules. Rather, to act ethically involved a process of self-reflection and developing self-awareness in relation to the existing moral code. This comprised both critically reflecting on the code and on the unwritten moral conventions and values that dominate, as well as how the self responds to them, particularly in moments of tension (Pringle & Hickey 2010).

Advocates of this Foucauldian stance define ethical coaching as the act of engaging in constant critique of knowledge and assumptions, specifically in relation to existing power relations and associated 'regimes of truth' (Denison 2007; Denison & Avner 2011; Foucault 1978). Such conduct involves considerable social and cultural appraisal, and an ongoing commitment to problematize every aspect of practice, both official and unofficial (Pringle & Hickey 2010; Shogan 2007). Doing so, according to Foucault (1992), has the power to transform a person into an 'ethical subject'. This occurs through the individual increasingly recognizing how the personal is enmeshed into wider political and social structures. The point here, however, is not to paint a passive picture of individuals resigned to their collective fate, 'trapped within a coercive sporting framework' (Pringle & Hickey 2010: 134). Rather, it is to give a sense of personal possibility and agency; to help coaches reflect on and realize how much power they actually have to think of practicing in 'other' ways (Markula & Pringle 2006).

Taken as such, a Foucauldian reading of sports coaching can be seen to be as much about innovation as a given ethical way of acting. However, this should not be envisaged as only devising new solutions to old problems, as simply 'pouring old wine in a new bottle' (Denison & Avner 2011: 218). What Denison and Avner (2011) call for here is a 'new flavour' to coaching practice, consisting of reframing or resetting difficulties and dilemmas. For example, rather than viewing an athlete's sudden inability to run faster through a physiological or a 'not-training-hard-enough' lens, it can alternatively be seen as a need for greater practice stimulation which could, in turn, be delivered through an array of differing perspectives (e.g. physical, mental, rhetorical or social). Similarly, again as illustrated by Denison and Avner (2011), a coach could reconceptualize power as being relational, or part of a prevailing social exchange (Blau 1964), as opposed to being embedded in him or herself. Such a heightened sensitivity about how problems are initially framed holds the potential for coaches to 'practice better'; with coaching itself being reconsidered as an ongoing 'process of learning, discovery and self-transformation' (Denison & Avner 2011: 224). Although this Foucauldian insight gives us some direction in relation to the process of coaching ethically, given Foucault's post-structuralist stance, it only limitedly engages with resulting actions. Consequently, it is to this, and more specifically to the work of Mike McNamee (1998, 2011), that we now turn.

## PROBLEMATIZING ETHICS: MOVING TOWARD VIRTUES-BASED CONDUCT (McNAMEE 2011)

Existing codes of professional practice are generally accepted to be necessary documents. Yet, some scholars have questioned whether they are entirely relevant (Carr 1998; McNamee 1998, 2011; Reddiford 1998). The concerns do not relate to the aims of such codes, but to their inadequacy in dealing with the ethically complex coaching environment, and to their view of morality as a set of clear regulations to be unproblematically followed. The absolutist lines they draw have been criticized for leading us to 'right–wrong' binary thinking, and to the false belief that we are successfully addressing moral difficulties when we are not (McNamee 2011). Although their clarity is often unquestioned in terms of outlining 'proper' human relationships in the coaching environment, such codes have been accused of inviting us to think of ethical life in terms of a series of rigid obligations. McNamee (1998: 148) views them as being reflective of moral conservatism, 'a flight back to the language of moral certainty, of duties, and rules', and to a 'culture of blame and punishment for perceived wrongdoing' (1998: 151). Such regulations maintain that rule adherence is at the heart of ethical conduct, and imply that if coaches follow rules then they must have a sense of moral maturity. Although such codes have been useful in identifying those who are unethical in their practice, thus enabling punishment, needless to say, we believe there is more to the development of moral maturity than that. This was a theme developed in a recent edition of the journal *Sport, Education and Society* (2013), where the issue of coaches' touching behaviour was discussed. Here, echoing the work of Piper & colleagues (Piper & Smith 2003; Piper & Stronach 2008; Piper *et al.* 2012), Jones *et al.* (2013) argued against a defensive policy discourse which positions all physical contact by coaches as being morally dubious. Rather, in borrowing from Noddings (1984: 648), they contended that 'pedagogical practice (which could well involve touching) should depend on a sensitivity to a constellation of situational conditions', interpreted from the perspective of both coach and athlete. The general point made was that such issues regarding physical contact, (e.g. hugging in joyful celebration or a consoling arm around the shoulder of a distraught athlete) and related decisions, could never be managed by the technical. Indeed, Reddiford (1998) considered 'given' instructive codes had little, if any, effect on the moral motivation of those who seek to make unjust gains, and that their existence merely leads to more sophisticated ways of cheating. McNamee (2011) also questioned the need for rules that outline obvious wrongdoings. For example, he asked:

> Why do we need a rule concerning sexual harassment in a code of conduct? Is it not clear that such actions are wrong, so why do we need a code to tell us this? We can no more sexually harass our colleagues or athletes than any other person in the street. The rule tells us nothing new.
>
> (McNamee 2011: 31)

Alternatively, he believed that the situations responsible for unacceptable behaviour need to be understood in order to ensure (as best we can) that they are not repeated. A climate of conduct that precludes such actions should, therefore, be constructed not because a rule book tells us that unethical behaviours are wrong, but because we sincerely believe them to be so. Finally, McNamee (2011) criticized the rule-based approach as being, by its very nature, under-determined. That is, he questioned how a set of regulations can anticipate or describe all the actions that may be considered unethical, or tell everyone what to do and what not to do in all circumstances. Plainly, it cannot. Such codes appear to leave many questions unanswered as they are simply unable to write out the particularity of quandary (McNamee 2011), or to assist coaches in addressing the infinite variety of moral issues they constantly face, once they have avoided obvious wrongdoings. Even when attempts have been made to achieve absolute rule clarity in terms of a certain act, judgement is often still needed in interpreting a possible unethical behaviour as fitting a given category (Reddiford 1998). Such codes then, are regarded as being too simplified to have much impact on behaviour, whilst being inadequate in preparing coaches to answer the morally fundamental recurring question of 'what will I do here in the light of what I consider myself to be?' (McNamee 1998).

To further illustrate the problematic nature of ethical decision-making in coaching, consider the following scenario, which has been adapted from the work of McNamee (1998).

> I am the coach of a middle-distance 16-year-old athlete, Rhys, who shows great promise. His parents are keen and supportive, both of his involvement in sport and of me as a coach. They want him to be pushed to fulfil his potential. However, at present, he is struggling with his interval training and just can't reach the agreed targets ('agreed' in terms of me suggesting a training schedule, and him just nodding!). In all probability, this is because he has not kept to the strict training regime laid out for him. This afternoon, he is tired after the morning run and looks distinctly unenthusiastic about the session ahead. How should I react, what should I do? A multitude of questions run through my mind. Should I make him run more intervals on the track? Is he too tired to do them properly? Is he self-motivated enough to do them properly? Have I done enough to prepare him for the forthcoming championships? Were they really agreed goals? Have I pushed him too hard? Do I have to toughen him up? These are everyday, ethically tinged questions for a coach that fall well outside the rule-governed jurisdiction of proclaimed codes of conduct. There are no rules to guide me here. After a minute's consideration, I decide that the only way to get Rhys to succeed is to push him harder; after all, that is what his parents want. I warn him that if the next set of sprints is not completed within a certain time, 'we'll be here all night till they are'. I tell him to 'harden up' and to 'tough it out'. In response, through great effort, he completes the set satisfactorily. I feel vindicated. I have proven to him what he's capable of if he is only prepared to work hard enough. I chastise him for his lack of will power and remind him of others' sacrifices that allow him this opportunity to explore and exploit his talent. Rhys walks away in an angry sulk, his animosity towards me obvious. To a degree, I understand his reaction. However, I am comforted in the knowledge that I have simply complied with the wishes of his parents, whilst demonstrating to him what he is capable of. I have engaged in no obvious wrongdoing, and merely kept to the agreed training schedule.

Although no rules as enshrined in a code of conduct were broken in the scenario described, it could be argued that the trust between the athlete and the coach has been violated, or at the very least placed under considerable strain. On the other hand, perhaps it was exactly what Rhys needed to make him value his talent. Such dilemmas highlight the complexity of coaching's ethical dimension, and the inadequacy of rules-based codes of conduct to help coaches deal with it. As there are no certainties here, such an issue as how hard young athletes should be pushed must be left to the discretion of the coach. In short, we just have to trust the coach to make the right decisions. To help coaches in this regard, coach education programmes should include a personal ethical component grounded in real issues as described above. For McNamee (1998), the main consideration within such a situation should not be 'whether I have broken any rules', but 'what should I do in light of what's best for my athlete and the claims I make for myself as a good person'. The immediate issue for coaches then, becomes how to determine what is right from wrong; that is, 'What do I believe qualifies as ethical behaviour and what does not?' and 'What is this decision based on?'

In relation to the wider issue of what qualifies as ethical behaviour, a common view in Western culture is to believe that moral perspectives are strictly a matter of preference (Sheilds & Bredemeier 1995). Although we acknowledge the role of context in deciding the most appropriate course of action, as stated in the introduction to the chapter, to abandon the debate to total relativity would leave coaches with no pilot or rudder by which to charter rough and dangerous seas.

In attempting to grapple with such thorny issues and subsequently progress related thinking, some academics have turned to Aristotelian concepts (e.g. Hemmestad *et al.* 2010; Standal & Hemmestad 2011), and in particular to that of *phronesis* for help (a notion briefly introduced in Chapter 1). In contrast to *episteme* (theoretical knowledge) and *techne* (technical knowledge), *phronesis* is postulated as a form of 'practical wisdom'; what Hardman and Jones (2011: 4) define as 'the ability to do the right thing in the right way at the right time'. Although such a sentiment sounds fine in practice, on deeper inspection, the question still remains of what guides us to identify what the 'right' thing is in the first place (i.e. how we ought to act). In this respect, phronesis, or the phronetic position, advocates that such decisions be guided by a framework of value-rationality. To combat the inevitable following question of who decides on the values we should follow, the general answer lies within the given prevailing social norms. Hence, and largely in line with the Foucauldian perspective outlined earlier, the criteria for ethical coaching judgments should come from the moral collective climate or common view among the group or culture under study (Hemmestad *et al.* 2010). Indeed, according to Flyvbjerg (2006: 375), a principal advocate of phronesis, 'sociality and history are the only solid foundation we have, the only solid ground under our feet'. This was a point recently echoed by McNamee (2011), who stated that a 'good life' can only be lived against a given background of cultural and historical traditions.

Although value is placed on given communal and cultural expectations, in agreement with Loland (2011), we also believe that the best coaches go further than merely reproducing existing normative schemes. Consequently, even though respectful of social structures, such coaches are stimulated by the need to innovate and create (albeit within a moral framework); qualities which have inspired coaches to be variously conceptualized as 'social orchestrators' (Jones & Wallace 2005, Jones *et al.* 2013), 'sophists' (Malloy & Rossow-Kimball 2007) and 'enlightened generals' (Loland 2011). The key is not to search for the ever-elusive 'edge' or 'X factor' at any cost, but to consider novel strategies in light of certain socially valued virtuous behaviours (e.g. justice, fairness and empathy). Here then, coaches need the reflective abilities to weigh and consider the evidence in light of their insights and interpretations in reasonable ways. What is required is a principled reflection, informed by a virtuous perspective on coaching practice, for the good of all concerned. In the words of Hemmestad *et al.* (2010: 455);

> [i]t is a perception of a pedagogue as one who should always be alert to see what
> habits and attitudes are being created and reinforced to discriminate between

experiences that are educative and mis-educative, and to be able to judge which attitudes are conducive to continued growth.

Although we believe it provides considerable guidance, for some, the concept of phronesis continues to fall short of providing real direction about how a good coach should act (Vetlesen 2007). As with many of the notions discussed in this book, such clarity is, without doubt, beyond the concept. However, in a fluid and dynamic activity such as coaching, this is better than promising too much (Standal & Hemmestad 2011). Alternatively, phronesis demands engagement by coaches for what they think is correct action, taking into account normative moral values. Doing so, enables coaches to consider both what they would like to do and what they are able to do within given cultural constraints.

A further way forward in this regard, albeit from a more individualistic standpoint, is to accept that while certain principles form the core of ethical action, they can, and should, remain flexible. Rokeach's (1968) work can help our understanding here, as he believed there were different kinds of values that could be classified by 'regions of the person'. The metaphoric language was used to highlight that some beliefs are more critical and more central to self-identity than others. Consequently, it appears that we are able to have principles and to treat them flexibly, particularly the more weakly held ones, without being considered inconsistent. In this way, we can be adaptable whilst constantly upholding certain moral standards. Sheilds and Bredemeier (1995: 13) liken it to a 'belief tree', where the roots equate to core beliefs, the branches are the intermediate beliefs, while the 'peripheral beliefs, like leaves, drop off easily in response to the shifting winds of life'. A related point was also made by Hardman *et al.* (2010). Here, the case was presented that, although variability and changing circumstances are a natural part and parcel of coaching life, coaches nevertheless need to conduct their flexible decision-making within a bounded morally-aware framework. Doing so, allows 'sensitivity to nuance *and* consistency of purpose and principled action [to be] protected' (2010: 353).

The ethical flexibility implied above falls broadly in line with the call of McNamee (1998, 2011) to educate coaches through a 'virtues' as opposed to a rule-based approach, thus ensuring that contextual decision-making takes place as opposed to rigid rule adherence. For him, ethics and ethical conduct cannot simply be reduced to the idea of rule responsibility. What is important is to develop coaches who genuinely follow the spirit of the rules, and not those whose behaviour merely equates to rule observance, where this means the avoidance of rule-breaking actions (McNamee 1998). Such a stance builds on the work of Kohen (1994) who believed that the professional must be given discretion, grounded in a highly internalized sense of responsibility, in order to effect context-sensitive ethical action. This sense of responsibility is crucial to answer the earlier cited recurring internal questions of 'in what do we ground our interpretations of what is right?' and 'what makes us confident of the rightness of our decisions?'

According to McNamee (1998), the answer is in developing a deeper moral code to live by, one based on personal virtue. Such a code seems particularly applicable to the sporting domain where coaches' goals, and the accompanying decisions they take, are both relative and absolutist, and usually complex. Unavoidably then, due to the inability of rules-based codes of conduct to cover all eventualities, the coach becomes someone in whom an element of trust and discretion must be invested. The least athletes (and others) can expect is that decisions affecting them are taken within a good ethical framework of responsibility to performer, self, and sport (McNamee 1998). Hence, we need to develop coaches who respect the rules to ensure that the contest is a fair and enjoyable one, as opposed to not breaking them from a fear of being caught and punished (McNamee 1998). We need coaches who adhere to the spirit of the game and not bend the rules as much as possible, who do not substitute codes of conduct in place of their own virtuous development, or who fear creatively engaging with the range of options open to them over and above the rules laid out. In trying to give flesh to such considerations, the question remains, 'what kind of person should such a coach be?'

In answer, and in line with a virtues-based approach, we believe that coaches should be individuals who conduct their lives consciously as moral agents. Such an account differs somewhat from the 'professionalized' view of coaching as a time-bounded activity, having a clear start and finish as reflected in formal coaching settings. Although in practice, we realize that there are (or should be) temporal and spatial boundaries to coaching practice, in terms of personhood (i.e. one's moral behaviour), the job of coaching really allows for no 'time off task' (Hardman *et al.* 2010). This may mean that coaches need to understand that how they behave and what they say outside immediate coaching contexts may be just as influential as the imparted technical and tactical information given within them.

We are not advocating here that coaches need to be overly sensitive and self-conscious of how their behaviour affects others. However, they do need to recognize that the impact they may have on athletes extends in a multitude of ways through a range of situations. This was a point made in Jones's (2009) autoethnographical paper where coaching was positioned within 'an ethic of care' (Noddings 1984). The featured tale highlighted the need for coaches to operate in the world of small realities; to take responsibility for all their actions, which often have far reaching (and unintended) consequences. Coaches thus, are encouraged to not only consider those purposeful actions intended to have a transforming effect, but also those many micro behaviours which often have lasting outcomes (Jones 2009).

## PERSONALIZING COACHES' ETHICAL BEHAVIOUR

Despite much having been written about morality (or the lack of it) in sport and the widespread production of rules-based codes, most coach education programmes continue to devote minimal or very superficial attention to ethical issues (Fernandez-Balboa 2000). Consequently, the coaches who pass through such programmes are unaware of the complexity or even of the existence of much unethical behaviour, nor are they mindful of how to deal with it. What is more, because they are not encouraged to critically think about such issues, many do not see the relevance of doing so when asked. Fernandez-Balboa (2000) neatly encapsulated the prevailing attitude in this regard: a situation we would argue remains as relevant today as when originally conceptualized:

> Spending a lot of time on ethics does not really apply to me. You see, I am (or am going to be) a coach, and my role is to teach physical skills to help athletes improve.

I will help many people this way, and that is a good thing, isn't it? Besides, I think I am a pretty good person. I get on well with people and some of my friends are from different ethnic backgrounds.

(Fernandez-Balboa 2000: 134)

He goes on to say that such a line of argument denotes great naivety with regard to unethical behaviour and its damaging consequences. While we may think ourselves to be basically good and try to do what we consider to be the right thing, unless we critically examine our beliefs and actions, we could be teaching and practising unethical behaviours without being aware of it (Dodds 1993). This is because coaching does not exist in an interpersonal vacuum, but in 'socio-cultural systems which have inherent discriminations and values attached to them' (Fernandez-Balboa 2000: 135). It is through the subsequent process of socialization that we acquire certain beliefs about others and ourselves and what is considered appropriate behaviour. It is also a process from which we invariably learn concepts such as 'us' and 'them'; that is, a dichotomous way of thinking and how to manifest such notions in actions of acceptance or rejection (Eckert 1989). The resulting behaviour often leads to stereotyping, stigmatization and the humiliation of others (Fernandez-Balboa 2000). Despite good intentions then, without critically reflecting upon knowledges and actions, we always run the risk of perpetuating what is damaging and degrading (Fernandez-Balboa 2000; Jones 2000). This is precisely why it is not enough to simply list ethical issues and consider the work of morally educating coaches to be done. Rather, we must critically engage with such issues at the personal level, so that we can deal with them as they appear in practice. It is through such engagement that we can aspire to base our coaching on virtuous ethical practice, which we sincerely believe to be right, as opposed to given rules.

Despite rhetoric to the contrary, there persists a hugely disproportionate emphasis within coaching on physical as opposed to ethical development. Hence, the enhancement of skills continues to be more important than matters of bigotry, discrimination and abuse (Fernandez-Balboa 2000). This is evident in both coach education programmes and coaching practice. For example, notwithstanding superficial self-reflective exercises, how often in coach education programmes do we encourage coaches to critique and deconstruct the assumptions that they live by in their coaching? How often do we ask them to question the myths that surround sport (e.g. 'participation builds character') with regard to the unethical behaviours that such assumptions engender? Do not the traits that appear so valued in competitive sport (e.g. prowess, dominance, aggressiveness) go against much moral reasoning and social responsibility? Similarly, does not the presumed meritocratic nature of sport encourage coaches to treat their athletes as convenient commodities that can easily be disposed of once they no longer fulfil their purpose? To address such issues, we need to examine and question our logic and recognize that even when it is well-intentioned, uncritical coaching has problematic and dangerous implications (Fernandez-Balboa 2000). This is precisely why it is important to consider our actions in light of what we deem to be virtuous. Such behaviour should be based on the well-being and development of the 'other', in balance with a degree of self-respect and a strong awareness of the consequences actions bring. The reflection that takes place is important as it keeps us vigilant in relation to our sentiments and practices, and encourages us to constantly ask if what we do denies the rights, choices and potentialities of others in any way (Dodds 1993).

According to Fernandez-Balboa (2000) a direct way to address the potential that we have to act unethically, and thus to develop a more virtuous approach, is to follow the systematic steps devised by Johnson (1996). These involve:

- Admitting the possibility that we have prejudices;
- Making honest attempts to identify what they are;
- Identifying specific actions that reflect those prejudices;
- Seeking support from others who may be able to help us in overcoming them.

Such a process is aimed at making us realize the limitations of our thinking and to help us recognize that our view of 'truth' may not be the only version. To contextualize the process into the coaching context, the questions we could ask relate to those ethical issues important to us. For example:

- Do I give athletes a range of choices that are agreeable to them?
- Are my comments and actions considerate of others' beliefs and life experiences?
- Do the athletes I work with fear me? If so, why?
- Do they respect me? If so, why?
- How well do I actually know the athletes I work with as people? What evidence do I have on which to base that belief?
- What is my first reaction when an athlete makes a mistake?
- Do I include athletes in the decision-making process? If so, how? If not, should I?
- Do I take the time to learn the perspectives of others?
- 'Does my physical presence confer dominance?' (Fernandez-Balboa 2000: 140)
- How much power do I have over the athletes I work with?

By critically engaging with such questions, we can expose some of the 'common sense', everyday actions of normal life, which can lead to unethical behaviour, and so aspire to develop a virtues-based framework through which 'better' coaching can occur.

## CONCLUDING THOUGHTS

In relation to fighting unethical issues in coaching, we agree with Fernandez-Balboa (2000) who concluded that the battle can never be considered over. This is because, not only is there a great deal to confront in the outside world, but much also remains embedded and embodied in ourselves. Consequently, it is a process that is both private and public. As coaches, we have numerous opportunities to deal with many ethical dilemmas on a daily basis. Therefore, it is important that we learn to recognize such predicaments and problems both within others and ourselves, and be able to deal with them.

Finally, and particularly in relation to the issue of personal scrutiny, coaches must also accept that they often exist as role models for their athletes. This is because they largely set and direct the ethical outlook and agenda of the context; a point recently made by

Hardman *et al.* (2010) in arguing that both a moral dimension and an emulation process exist within coaching. Consequently, 'coaches should focus greater attention on the ethical implications of their actions, and how such behaviours are understood and impact upon those they wish to influence' (2010: 350). This not only requires sensitivity about what one considers fair, about human relations, social conventions and role obligations, but also the capacity to 'engage with an athlete's personal attempt at self construction and representation' (Hardman *et al.* 2010: 354). In conclusion then, if we accept that unethical behaviours are not natural but learned, and can permeate many areas of our lives, we can accept that through critical vigilance and reflection, there are ways to break the cycle and the 'traps of our own reasoning and conditioning' (Fernandez-Balboa 2000: 142).

## END-OF-CHAPTER TASKS

Consider and respond to some or all of the questions presented towards the end of the chapter as developed from the work of Johnson (1996) (which are reproduced below);

- Do I give athletes a range of choices that are agreeable to them?
- Are my comments and actions considerate of others' beliefs and life experiences?
- Do the athletes I work with fear me? Why?
- Do they respect me? Why?
- How well do I actually know the athletes I work with as people? What evidence do I have on which to base that belief?
- What is my first reaction when an athlete makes a mistake?
- Do I include athletes in the decision-making process? If so, how? If not, should I?
- Do I take the time to learn the perspectives of others?
- 'Does my physical presence confer dominance?' (Fernandez-Balboa 2000: 140);
- How much power do I have over the athletes I work with?

## REFERENCES

Blau, P.M. (1964). *Exchange and Power in Social Life.* New York: John Wiley and Sons.

Carr, D. (1998). What moral educational significance has physical education? A question in need of disambiguation. In M. McNamee & J. Parry (eds.) *Ethics and Sport.* London: E and FN Spon.

Denison, J. (2007). Social theory for coaches: A Foucauldian reading of one athlete's poor performance. *International Journal of Sport Science and Coaching,* 2: 369–383.

Denison, J. & Avner, Z. (2011). Positive coaching: Ethical practices for athlete development. *Quest,* 63: 209–227.

Dodds, P. (1993). Removing the ugly 'isms' in your gym: Thoughts for teachers on equity. In J. Evans (ed.) *Equality, Education and Physical Education.* London: Falmer Press.

Eckert, P. (1989). *Jocks and Burnouts: Social Categories and Identity in the High School*. New York: Teachers College Press.

Fasting, K. & Brackenridge, C. (2009). Coaches, sexual harassment and education. *Sport, Education and Society*, 14(1): 21–35.

Fernandez-Balboa, J-M. (2000). Discrimination: What do we know and what can we do about it? In R.L. Jones & K.M. Armour (eds.) *Sociology of Sport: Theory and Practice*. London: Longman.

Flyvbjerg, B. (2006). Making organization research matter: power, values and phronesis'. In S.R. Clegg, W.R. Nord & C. Hardy (eds.) *The Sage Handbook of Organization Studies*. London: Sage.

Foucault, M. (1978). *The History of Sexuality: An Introduction*. New York: Vintage Books.

Foucault, M. (1992). *The Use of Pleasure: History of Sexuality: Vol 2*. New York: Pantheon.

Giardina, M.D. & Denzin, N.K. (2012). Policing the Penn State crisis: violence, power, and the neoliberal university. *Cultural Studies <=> Critical Methodologies*, 12(4): 259–266.

Giroux, H.A. & Giroux, S.S. (2012). Universities gone wild: Big money, big sports, and scandalous abuse at Penn State. *Cultural Studies <=> Critical Methodologies*, 12(4): 267–273.

Hardman, A. & Jones, C.R. (2011) Introduction. In A. Hardman & C.R. Jones (eds.) *The Ethics of Sports Coaching*. London: Routledge.

Hardman, A., Jones, C.R. & Jones, R.L. (2010). Sports coaching, ethics and the virtues of emulation. *Physical Education and Sport Pedagogy*, 15(4): 345–359.

Hemmestad, L.B., Jones, R.L. & Standal, Ø.F. (2010). Phronetic social science: a means of better researching and analysing coaching? *Sport, Education and Society*, 15(4): 447–459.

Johnson, D.W. (1996). *Reaching Out: Interpersonal Effectiveness and Self-actualisation*, 6th edn. Needham Heights, MA: Allyn and Bacon.

Jones, R.L. (2000). Toward a sociology of coaching. In R.L. Jones & K.M. Armour (eds.) *The Sociology of Sport: Theory and Practice*. London: Addison Wesley Longman.

Jones, R.L. (2006). How can educational concepts inform sports coaching? In R.L. Jones (ed.) *The Sports Coach as Educator: Re-conceptualising Sports Coaching*. London: Routledge.

Jones, R.L. (2009). Coaching as caring (The smiling gallery): Accessing hidden knowledge. *Physical Education and Sport Pedagogy*, 14(4): 377–390.

Jones, R.L. & Wallace, M. (2005). Another bad day at the training ground: coping with ambiguity in the coaching context. *Sport, Education and Society*, 10(1): 119–134.

Jones, R.L., Armour, K.A. & Potrac, P.A. (2004). *Sports Coaching Cultures: From Practice to Theory*. London: Routledge.

Jones, R.L., Bailey J. & Santos, S. (2013). Coaching, caring and the politics of touch: a visual exploration. *Sport, Education and Society*, 18(5): 648–662.

Jones, R.L., Bailey, J. & Thompson, I. (2013). Ambiguity, noticing, and orchestration: Further thoughts on managing the complex coaching context. In P. Potrac, W. Gilbert & J. Denison (eds.) *The Routledge Handbook of Sports Coaching*, London: Routledge.

Kidd, B. & Donnelly, P. (2000). Human rights in sport. *International Review for the Sociology of Sport*, 35: 131–148.

Kohen, D. (1994). *The Ground of Professional Ethics*. London: Routledge.

Kretchmar, R.S. (1994). *Practical Philosophy of Sport*. Champaign, IL: Human Kinetics.

Loland, S.L. (2011). The normative aims of coaching: The good coach as an enlightened generalist. In A. Hardman & C.R. Jones (eds.) *The Ethics of Sports Coaching*. London: Routledge.

Lyle, J. (2002). *Sports Coaching Concepts. A Framework for Coaches' Behaviour*. London: Routledge.

Malloy, D.C. & Rossow-Kimball, B. (2007). The philosopher-as-therapist: The noble coach and self awareness. *Quest*, 59: 311–322.

Markula, P. & Pringle, R. (2006). *Foucault, Sport and Exercise: Power, Knowledge and Transforming the Self*. London: Routledge.

McNamee, M. (1998). Celebrating trust: virtues and rules in the ethical conduct of sport coaches. In M. McNamee & J. Parry (eds.) *Ethics and Sport*. London: E and FN Spon.

McNamee, M. (2011). Celebrating trust: Virtues and rules in ethical conduct of sports coaches. In A. Hardman & C.R. Jones (eds.) *The Ethics of Sports Coaching*. London: Routledge.

Noddings, N. (1984). *Caring: A Feminine Approach to Ethics and Moral Education*. Berkeley, CA: University of California Press.

Piper, H. & Smith, H. (2003). 'Touch' in educational and child care settings: Dilemmas and responses. *British Educational Research Journal*, 29(6): 879–894.

Piper, H. & Stronach, I. (2008). *Don't touch! The educational story of a panic*. London: Routledge.

Piper, H., Taylor, B. & Garratt, D. (2012) Sports coaching in risk society: no touch! no trust! *Sport, Education and Society*, 17(3): 331–345.

Pringle, R.G. & Hickey, C. (2010). Negotiating masculinities via the moral problematisation of sport. *Sociology of Sport Journal*, 27: 115–138.

Reddiford, G. (1998). Cheating and self-deception in sport, in M. McNamee & J. Parry (eds.) *Ethics and Sport*. London: E and FN Spon.

Rokeach, M. (1968). *Beliefs, Attitudes and Values*. San Francisco: Jossey-Bass.

Sheilds, D. & Bredemeier, B. (1995). *Character Development in Physical Activity*. Champaign, IL: Human Kinetics.

Shogan, D. (2007). *Sport Ethics in Context*. Toronto: Canadian Scholars' Press.

*Sport, Education and Society* (2013). 18(5).

Standal, Ø. & Hemmestad, L. (2011). Becoming a good coach: Coaching and phronesis. In A. Hardman & C.R. Jones, (eds.) *The Ethics of Sports Coaching*. London: Routledge.

Vetlesen, A.J. (2007). *Hva er etikk?* (What is ethics?). Oslo: Universitetsforlaget.

## CHAPTER 4

# Coaching as a (micro)political activity

## INTRODUCTION

> I've learnt that how you deal with the political side of the job can really impact upon how successful you can be as a coach … You can't do it without support. You need to recognise what relationships and interactions you have with people. The more you know about that side of things, the more you can do with your coaching knowledge and practical skills. It has certainly made me more thoughtful about how and why I engage with the people I work with.
>
> (Thompson *et al.* 2013: 11)

> It was great getting the job. A bit like a politician getting elected. Now I was in the position, I wanted to keep it. I also wanted to do what I thought was good for the club and the players. The only way to do that was to get the support of the 'big hitters' [most influential people] at the club. I had to do that if I was going to survive. I had to convince them, the electorate you might say, that what I had to offer was good for them. I had to persuade the players, board, and fans at the club. Not an easy task, and not something you coach education people often talk about on your courses!
>
> (Potrac & Jones 2009a: 565)

Scholars of coaching science have increasingly questioned the sanitized and functionalistic representation of coaching that has historically dominated the literature (e.g. Jones & Wallace 2005; Potrac & Jones 2009a 2009b; Potrac *et al.* 2013a). The suggestion that coaching is a linear and straightforward activity practiced in relation to bio-scientific, technical, and tactical knowledge and methods no longer appears to hold water. This is because a growing body of evidence (see Matthews *et al.* 2013; Potrac *et al.* 2013b; Purdy & Jones 2011, among others) has illustrated how coaching is essentially characterized by ideological diversity, poor coordination, and 'riven with actual or potential conflict' (Ball 1987: 19). Such inquiry has detailed how 'coaches work with a diverse range of individuals (such as athletes, assistants, consultants, and administrators), who may not only bring different traditions and goals to the workplace, but would also not hesitate to act on their beliefs if the opportunity arose to do so' (Potrac & Jones 2009b: 566). Similar to the everyday realities of organizational life in other settings (see Kelchtermans 2011; Kelchtermans & Ballet 2002a, 2002b; Buchanan & Badham 2008), obtaining, maintaining, and advancing the support or 'buy-in' from key contextual stakeholders arguably lies at the heart of a coach's endeavours (Jones *et al.* 2004; Jones *et al.* 2011; Purdy *et al.* 2013). Consequently, it is important for coaches to actively consider and reflect upon the ways in which their working relationships and accompanying interactions may influence the time, space and resources that are afforded to them, as well as the climate in which they seek to achieve their coaching goals.

This chapter aims to not only outline why we should consider coaches' work as inherently (micro)political in nature, but also to introduce some theoretical ideas and concepts that could be utilized to help our thinking about this particular feature of coaching. The chapter initially outlines the centrality of (micro)politics in everyday life. Attention subsequently shifts to exploring why coaches and key contextual stakeholders may engage in political actions. Following this, a brief overview of the (micro)political realities of practice evidenced in the coaching literature is provided. Finally, the chapter concludes by considering the utility of conceptualizing coaches as '(micro)political performers'.

## WHAT IS (MICRO)POLITICS?

According to Leftwich (2005: 101), politics is a 'timeless process which organizes and expresses the interaction of people, resources, and power'. He argued that politics consists of the three key interactive ingredients of people (who often have different ideas, interests, and preferences), power (which is the ability of an individual to achieve a desired outcome), and resources (which may be material or non-material in nature, and frequently scarce in terms of availability). Examples of material resources include physical objects such as land, money and equipment. In contrast, non-material resources can be facets such as time, status, support and opportunity (Leftwich 2005).

This definition of politics enables us to recognize how it is a generalized feature of social life that exists whenever two or more people engage in any form of collective activity in informal, formal, public or private settings (Leftwich 2005). In doing so, it challenges the popularly held view that politics is the limited preserve of public institutions, politicians and policymakers, with other aspects of social life (such as coaching) being seen as largely apolitical in nature (Leftwich 2005). In particular, Leftwich (2005: 107) reminds us that, given the social character of our existence, politics is not 'simply an unnecessary, temporary' or, indeed, a 'distasteful phenomenon that we could do without'. Instead, it is an 'absolutely intrinsic, necessary and functional feature of our social existence' (Leftwhich 2005: 107).

To illustrate his point regarding the pervasiveness of politics, Leftwhich (2005) used the example of two people riding a tandem who disagree about whether to turn left or right at a crossroads. He described how this situation encapsulates all of his key components of politics. For example, there are people (two of them in this case) with different interests and ideas about which way to go, resources in the form of the tandem (which is only capable of going in one direction), and power which may be determined by who is on the tandem. With regard to the latter he questioned,

> If a man and woman, what is the configuration of the power relations between them? If a parent and child, does the former decide in virtue of his or her status or authority? Or does he forgo that power in order to please the child, and does that transfer power to the child? Will age be a factor? If one person owns the tandem, does that or should that give her greater power over which way to go?
>
> (Leftwhich 2005: 104)

Equally, Leftwhich (2005) recognized that the two individuals may not differ over choice of direction but could disagree over when to stop and rest, or may complain about who is putting more or less effort into the riding of the tandem. There are perhaps two important messages to take from this example. The first is that 'the conflict of interests and ideas about how to use or distribute resources, in the context of different amounts of power, is what inevitably makes the activities to do with arranging the use or distribution of such resources so political' (Leftwhich 2005: 107). Secondly, such micro-level acts of conflict, negotiation and collaboration illustrate the extent to which politics permeates our everyday lives, be it at work or in recreational settings.

The examination of these micro-level political interactions in a variety of organizational contexts (e.g. schools, companies, universities and sports clubs) has given life to the study of micropolitics (Ball 1987; Blase 1991; Kelchtermans 2002a, 2002b; Lindle 1994). While no single definition of micropolitics is considered definitive, the most frequently utilized one is that developed by Blase (1991: 11):

> [m]icro-politics refers to the use of formal and informal power by individuals and groups to achieve their goals. In large part, political actions result from perceived differences between individuals and groups, coupled with a motivation to use power and influence and/or to protect ... Both co-operative and conflictive actions and process are part of the realm of micopolitics [while] the macro and the micro frequently interact.

According to Blase and Anderson (1995), the theoretical and empirical exploration of micropolitics did not begin until the 1980s, with such work being primarily conducted within education and management settings. Furthermore, on the rare occasion when micropolitical activity was acknowledged, it was often 'recast deliberately as poor climate, bad management, or an indicator of incompetence' on behalf of the individuals involved

(Lindle 1999: 2). The accompanying reluctance to recognize micropolitical aspects of organizational life is not only inconsistent with the experiences of many people, but has also stunted our understanding of its components and the interactions that occur between different stakeholders under varying circumstances (Leftwhich 2005; Lindle 1994).

Although the academic study of micropolitics has a relatively short history, it has undoubtedly provided some rich and constructive insights into the frequently turbulent nature of organizational life. For example, within the fields of education and management it has highlighted the limitations of viewing organizations as only consisting of coherent and cohesive social networks, where trust, openness, collaboration, and rationality dominate (Ball 1987; Buchanan & Badham 2008; Eilertsen *et al.* 2008; Malen & Cochran 2008; Wallace 2003). Instead, such work has illuminated how organizations may be vulnerable to the often-conflicting ideologies of those individuals that comprise them and, as such, 'competition may sit alongside competition' with acts of informal backstaging (and sometimes backstabbing) often supporting public action (Buchanan & Badham 2008: 2).

While the emphasis of micropolitical inquiry is clearly about exploring individuals' interests, behaviours and interactions, it is important to recognize that such action does not exist in a social or cultural vacuum. That is, a symbiotic relationship exists between micropolitics and the wider societal (or macro) context in which it occurs (Taylor-Webb 2005, 2006, 2008). In emphasizing this point, Lukes (1977: 29) argued that organizational life:

> can only properly be understood as a dialectic of power and structure, a web of possibilities for agents, whose nature is both active and structured, to make choices and pursue strategies within given limits ... Any standpoint or methodology which reduces that dialectic to a one-sided consideration of agents without ... structural limits or structures without agents, or which does not address the problem of their interrelation, will be unsatisfactory.

Recent inquiry in the sociology of education has highlighted the interrelationship between neo-liberal values, macro-level educational policy, and the ways in which managers, administrators and teachers variously seek to enforce, support, resist or begrudgingly comply with particular strategic-related processes and objectives within their respective school settings (Ball 2000, 2003; Taylor-Webb 2008). Such accounts serve to illustrate Deleuze and Guattari's (1988: 213) assertion that 'everything is political, but every politics is simultaneously a macropolitics and a micropolitics'.

## WHY MIGHT (MICRO)POLITICAL ACTIVITY OCCUR IN COACHING SETTINGS?

In addition to understanding what (micro)political action is, it is perhaps also useful to reflect on the reasons why social actors (e.g. athletes, coaches and administrators, among others) may engage in such actions. Ball (1987) challenged us to consider how issues of goal diversity and ideological disputation regarding organizational philosophy, practices, and/or the deployment of resources may lead individuals (or groups) to engage in skilled strategic action. The purpose of such political activity is often cited as being to gain situational jurisdiction, whilst containing varying levels of conflict, collaboration and negotiation. Similarly, Kelchtermans (2009, 2011) suggested that (micro)political action is frequently the result of behaviour within an organizational setting which often revolves around an individual striving for what he or she considers desirable working conditions. Desirable working conditions, he argued, can be understood both in terms of an individual's effectiveness in achieving outcomes, and of experiencing work-place satisfaction in a personal sense. The notions of goal diversity and ideological disputation among coaches, athletes, and administrators, as well as the related desire to achieve effective and satisfying working conditions, will be explored in the following section of this chapter.

Within this micropolitical framework, Kelchtermans and colleagues (Kelchtermans 2007, 2009; Kelchtermans & Ballet 2002a, 2002b) also identified a variety of interests that might influence (micro)political action. These include self-interests, material interests, cultural-ideological interests, and, finally, socio-professional interests. While we consider each of these interests in turn for analytical purposes, it is important to recognize that they frequently intertwine within the context of an individual's experiences and understandings of everyday organizational life. According to Kelchtermans and Ballet (2002a, 2002b), self-interests primarily relate to issues of professional self-understanding and social recognition in the workplace. They noted that (micro)political action can occur when an individual's self-understanding, inclusive of the facets of self-esteem (i.e. the individual's appreciation of his or her actual job performances), self-image (i.e. the way an individual typifies his or her self in a role), job motivation (the motives that make a person want to take up a particular role, remain in it, or leave it), future perspective (i.e. a person's expectations about his or her future career trajectory), and task perception (i.e. a person's views on the tasks that should be performed in order to fulfil a particular role in a positive fashion), is believed to be threatened. Such issues have been increasingly recognized in the coaching literature, especially in terms of an individual seeking to have his or her competencies recognized by respective significant others (Cushion & Jones 2006; Jones 2006; Potrac & Jones, 2009a).

Material interests refer to the ability to obtain equipment, infrastructure, funds, time and opportunities to secure personal goals and aspirations. In a coaching context, this could relate to a coach's ability to access materials that provide a good (and satisfying) job performance. Kelchtermans (2007, 2009) noted that obtaining such resources is often a significant feature of (micro)political activity, as failure to do so can result in feelings of vulnerability. This vulnerability cannot only stem from a coach's belief that he or she is not able to produce the desired level of performance, but also concern that they are regarded negatively by various significant others (e.g. athletes, administrators, other coaches and support staff, and parents).

With regards to material interests, Kelchtermans and Ballet (2002a, 2002b) highlighted how the energy teachers invested in planning lessons and developing creative pedagogical materials were not only driven by concerns of pupil learning, but also 'for strategic reasons of becoming visible as competent, creative, and hardworking professionals' (Kelchtermans & Ballet 2002b: 112). Similarly, a coach's use of particular pedagogical methods and materials could be used to serve wider (micro)political purposes in addition to facilitating athlete learning. While such notions have been hinted at by Potrac and Jones (2009a, 2009b), the exploration of the symbolic meaning attached to pedagogical materials remains considerably unexplored and thus a potentially fruitful topic for future study.

Kelchtermans (2007, 2009) considers organizational interests to consist of the procedures, positions, roles, contract conditions, and formal task descriptions in any organization. As an example, Kelchtermans and Ballet (2002a, 2002b) highlighted how moving from a temporary contract to a permanent contract was frequently at the heart of neophyte teachers' (micro)political concerns. Their work provides examples of teachers acting strategically to achieve this particular outcome. Here, teachers' actions included taking on extra duties to impress their superiors, as well as avoiding any conflicts with existing staff. Although micropolitical action in relation to such interests has received scant attention within coaching, Gale (2014) did illustrate how community coaches engaged in efforts to ensure that employment contracts were renewed and, when and where opportunity permitted, access to more senior positions was secured. Equally, Potrac *et al.* (2013a) provided an example of a coach choosing not to challenge his superior over a perceived injustice for fear of damaging his chances of continued employment.

Cultural-ideological interests are principally concerned with 'the more or less explicit norms, values, and ideas' acknowledged in an organization as 'legitimate and binding elements of culture' (Kelchtermans & Ballet 2002b: 114). Kelchtermans (2007, 2009) argued that these types of interests frequently relate to the issue of more or less collectively shared ideas about 'good education' and, by extension, 'good teaching'. While there are legal prescriptions about issues relating to staffing, funding and curriculum, the goals, values and priorities of everyday life in schools can be open to negotiation and definition. For example, Kelchtermans (2007, 2009) noted how cultural-ideological contestation occurred when the teachers observed a disjuncture between their own personal motivations, beliefs, and task perceptions and those of the dominant school culture. In terms of coaching, this closely relates to the (micro)political action that may occur as a consequence of an individual's subscription, or resistance, to the dominant discourses regarding 'good coaching'.

Finally, socio-political interests relate to the quality of interpersonal relationships that an individual has in, and around, an organization (Kelchtermans & Ballet 2002b). Interestingly, Kelchtermans and Ballet (2002b) highlighted how good working relationships with colleagues was important to neophyte teachers, who considered opportunities to discuss pedagogical issues, share questions and concerns, as well as collaborating with colleagues as vital to their professional success and development. Socio-professional interests then appear significant in teachers' decision-making and subsequent actions, with many describing their readiness to endure unconstructive conditions (i.e. a conflict of cultural-ideological interests) rather than risk troubled relationships with colleagues. Similar lines of thought could be used to understand the value individuals attach to interpersonal relationships in coaching, and the degree, if at all, these relationships are managed alongside other pressing, sometimes conflicting, issues (Potrac & Jones 2009a, 2009b).

While the works of Ball (1987) and Kelchtermans and colleagues (Kelchtermans 2009; Kelchtermans & Ballet 2002a, 2002b) are useful in terms of considering 'how' and 'why' individuals engage in (micro)political actions in coaching settings, our understanding may be enhanced by considering such behaviour in relation to wider cultural trends. For example, Potrac *et al.* (2013a) made sense of the 'gritty' realities of coaching, inclusive of various acts of uncaring and selfish behaviour through Roderick's (2006a, 2006b) writings on the culture of football and Bauman's (1996, 2000, 2003, 2007) theorizing on *Liquid Times*. Here, a coach's actions were not only understood to have occurred in a sporting subculture characterized by insecurity and constant scrutiny (Roderick 2006a, 2006b), but also in relation to wider norms reflective of 'individualisation, uncertainty, precariousness and privatization' (Potrac *et al.* 2013a: 86; Bauman, 2007). With regard to the latter, Bauman (2007) argued that our everyday lives have been increasingly subject to an erosion of human bonds, with self-interest and the maintenance of individual status and standing being at the forefront of social life. The end result is 'people living separately side by side' (Bauman 1996: 18). In a similar vein, Gale (2013) contextualized community coaches' understandings of the (micro)politics they encountered, and participated in, within their respective work places in relation to a variety of neo-liberal, performance-driven policy directives (Ball 2003; Houlihan & Green 2009). In particular, her research illustrated how participant coaches' understood the funding mechanisms to have been realigned so that only successful performance in terms of 'hitting' increasingly challenging KPIs was rewarded. This resulted in a climate of increased insecurity, which, perhaps unsurprisingly, led coaches to practice in a defensive and protective manner.

## (MICRO)POLITICAL ACTION IN COACHING: AN UNFOLDING STORY

During the last decade, research in sports coaching has increasingly illustrated the role of (micro)political action in practice (e.g. Cassidy & Kidman 2010; Consterdine *et al.* 2013; Potrac *et al.* 2013a; Purdy & Jones 2011; Purdy *et al.* 2013). Much of this work has focused on coaches' efforts to 'win-over' the athletes they work with. For example, the elite coaches interviewed by Jones *et al.* (2004) used a variety of strategies to gain athlete support for their respective coaching agendas and programmes. These included using 'white lies', presenting humorous and friendly personas, and engaging in constant 'face-work' (See Chapter 7 The coach as a pedagogical performer). Similarly, Potrac *et al.* (2002) and Cushion and Jones (2006) described how practitioners felt obliged to act in 'coach appropriate ways'. Not only did they perceive such behaviour to be an occupational demand, but also felt that to do otherwise would be to risk losing the respect of the players they coached. Equally, Gale (2014) provided insights into community coaches' understandings of the face-work and emotional labour undertaken in their quest to obtain favourable feedback from those they coached. The coaches here not only felt that high ratings represented a major means by which their 'effectiveness' was judged, but, relatedly, shared a view that these evaluations had significant implications for their continued employment. For example:

> Our efforts do get monitored from numbers going through the sessions and customer satisfaction. I am aware that people will get asked how my service is; therefore, it is

something that you are always aware of ... If we don't get the numbers or the right levels of customer satisfaction, then we risk having our hours cut and I can't afford that to happen.

(Gale, 2013; 226–227)

This is not to say that the coaches cited above peddled false impressions without conscience. Rather, it reflected their understandings of the ways in which social power is exercised. Indeed, failure to obtain and maintain the support of the athletes or participants they worked with was seen as tantamount to failure.

In a related vein, Potrac and Jones (2009a) provided an example of a coach dealing with vociferous resistance from a senior and influential player in a semi-professional football team. Here, the coach described how he initially avoided engaging in direct retaliatory action and, instead, focused on manipulating situations that would result in him being accepted and supported by the majority of the players. Having initially failed to win-over the resistant player, the coach explained how he set about systematically recruiting a small cadre of supportive players, as well as purposefully engineering training situations that publicly exposed the resistant player's shortcomings. The result was a reduction in the latter's status and standing among other players and members of the coaching staff.

In addition to highlighting the strategic and (micro)political actions of coaches, such inquiry has also shed light on the ways in which athletes choose to resist coaches' authority and methods. Purdy and colleagues (Purdy *et al.* 2008; Purdy *et al.* 2009; Purdy & Jones 2011) provided examples of rowers opposing what they felt were poor coaching practices. Such resistance included openly challenging coaches, the use of general scorn and a derogatory nickname for one coach in particular, informal but regular complaints to senior club administrators, as well as the withdrawal of best effort in training sessions. The flowing journal entry illustrates an example of such action.

*Journal Entry: February 2015*
I have to admit that I was deliberately awkward at practice this morning. When coxing the eight she [the coach] asked me to switch from the drill I was doing to another. I was still mad at her for telling me that I'd have to trial for my seat, but there was something about her tone that put me off. She was barking orders, but she has hardly been coaching us all week. Why should we suddenly listen to her? ... I kept going, ignoring her request. After a few strokes she yelled at me again to switch drills. I stared at Matt, who was stroking the boat. He gave me a knowing grin, I nodded my head, and counted five more strokes before I switched the drill. And for those five strokes there was nothing she could do. She could yell until she was going blue in the face, I wasn't going to give in and, from Matt's grin, I knew the crew would support me. Today, I wanted control. I wanted to show her that she couldn't run everything. It was our showdown and for five short strokes I felt I had won.

(Purdy *et al.* 2008: 327)

Similar practices were illustrated in Cushion and Jones' (2006) study of a coaching culture in elite youth football. While the players here were not as vocal or as daring as the rowers in Purdy *et al.*'s (2008) paper, they also sometimes chose to withdraw best effort as a means of exercising some – albeit limited – control over what they considered to be a harsh coaching environment.

More recently, Potrac *et al.* (2013a) explored the sometimes competitive, calculating, and uncaring relationships that can exist between coaches who are required to work together. This study sought to delve beneath the functionalistic portrayal of collegiality by considering how such working relationships may be influenced by each coach's 'motivations, goals, fears, and wishes to … generally keep a job' (Potrac *et al.* 2013a: 83). In particular, they unearthed the individualized nature of a particular coach's thinking regarding his career goals, as well as related efforts to advance status within a 'ruthless' coaching environment characterized by low level job-security. Here, the coach described how he utilized a number of reactive and proactive strategies as well as his perceptions related to being on the receiving end of other coaches' (micro)political actions. For example:

> I stood, arms folded, on the sideline while Steve led the players through a passing activity. I'd noticed that the practice was incorrectly set-up and that it would soon grind to a halt. The practice was flawed. A part of me wanted to let him know, so he could avoid the 'crash'. I didn't though. As anticipated, the session didn't work. The players seemed confused. Everyone looked at Steve. He was silent, unable to comprehend the dysfunction. I saw a chance … 'I can sort this out' I offered whilst curtailing my enthusiasm at the unfolding situation. I explained to the players where they should be for the exercise to work. But that wasn't enough. Calmly and with ruthless calculation, I pulled the trigger adding 'It was always going to fail with that set-up. It never had a chance of working'. It was a low shot. Sorry, Steve, but you know that's just how it is. I turned to him, 'They're all yours now, mate'. Steve continued but not with his usual confidence. His body language said it all; flat and fragmented.
>
> (Potrac *et al.* 2013a: 82)

Purdy *et al.* (2013) illustrated the notion of (micro)political conflict between coaches and administrators by utilizing ethnographic fiction to illustrate the dynamics of trust and distrust in coaching settings. The paper focused on the tensions and dilemmas a coach faced as he attempted to navigate a social terrain that was comprised of, and subject to, the conflicting philosophies, demands, and agendas of individual coaches, players, and administrators. For example:

> The game had finished in a 2-2 draw … Rather than accompany the team into the dressing room straight after the game, as was my usual practice, I had to pop up to the stadium lounge/viewing area to thank the two university students who had video-taped the game for me to watch and digest in the following days. The last thing I expected to see was the Club Chairman loudly complaining of the 'substandard coaching!' 'all this 4-3-3 stuff is a load of bollocks!' Not only were his comments clearly audible to his colleagues at the table but to just about all the parents and other people in the room. We looked at each other for a few seconds, and then we both

continued with our business as if nothing had happened. However, for those few seconds our eyes met, I knew we were confirming what we already felt and knew. We don't like or trust each other ... Regardless of the results, I came to the conclusion that he was looking forward to ending my tenure as head coach after the tournament. If nothing else, it made me want to do well with and for the team. I had to do well to protect my reputation.

(Purdy *et al.* 2013: 314)

Finally, in this section, it is important to recognize the contribution of Garratt, Piper and Taylor (Garrat *et al.* 2013; Piper *et al.* 2013a; Piper *et al.* 2013b; Piper, Taylor & Garratt 2012), which illustrated the (micro)politics surrounding the notion of touch and related behaviours (such as being alone with athletes) in coaching practice. This work illuminated some of the ways in which coaches adopt defensive stances on touch in order to maintain positive coaching relationships, as well as protect their respective careers (Piper *et al.* 2012). In particular, they argued that the dominant discourses, moral panic, and related policy measures regarding child protection have increased the scrutiny and surveillance which coaches are subjected to. Drawing upon Foucault's theorizing, they reasoned that 'the guidelines and training stemming from the dominant discourse, for the most part initiated by the NSPCC's Child Protection in Sport Unit, create an environment in which many coaches and PE teachers are confused and fearful, and consequently unsure of how to *be* around the children and young people they teach and coach' (Piper *et al.* 2013a: 583). The following cites a contextual example taken from an interview with a female swimming coach:

Her child came out of the water after a lesson and had marks on her tummy and [the mother] thought this student [Coach] had been responsible for this in some way. It turns out that he wasn't, and she'd [the child] done something at school but she [the parent] reported the student ... and the [University] Dean heard about it and the student was suspended from uni for a while, it was all investigated by the Police ... and in the end the school phoned up and said that she [the child] had fallen down ... this bruising was from school. But this poor student though, has now got this on his academic record, being suspended for a term, and he wanted to go into teaching ... and he couldn't go into teaching even though he was proved innocent.

(Piper *et al.* 2012: 339)

Although the selected examples presented in this chapter largely emphasize conflict and problematic issues (rather than those of negotiation and collaboration), we are certainly not advocating that coaching is only characterized by political strife and dispute. Indeed, Fry (1997) shows us how political actions can also be constructive in nature and outcomes. Nevertheless, by illustrating some of the grittier aspects of coaching, the intention here was to illustrate how working with other people may not always be the exclusively unifying, functional, and convergent activity that it has often been portrayed to be in the coaching literature.

## CONCLUDING THOUGHTS

In concluding this chapter, we encourage readers to consider the degree to which coaches will, in all likelihood, be required to engage in a variety of proactive and reactive micro-political actions. These may include gaining support from contextual stakeholders (e.g. athletes, fellow coaches, administrators and parents), and persuading them of the merits of a particular coaching agenda and philosophy and, relatedly, dealing with resistance from one or more of these parties. Political actions could also stretch to negotiating access to resources required to achieve effective working conditions. This dynamic and fluid process of forging and re-forging alliances and working relationships is likely to entail considerable 'face-work' as well as an ability to read and interpret the (micro)political nature of a coaching environment (Potrac & Jones 2009a). Indeed, coaches' successes or failures, however they are determined, may be closely related to their capacity to write themselves into social landscapes that are comprised of various degrees of ambiguity, pathos, struggles of interest, and processes of power (Jones & Wallace 2005; Jones *et al.* 2013; Potrac & Jones 2011).

Finally, it is also perhaps worth highlighting how a coach's engagement in (micro) political activity may be a thoroughly emotional affair (see also Chapters 6 and 7 for further discussion). Indeed, in attempting to navigate the challenges, opportunities and dynamics of context, coaches may experience a variety of strong emotions, both positive and negative (Potrac *et al.* 2013a, 2013b; Potrac & Marshall 2011). These may include joy, satisfaction, guilt, anger and fear. Equally, in their relationships with others, coaches may also need to consider which emotions can be shown or should remain hidden, as well as the degree to which they should be displayed (Potrac *et al.* 2013a, 2013b; Potrac & Marshall 2011). Consequently, the emotions a coach shows, or hides are important aspects of the (micro)political engagements with athletes, assistants, administrators and parents (Nelson *et al.* 2014). Unfortunately, one of the shortcomings of the coaching literature at the time of writing is the limited consideration given to the ways in which 'emotion and cognition, self and context, ethical judgment and purposeful activity are intertwined in the complex reality of coaching' (Potrac *et al.* 2013: 243). This is certainly something that we and, hopefully, other coaching scholars will seek to address in the continued quest to develop a more complete and multi-layered understanding of coaching.

## END-OF-CHAPTER TASKS

Before answering the questions below, you should read this chapter and at least one of the readings associated with it. Having completed the readings, watch the *Remember the Titans* movie and consider the questions below. Equally, you may also wish to consider these questions within a sporting setting of your choice (e.g. amateur netball, high performance track and field athletics).

1 Identify the key individuals and groups that had an influence on the coach's practice, environment, and the resources available to him. Describe the actual and

potential impact that these people might have upon the coaching environment. (Link your response to the readings).

2 Describe and discuss the different strategies that the coach used in an effort to access required resources and ensure that different individuals and groups bought into his coaching programme. What did you think the coach did well? What would you have done differently if you were the coach? When? How? Why? What would you have avoided doing? When? Why? (Make links from what you have read to your thoughts, choices, and actions).

## REFERENCES

Ball, S. (1987). *The Micro-politics of the School*. London: Methuen.

Ball, S. (2000). Performativities and fabrications in the education economy: Towards the performative society? *The Australian Educational Researcher*, 27(2): 1–23.

Ball, S. (2003). The teacher's soul and the terrors of performativity. *Journal of Education Policy*, 18(2): 215–228.

Bauman, Z. (1996). *Alone Again: Ethics After Certainty*. London: Demos.

Bauman, Z. (2000). *Liquid Modernity*, Cambridge: Polity Press.

Bauman, Z. (2003). *Liquid Love: On the Frailty of Human Bonds*. Cambridge: Polity Press.

Bauman, Z. (2007). *Liquid Times: Living in an Age of Uncertainty*. Cambridge: Polity Press.

Blase, J. (1991). *The Politics of Life in Schools: Power, Conflict, and Cooperation*. Newbury Park, CA: Corwin Press.

Blase, J. & Anderson, G. (1995). *The Micropolitics of Educational Leadership: From Control to Empowerment*. New York, NY: Teachers College Press.

Buchanan, D. & Badham, R. (2008). *Power, Politics, and Organizational change: Winning the Turf Game*. London: Sage.

Cassidy, T. & Kidman, L. (2010). Initiating a national coaching curriculum: A paradigmatic shift? *Physical Education and Sport Pedagogy*, 15(3): 307–322.

Consterdine, A., Newton, J. & Piggin, S. (2013). 'Time to take the stage': A contextual study of a high performance coach. *Sports Coaching Review*, 2(2): 124–135.

Cushion, C. & Jones, R.L. (2006). Power, discourse, and symbolic violence in professional youth soccer: The case of Albion Football Club. *Sociology of Sport Journal*, 23(2): 142–161.

Deleuze, G. & Guattari, F. (1988). *A Thousand Plateaus: Capitalism and Schizophrenia*. New York, NY: Bloomsbury Publishing.

Eilertsen, T.V., Gustafson, N. & Salo, P. (2008). Action research and the micropolitics in schools. *Educational Action Research*, 16(3): 295–308.

Fry, J. (1997). Dealing with the powers that be. *Sport, Education and Society*, 2(2): 141–162.

Gale, L. (2013). Community coaches' experiences of practice: A narrative biographical study, unpublished PhD thesis, University of Hull, United Kingdom.

Gale, L. (2014). The everyday realities of community sports coaching, unpublished PhD thesis, University of Hull, United Kingdom.

Garratt, D., Piper, H. & Taylor, B. (2013). 'Safeguarding' sports coaching: Foucault, genealogy and critique. *Sport, Education and Society*, 18(5): 615–629.

Goffman, E. (1959). *The Presentation of Self in Everyday Life*. London: Penguin.

Houlihan, B. & Green, M. (2009). Modernization and sport: The reform of Sport England and UK Sport. *Public Administration*, 87(3): 678–698.

Jones, R. (2006). Dilemmas, maintaining 'face' and paranoia: An average coaching life. *Qualitative Inquiry*, 12(5): 1012–1021.

Jones, R.L. & Wallace, M. (2005). Another bad day at the training ground: Coping with ambiguity in the coaching context. *Sport, Education and Society*, 10(1): 119–134.

Jones, R., Armour, K. & Potrac, P. (2004). *Sports Coaching Cultures: From Practice to Theory*. London: Routledge.

Jones, R., Potrac, P., Cushion, C. & Ronglan, L.T. (2011). *The Sociology of Sports Coaching*. London: Routledge.

Jones, R., Bailey, J. & Thompson, A. (2013). Ambiguity, noticing, and orchestration: Further thoughts on managing the complex coaching context. In P. Potrac, W. Gilbert & J. Dennison (eds.) *The Routledge Handbook of Sports Coaching*. London: Routledge.

Kelchtermans, G. (2007). Macropolitics caught up in micropolitics: The case of the policy on quality control in Flanders (Belgium). *Journal of Education Policy*, 22(4): 471–491.

Kelchtermans, G. (2009). Career stories as gateway to understanding teacher development. In M. Bayer, U. Brinkkjær, H. Plauborg & S. Rolls (eds.) *Teachers' career trajectories and work lives*. The Netherlands: Springer.

Kelchtermans, G. (2011). Vulnerability in teaching: The moral and political roots of a structural condition. In C. Day & J. Lee (eds.) *New Understandings of Teacher's Work*. The Netherlands: Springer.

Kelchtermans, G. & Ballet, K. (2002a). Micropolitical literacy: Reconstructing a neglected dimension in teacher development. *International Journal of Educational Research*, 37: 755–767.

Kelchtermans, G. & Ballet, K. (2002b). The micropolitics of teacher induction: A narrative-biographical study on teacher socialization. *Teaching and Teacher Education*, 18(1): 105–120.

Leftwhich, A. (2005). The political approach to human behaviour: People, resources and power. In A. Leftwhich (ed.) *What is politics?* Cambridge: Polity Press.

Lindle, J. (1999). What can the study of micropolitics contribute to the practice of leadership in reforming schools? *School Leadership and Management*, 19(2): 171–178.

Lukes, S. (1977). *Essays in Social Theory*. London: Macmillan.

Malen, B. & Cochran, M.V. (2008). Beyond pluralistic patterns of power: Research on the micropolitics of schools. In B. Cooper, J. Cibulka & L. Fusarelli (eds.) *Handbook of Education Politics and Policy*. London: Routledge.

Matthews, N., Fleming, S. & Jones, R. (2013). Sociology for coaches. In R. Jones & K. Kingston (eds.) *An Introduction to Sports Coaching*, 2nd edn. London: Routledge.

Nelson, L., Potrac, P., Gilbourne, D., Allanson, A., Gale, L. & Marshall, P. (2014). Thinking, feeling, acting: The case of a semi-professional soccer coach. *Sociology of Sport Journal*, 19(1): 19–40.

Piper, H., Garratt, D. & Taylor, B. (2013a). Child abuse, child protection, and defensive 'touch' in PE teaching and sports coaching. *Sport, Education and Society*, 18(5): 583–598.

Piper, H., Garratt, D. & Taylor, B. (2013b). Hands off! The practice and politics of touch in physical education and sports coaching. *Sport, Education and Society*, 18(5): 575–582.

Piper, H., Taylor, B. & Garratt, D. (2012). Sports coaching in risk society: No touch! No trust! *Sport, Education and Society*, 17(3): 331–345.

Potrac, P. & Jones, R. (2009a). Micro-political workings in semi-professional football coaching. *Sociology of Sport Journal*, 26: 557–577.

Potrac, P. & Jones, R. (2009b). Power, conflict and co-operation: Towards a micro-politics of coaching. *Quest*, 61: 223–236.

Potrac, P. & Jones, R. (2011). Power in coaching. In R. Jones, P. Potrac, C. Cushion & L.T. Ronglan (eds.) *The Sociology of Sports Coaching*. London: Routledge.

Potrac, P. & Marshall, P. (2011). Arlie Russell Hochschild: The managed heart, feeling rules, and emotional labour: Coaching as an emotional endeavour. In R. Jones, P. Potrac, C. Cushion & L.T. Ronglan (eds.) *The Sociology of Sports Coaching*. London: Routledge.

Potrac, P., Jones, R. & Armour, K. (2002). 'It's all about getting respect': The coaching behaviours of a top-level English football coach. *Sport, Education and Society*, 7(2): 183–202.

Potrac, P., Jones, R., Gilbourne, D. & Nelson, L. (2013a). 'Handshakes, BBQs, and bullets': self-interest, shame and regret in football coaching. *Sports Coaching Review*, 1(2): 79–92.

Potrac, P., Jones, R., Purdy, L., Nelson, J. & Marshall, P. (2013b). Coaches, coaching, and emotion: A suggested research agenda. In P. Potrac, W. Gilbert and J. Denison (eds.) *The Routledge Handbook of Sports Coaching*. London: Routledge.

Purdy, L. & Jones, R. (2011). Choppy waters: Elite rowers' perceptions of coaching. *Sociology of Sport Journal*, 28(3): 329–346.

Purdy, L., Potrac, P. & Jones, R. (2008). Power, consent and resistance: An autoethnography of competitive rowing. *Sport, Education, and Society*, 13(3): 319–336.

Purdy, L., Jones, R. & Cassidy, T. (2009). Negotiation and capital: Athletes' use of power in an elite men's rowing program. *Sport, Education and Society*, 14(3): 321–338.

Purdy, L., Potrac, P. & Nelson, L. (2013). Trust, distrust and coaching practice. In P. Potrac, W. Gilbert & J. Denison (eds.) *The Routledge Handbook of Sports Coaching*. London: Routledge.

Roderick, M. (2006a). *The Work of Professional Football: A Labour of Love?* London: Routledge.

Roderick, M. (2006b). A very precarious profession: Uncertainty in the working lives of professional footballers. *Work, Employment and Society*, 20(2): 245–265.

Taylor-Webb, P. (2005). The anatomy of accountability. *Journal of Education Policy*, 20(2): 189–208.

Taylor-Webb, P. (2006). The choreography of accountability. *Journal of Education Policy*, 21(2): 201–214.

Taylor-Webb, P. (2008). Re-mapping power in educational micropolitics. *Critical Studies in Education*, 49(2): 127–142.

Thompson, A., Potrac, P. & Jones, R. (2013). 'I found out the hard way': Micro-political workings in professional football. *Sport, Education and Society* (ahead-of-print): 1–19.

Wallace, M. (2003). Managing the unmanageable? Coping with complex educational change. *Educational Management Administration and Leadership*, 31(1): 9–29.

## CHAPTER 5

# The professionalization of sports coaching

## INTRODUCTION

The landscape of professionalism in relation to sports coaching has been subject to many pressures and tensions over the last decade (Taylor & Garratt 2010a, 2010b). A principal reason for this has been the absence of accord about what actually constitutes the activity; that is, agreement as to coaching's 'particular traditions, cultures and practices' (Taylor & Garratt 2010a: 125). Although a call for such consensus has recently appeared in the literature (Jones *et al.* 2014; North 2013; Taylor & Garratt 2010b), developments to date have only limitedly succeeded in affecting the emergence of sports coaching as a profession. This lack of progress has been exacerbated by more general unsuccessful attempts to 'clarify the differences between professions and other occupations, and identifying what makes professions distinctive' (Evetts 2012: 2). Consequently, for coaching to be considered a profession, a unique identity and discourse is required. It is only be virtue of progressively engaging with related attributes that coaches can be considered professionals and coaching a profession. Of crucial importance, however, is that such a discourse should go well beyond limited categorization and prescription of practice. Rather, it should be explicitly grounded in the critical scrutiny of ideas, theories, ethical values and empirical evidence.

The aim of this chapter is to revisit and develop recent writings into the professionalization of sports coaching. Not only is this in relation to current issues and debates (Duffy *et al.* 2011; Taylor & Garratt 2010a, 2010b), but also to further examine the nature of coaching and how it could be envisioned and developed as a profession. In doing so, it borrows heavily from Taylor and Garratt's work (2010a: 122) in seeking to 'bring a sharper and more critical perspective' to understanding the professionalization of sports coaching. The significance of the chapter lies both in building on Evetts's (2011, 2012) critique of managerialist tendencies within the professionalization movement more broadly, and Taylor and Garratt's (2010a) specific appraisal of such a drive within the field of coaching. Through such an assessment, an alternative way of conceiving coaching as a profession is considered. This includes a return to historical notions of 'occupational value' and, perhaps rather strangely on first reading, to an accompanying philosophy of amateurism. In terms of structure, following this brief introduction, an outline of recent writings and positions concerning the professionalization of coaching is given. Primacy is afforded here to the critical work of Taylor and Garratt (2010a, 2010b), who argued that each element of coaching can only be understood in relation to others. Although they rightly claim that precise definitions of what counts as a 'profession' remain elusive (Evetts 2012), the case is made that more instrumental considerations evident in various recently produced position papers lack the critical and conceptual depth required for professional status. This is largely because the 'positions' taken reflect a fracture from traditional notions of good practice (Day 2014), thus failing to question the relationships between education, socialization and practice. Here, then, we argue for the professionalization of coaching to somewhat return to a historical emphasis on 'occupational value' as opposed to organizational bureaucracy (Evetts 2011, 2012). Relatedly, we also contend that coaching should be less considered professional than amateur. Although on first glance this may be conceived as a confusing contradiction, amateurism, in this instance, is not disparagingly conceived as a non-specialist, below par activity. Rather, an amateur is considered in the alternative sense as a 'lover of'; as a person passionately and intrinsically attached to a particular pursuit. This is specifically in terms of viewing coaching as a relationally caring act and process engaged in for its own sake. As in other similar 'service' professions, expertise within it becomes manifest, not through the precise demonstration of given competencies, but through sensitivity to context and momentary imaginative judgements sourced from tacit knowledge. Finally, a reflective conclusion summarizes the principal points made.

## RECENT MOVEMENTS AND POSITIONS

In recent years, numerous governments have expressed a desire for influence and account-ability in many employment related sectors (Stronbach *et al.* 2012); a tendency, which has affected what counts as legitimate knowledge, organizational structures and practices. In particular, the concept of professionalization appears of added importance to those newly emerging occupations (e.g. IT consultancy, human resources management and psychology) 'seeking status and recognition'; a status often sought through the 'standardization of [related] education, training and qualifications' (Evetts 2012: 3). Indeed, the language of professionalism has clearly entered the managerial literature in many ways, and vice versa. Unsurprisingly, coaching has not been exempt from such managerialist tendencies and pressures (Taylor & Garratt 2010a). In the UK, for example, this has been most obviously seen through numerous ongoing initiatives to sharpen the recruitment and further support of coaches, thus establishing an impetus for a coaching profession (Taylor & Garratt 2010a, 2010b). Similar developments have also taken place in Canada and Australia (Duffy *et al.* 2011). It reflects an undertaking towards an 'ideal type' of coach, possessive of quintessential characteristics inclusive of a distinct knowledge base (Taylor & Garratt 2010b); of an officially sanctioned orthodox identity constructed from systematic certification. Evetts (2011: 412) views such an occurrence as re-defining professionals as managers, who then 'manage by normative techniques'. It is a functionalist approach, which considers a profession as comprising a definite list of 'traits'. Taylor and Garratt (2010a: 128) regard such tendencies and associated discourse as being reflective of 'a neo-liberal mode of organisational arrangement'. It is an arrangement which, while inviting inclusiveness to a given certified 'club' of qualified members, also excludes and diminishes the voices of experienced practitioners 'lost to the language of change' (2010a: 128). Here, occupational regulation and control are explained and justified as means to establish and improve 'professionalism' (Evetts 2012). Such control, however, is illustrative of a professionalism being imposed from above which, in turn, promotes a selective discourse and practice reflective of standardization, managerialism and assessment (Evetts 2011). In the words of Evetts (2011: 408), 'organization objectives regulate and replace occupational control in practitioner-client interactions thereby limiting the exercise of discretion and preventing the service ethic that has been so important in professional work'.

The resultant loss of autonomy, discretion and identity among some coaches has fuelled frustration, anger and resentment (Taylor & Garratt 2010b). What is more, many coaches have increasingly found themselves subject to regimes of discursive and behavioural control; regimes which 'complicate existing practices whilst simultaneously conflating professional roles and responsibilities' (Taylor & Garratt 2010: 124). An example of this tendency lies in the International Council for Coaching Excellence's (ICCE) subsequent adoption of its own Magglingen Declaration, which 'stressed the need for the identification of [given] coaching competencies' (Duffy *et al.* 2011: 96). This built on the European Coaching Council's (2007) proposal that a licensing system for coaches be established as part of a regulatory professional process. In response, many sporting federations, both national and international, have adopted a variety of accreditation processes and products, while self-proclaimed international organizations have continued the clamour for foundations to be laid recognizing coaching as a profession (e.g. ICCE 2010). In many ways, this can be conceived as bureaucratic managerialism attempting to exercise control over idiosyncratic relational activity. In doing so, a form of moral community is constituted based on membership and compliance. A connected development resides with the drive for the identification of clear, discrete and, therefore, measurable competencies; a process, according to Evetts (2011: 407), driven by the 'logics of the organization'. Although in one way, this can be viewed as an effort to clarify some of coaching's inherent complexity, the upshot has been a considerable decontextualization and superficial portrayal of practice. Additionally, as recently pointed out by Taylor *et al.*;

> as a result of the claim to specialist expertise, many of these documents receive little, if any, critical comment or review and are taken as authoritative declarations, so providing a powerful underpinning of the prevailing discourse and adding to the network of governmentality.

> (Taylor *et al.* 2014: 6)

The upshot of managerialist and similar claims on coaching has been a portrayal of the practitioner as virtuoso, allowing clear demonstration of skills and distinctive know-how that, in turn, produce observable and measurable outcomes (Davies 1985). Within the caring professions, such skills can be considered 'curing' as opposed to the more general notion of 'tending' (Davies 1985). What, of course, is not engaged with here is the often problematic, insecure and everyday 'dirty' work of coaching. These are the necessary invisible tasks that allow the apparent clean planning and pedagogic delivery to take place; tasks which are not 'susceptible to codification and representation as explicit rules and recipes' (Atkinson and Delamont 1985: 316).

In terms of achieving certified status, it has been found that coaches have responded by feeling the need to actively demonstrate required competencies no matter the context or their appropriateness in order to pass the course (Chesterfield *et al.* 2010; Piggott 2012). Here, coaches have been found to act in line with the views and methods promoted by course educators, without subscribing to them in any depth or sincerity. Eventual practice then, entails a reversion to previously held beliefs (Chesterfield *et al.* 2010). Indeed, according to Piggott (2012) among others, national coaching policies and guidelines are frequently being actively, yet covertly, resisted at local level. Furthermore, a recent (large scale) study by Nash *et al.* (2012) found that over 60 per cent of the coaches questioned felt unsupported by their national governing bodies (NGBs), leading to a considerable degree of cynicism amongst them for such bodies and other related coaching organizations. It is, therefore, unsurprising that the current aspiration to professionalize coaching 'through technologies of certification, benchmarking standards and formal accreditation (e.g. coaching 'quality marks') appear to be, at best, problematic' (Piggott 2012: 537).

Although such a quandary has been well documented, many 'position papers' continue to be produced in relation to the professionalization of coaching (e.g. Duffy *et al.* 2011). This is despite the persistent absence of the aforementioned foundational step of really examining and developing agreement about the core business of the activity. Indeed, according to Cruess *et al.* (2004: 76) 'it seems axiomatic that an educational activity aimed at teaching an abstract concept should begin by defining the concept'. This was a point made earlier by Taylor and Garratt (2010b), who lamented the lack of clarity surrounding coaching's conceptual boundaries as a requisite to any professional identity being developed. Hence, although we believe that some consensus is emerging around the notion of coaching as a complex relational activity (e.g. as developed in the first edition of this book), one that extends beyond individual or interactional concepts to engulf socio-historical and cultural ones, further progress needs to be made. Perhaps what is required here is an improved appreciation that ideas and actions arise in, and are shaped by, particular social circumstances; that is, they are based on a historically grounded system of social relations (Daniels 2010; Jones *et al.* 2014). Such recognition of the 'setting of development' and how the broader milieu and background produces and re-produces action (Daniels 2010) takes issue with the two-dimensional managerialist tendencies which have tended to dominate the professionalization of coaching. Not only does such a rationalistic inclination reflect a fracture from traditional notions of good practice, it also denies a group the historical basis of its identity construction (Evetts 2011). This was an issue recently engaged with by Day (2014) who, in tracing coaching's historical roots, claimed that nineteenth-century practitioners continually experimented in applying emerging knowledge. In doing so, they intuitively accepted or rejected appropriate material. In the words of Day

> In contrast to 'professional knowledge', this craft knowledge was 'knowing in action'; a feel for coaching developed with and from experience which appears to have been embedded within informal structures created by coaches engaging in a process of collective learning.
>
> (Day 2014: 151)

Consequently, although a continual demand from coach educators for practitioners to 'reflect' on experience is certainly evident, such reflection is often superficial in both nature and scope, focusing more often than not on what does and does not work. Alternatively, 'the process of employing historical perspectives to inform and develop the broader coaching landscape' has rarely been utilized, if at all (Day 2014: 151). This would appear to be slightly ironic if not wasteful, as the practice of coaching (i.e. supporting and improving athletic performances) long predates attempts at organizing it into a formal occupation. Indeed, for Day (2014), this neglect has direct implications for the current professionalization of coaching, the advocates of which should, at the very least, consider the relative importance of traditional elements of coaching before driving forward with prescriptive certified practice. Furthermore, although attempts are now being made to replicate many aspects of craft coaching, such as 'communities of practice' and 'mentors', their effectiveness and credibility can be questioned in terms of their imposition from above as opposed to organic growth (Day 2014). Additionally, given tacit or craft knowledge's often abstract nature, it is hard to see how such erudition can 'be formally transmitted or assessed, however much coach educators try to make it more explicit' (Day 2014: 160). Unsurprisingly then, the current managerialism of coaching, as discussed above, has inevitably led to the devaluation of carefully developed craft perception and sagacity; such knowledge being replaced by certification and an institutionalization of practice in the name of 'professionalization'.

## AN ALTERNATIVE CONCEPTUALIZATION: 'OCCUPATIONAL VALUE' AND NOTIONS OF AMATEURISM

In an effort to develop and progress the issue of coaches' and coaching's professionalization, we invoke the twin concepts of 'occupational value' and amateurism. The point of doing so is not to hark back and reconstruct some idealized or distorted sporting (or coaching) age, when bureaucratic certification was not considered. Rather, it is to better position the core value of coaching as a socio-pedagogic activity; a relational process enacted with care, passion and consideration (Jones *et al.* 2013). Doing so, helps better outline the nature of coaching and the subsequent notions around which its development as a profession can be built.

The notion of occupational value (Evetts 2011) is founded on the belief that expert judgment and professional discretion are aspects worth guarding and preserving. However, this should not be viewed as some protector of jurisdiction and privilege, or a conservative bulwark against reformist considerations. In fact, quite the opposite, it is a stance invoked in the spirit of progressive flexibility and adaptations to emerging challenges. Occupational value then, emphasizes a shared identity and understanding in relation to the work carried out (often based on education and 'apprenticeship socialisation' (Evetts 2011: 409). Although this can well be guaranteed by licensing, we view it as being primarily founded on respect for the trust infused practitioner-client relationship, as opposed to the managerial hierarchy of bureaucratic organizations (Evetts 2011). While we acknowledge that nonfigurative notions as 'relational trust' can be viewed as problematic, we take a lead from Friedson (2001: 34–35) who stated that

> [t]he ideal typical position of professionalism is founded on the official belief that the knowledge and skill of a particular specialisation requires a foundation in abstract concepts and [their] formal learning.

This resonates with the much earlier thinking of William James (1908), who championed vagueness through equating it with contextual richness, vitality and intensity, as opposed to the search for certainty and the instrumental application of precision. Indeed, James's (1908) advocacy of vagueness was founded on a perception of social life as complex, dynamic, pluralistic and always unfinished; concepts which certainly can be used to describe sports coaching. Such a notion was also used by Potrac *et al.* (2013), who, in borrowing from Schofield (2003), defined the vagueness of coaching as possessing generative potential, a place where novel activity can be engaged and experimented with. Vagueness thus, is considered as a condition of uncertainty or 'open possibility'. This is not to say that vagueness should somehow replace the notion of precision. Rather, it should exist in a state of dynamic tension with it; to counter the latter's drive for ever increasing levels of clarity which can lead to rigidity and the hampering of open-ended inquiry (Schofield 2003). In the words of Schofield (2003: 327), '"thinking vaguely" forces us to be aware of alternative options and possibilities that are always latent within any sphere of organization'. Consequently, although a degree of structure and conceptual boundaries are no doubt necessary, the point we wish to make is that precision, categorization and professionalism should not be always considered as conjoined entities.

According to Evetts (2011), aspects of professionalism which embrace occupational value generally, although not exclusively, include: control of work processes and priorities; common and lengthy periods of shared education; collegial authority and mutual support; a strong sense of occupational identity; a sense of purpose and contribution; discretionary judgement in highly complex situations; and, relations with clients characterized by trust and confidence. Such aspects, however, should not be regarded as rigidly defining characteristics, but ideals to aspire towards and with which to engage. Although Evetts (2011) presented such aspects as part of the ideological appeal of professionalization, we consider them crucial notions for a better conceptualization of coaching as a profession. Such aspects, and their processual engagement, stand in principled opposition to the explicit requirement to audit, account for, and evidence given 'professional' competencies.

Another concept related to occupational value worth further examination and engagement in this context is that of amateurism. As touched upon earlier, the spirit of amateurism is invoked in this instance, not in terms of shoddy or inadequate work, but in undertaking practice for its intrinsic value – for the 'love of the game'. In this respect, amateur is returned to its original Latin meaning of 'lover of', as a person avidly and ardently attached to a particular pursuit. This is not to say that all coaches are, or should be, totally driven by altruistic motivations. Neither should they shun financial reward for (good) work done. Rather, the point lies in recognizing that coaching should be viewed more as a vocation, a passion, as a complex, negotiated activity engaged in primarily for its intrinsic rewards linked to the challenge of generating learning through sensitive pedagogical action.

Such a sentiment echoes that of Brint (2012) who concurred that all work, not just so-called professional work, has elements of moral responsibility. This is particularly in relation to carrying out duties, whatever they may be, with integrity, commitment, and to the best of one's abilities. In borrowing from the work of William Sullivan (2005), Brint (2012: 23) defined this as 'the stance of intelligent responsiveness to expectations of social relationships'. What can support such a stance is an apprenticeship into the values and social responsibilities of the work involved. Here, trust, as in earlier defined professions, was deemed a naturally important part of the relationship between professional and client. R.H. Tawney (1920), the social critic and advocate of adult education, famously attempted to generalize this relationship by declaring the role of professionals as 'social trustees'. Here, the meaning or purpose was not to make money (even though engagement in some professions can undoubtedly make one rich), but that individuals should 'practice well', whatever that practice may be. Such ideas, of course, reflect notions of larger social purpose, which link into the earlier mentioned altruistic notions of coaching.

However, this doesn't mean that the 'social responsibility' felt by a coach should dominate the quality and sensitivity of his or her pedagogical actions. For example, it is fine for a coach to be a kind, considerate high-minded idealist, but if athletes learn little from poor pedagogical practice, then the objective of the exercise is lost. Similarly, and on the other hand, if a brilliant technical coach's sense of social responsibility stretches no further than lucid instruction, mechanical feedback and motivation within the confines of given sessions, then again, we would argue that the purpose of the work is not realized. Alternatively, there should be a dynamic balancing act between the instrumental and the intrinsic. Unsurprisingly, this dilemma or tension leads us again to the question of 'responsibility for what' should coaches have? The answer for us, of course, lies in the realms of the social and pedagogical; a view that has slowly gathered strength since this book first appeared (e.g. Nelson et al. 2012; Kirk 2010; Taylor & Garratt 2010b).

Although it is somewhat gratifying that the perspective has gained increasing recognition, the notion that the essence of coaching should be grounded in socio-pedagogy is not altogether new, and certainly not new to coaches. Indeed, such views were directly expressed, and tentatively engaged with, over a decade ago by Jones et al. (2004). Here, a number of coaches professed to the committed professional immersion alluded to, which was theorized as self-actualization; that is, of realizing the self in and through the coaching role. This is where the role becomes something intrinsically worth doing for the individual; an activity which is 'endowed in rightness' for him or her (Raffel 1998). Illustrating the stance, respective World Cup winning coaches Bob Dwyer (rugby union) and Lois Muir (netball) proclaimed that 'the role of the coach is to give, give and give to the players'; and 'you've got to give everything you've got; a total commitment' (Jones *et al.* 2004: 130). These findings laid the foundation for recent work, which related coaches' practice to an 'ethic of care' (Jones *et al.* 2013). Hence, although coaches can be considered to both care for and about various things (e.g. the athletic performances of athletes, their role in constructing a desired environment), what appears to often override such concerns is a deep passion to continually give their best in the service of the athletes they work with. Such care reflects a level of human and relational concern, which stretches well beyond the relatively narrow confines of recently defined professional thoroughness. Without such care, so-called professionalism is often restricted to an officious checking procedure of watchfulness; a managerial certification which encourages unreflective action.

This care-ful view of coaching is not so far removed from earlier conceptualizations of professions in general. For example, Cruess *et al.* (2004) defined a profession as a kind of 'social contract' with society; with its workings tied to specialized complex knowledge carried out in the interests of others. In this respect, it also concurs with those who claim a profession should 'have a crucial social function' in terms of 'doing something for society' (Duffy *et al.* 2011: 104). Recognizing that coaching (like teaching) is other-related, goes some way to address the 'social contract' and altruistic orientated criteria for professional status (Cruess *et al.* 2004). Here, then, we believe that emphasis be placed on coaching's caring nature, inclusive of attention to related ethical issues and responsibilities within existing socio-pedagogical norms and strategies (Noddings 1984). Such a conceptualization supports, and builds upon, the case made by Taylor and Garrett (2010b: 101), who consider coaching to be a culturally embedded educational activity, where related ideology should be used to 'mould and guide practice'. This contrasts with a view of coaching as underpinned by, and evaluated against, managerial and leadership notions that inevitably measure practice against some defined list of core competencies.

As opposed to deciding upon closely defined categorizations, a 'one size fits all' which simply cannot serve coaching's current aspirations, such an approach appears both more realistic and meaningful to establishing coaching as a profession. Perhaps what we should be aiming for is to differentiate between professionalization 'from within' (i.e. successful manipulation of the market by the occupational group) and 'from above' (domination of forces external to the occupational group) (Evetts 2012; McClelland 1990). The latter is seen as control of the work not by workers, but by organizational managers, policymakers and supervisors. So, how do we go about developing such professionalization 'from within'? Although no doubt it has to be embedded in the mindset of individuals, it also has to be woven into the fabric of organizational contexts. In this instance, policymaking organizations should create the conditions for trust that allow, and not restrict, professionals to do their job effectively and creatively. For coaching, this means moving away from a culture of managerialism and competencies, to fully accept, embrace and further develop the socio-pedagogic nuance required for athlete learning. In terms of action, increasing credence should be given to Day's (2014) earlier discussed call to better respect carefully developed craft knowledge. This is where the appeal to professionalism is made and used by the occupational group itself, 'from within', and from where the returns can be substantial. These returns include the development of a particular discourse which, in turn, can be used to construct coaching's occupational identity, whilst also promoting its image both in its own interests, and as a way of protecting the public interest (Evetts 2012).

Having said that, it is important to echo the earlier mentioned note of caution that the case made is not to counter reform or to construct an overtly romantic view of craft knowledge. Rather, it is to better respect and allow for judicious decision-making in relation to 'how, when and for whom' when considering both established and evolving knowledge. Indeed, according to Bruner (1996: 44), 'the challenge is always to situate our knowledge in the living context'; a challenge which characterizes insightful professional practice. Although traditional craft knowledge serves as a valuable 'stock', no doubt this needs considerable deconstruction if its implications are to be appreciated. Uncritically accepting and transplanting such knowledge without contextual considerations is as bad as indiscriminately applying a managerial competency framework. Furthermore, although coaches often know more than they can immediately verbalize (as developed through practising the 'craft'), more still is stored in other places, which needs to be made explicit (Bruner 1996).

What is argued for in our case for developing coaching as a profession is the required space for active interpretation; that professional coaching knowledge should not be grounded in a clear specification of what is to be learned and given standards for assessing its achievement, but in 'discourse, collaboration and negotiation' (Bruner 1996: 57). However, such an epistemology is not a call for some 'free for all' relativism, or for assumed traditional traits. Rather, professional coaching knowledge should reflect a workable consistency or 'agreed general principles' in relation to practice; what Schütz (1972), in another context, termed 'intersubjective agreements'. Any revision then, should be taken with care and restraint, with a balance between 'indeterminate' and technical knowledge being respected. Subsequently, a professional coach should not only be able to distinguish between what 'is known canonically and what they know personally' (Bruner 1996: 61), but also to determine how to meld both to meet the needs of a particular context.

## CONCLUDING THOUGHTS

In this chapter, current developments towards the professionalization of sports coaching have been critiqued, while an alternative one, based principally on the idea of occupational value (Evetts 2011) and related notions of amateurism, has been proposed. This is not to say that both discourses (i.e. the more instrumental and the more intrinsic) should be viewed as mutually exclusive. Indeed, both seek to demystify aspects of professional knowledge, protect against malpractice and 'unprofessional' behaviour, while striving to improve the process and act of coaching itself. Similarly, it is important to remember that more recent definitions of professionalism (and its links with management) bring opportunities as well as sizeable challenges. However, we differentiate from previous and ongoing professionalization agendas (e.g. Duffy *et al.* 2011) (although remaining in agreement with Taylor & Garratt 2010a, 2010b) in two principal ways. First, in our fundamental belief that coaching is a pedagogic, relational activity; a definitional necessary step before any professionalization of activity can truly begin. Second, that professional practice demands a space for sagacious and discriminating decision-making based on the aforementioned consensus as to the nature of the activity. Consequently, rather than emphasizing unquestioning compliance to given competencies, certification and standardization, the focus in relation to the professionalization of sports coaching should lie on judicious qualitative care and constructivist notions of pedagogy. Such a development would protect against the institutionalism and decontextualization of practice.

## END-OF-CHAPTER TASKS

1 The recent move to professionalize sports coaching reflects a tendency towards managerialism and certification. Consider this statement in light of the critique offered in this chapter.
2 Harking back to a perceived 'golden age' of craft practice is neither productive nor progressive to further develop coaching as a bona fide profession. Consider this statement in light of the work of Evetts, and Taylor and Garratt, among others.
3 How should coaching be defined as a profession? Subsequently, how would you educate coaches as professionals?

## REFERENCES

Atkinson, P. & Delamont, S. (1985). Socialisation into teaching: the research which lost its way. *British Journal of Sociology of Education*, 6(3): 301–322.

Bellah, R.N., Madsen, R., Sullivan, W.M., Swidler, A. & Tipton, S.M. (2007). *Habits of the Heart: Individualism and Commitment in American Life*. UC Press: Oakland, CA.

Brint, S. (2012). Professional responsibility in an age of experts and large organisations. Available at http://www.higher-ed2000.ucr.edu/documents/ProfessionalResponsibility BrintJanuary102014.pdf.

Bruner, J. (1996). *The Culture of Education*. Cambridge Mass: Harvard University Press.

Chesterfield, G., Potrac, P. & Jones, R.L. (2010). 'Studentship' and 'impression management': Coaches' experiences of an advanced soccer coach education award. *Sport, Education and Society*, 15(3): 299–314.

Cruess, S., Johnston, S. & Cruess, R. (2004). Profession: A working definition for medical educators. *Teaching and Learning in Medicine*, 16(1): 74–76.

Daniels, H. (2010). Situating pedagogy: Moving beyond an interactional account. *Pedagogies: An International Journal*, 5(1): 27–36.

Davies, M. (1985). *The Essential Social Worker*, 2nd edn. Aldershot: Gower.

Day, D. (2014). Victorian coaching communities: Exemplars of traditional coaching practice. *Sports Coaching Review*, 2(2): 151–162.

Duffy, P., Hartley, H., Bales, J., Crespo, M., Dick, F., Vardhan, D., Nordmann, L. & Curado, J. (2011). Sports coaching as a 'profession': Challenges and future direction. *International Journal of Coaching Science*, 5(2): 93–123.

Evetts, J. (2011). A new professionalism? Challenges and opportunities. *Current Sociology*, 59(4): 406–422.

Evetts, J. (2012). Professionalism in turbulent times: Changes, challenges and opportunities, paper presented at Propel International Conference, Stirling 9–11 May.

Friedson, E. (2001). *Professionalism: The third logic*. Cambridge: Polity Press.

James, W. (1908). *Psychology: A Briefer Course*. London: Macmillan.

Jones, R.L., Armour, K. & Potrac, P. (2004). *Sports Coaching Cultures: From Practice to Theory*. London: Routledge.

Jones, R.L., Bailey J. & Santos, S. (2013). Coaching, caring and the politics of touch: A visual exploration. *Sport, Education and Society*, 18(5): 648–662.

Jones, R.L., Edwards, C. & Viotto Filho, I.A.T. (2014). Activity theory, complexity and sports coaching: An epistemology for a discipline. *Sport, Education and Society*. DOI:10.1080/13573322.2014.895713.

Kirk, D. (2010). Towards a socio-pedagogy of sports coaching. In J. Lyle & C. Cushion (eds.) *Sports Coaching: Professionalization and Practice*. London: Elsevier.

McClelland, C.E. (1990). Escape from freedom? Reflections on German professionalization 1870–1933. In R. Torstendahl & M. Burrage (eds.) *The Formation of Professions: Knowledge, State and Strategy*. London: Sage.

Nash, C., Sproule, J., Hall, E. & English, C. (2012). *Coaches Outside the System*. Research report for sports coach UK.

Nelson, L., Cushion, C., Potrac, P. & Groom, R. (2012). Carl Rogers, learning and educational practice: Critical considerations and applications in sports coaching, *Sport, Education and Society*, 1–19 iFirst Article.

Noddings, N. (1984). *Caring: A Feminine Approach to Ethics and Moral Education*. Berkeley, CA: University of California Press.

North, J. (2013). Philosophical underpinnings of coaching practice research. *Quest*, 65: 278–299.

Piggott, D. (2012). Coaches' experiences of formal coach education: A critical sociological investigation. *Sport, Education and Society*, 17(4): 535–554.

Potrac P., Jones, R.L., Gilbourne, D. & Nelson, L. (2013). Handshakes, BBQs and bullets: Self-interest, shame and regret in football coaching. *Sports Coaching Review*, 1(2): 79–92.

Raffel, S. (1998). Revisiting role theory: Roles and the problem of the self. *Sociological Research Online*, 4(2). Available at www.socresonline.org.uk/4/2/raffel.html.

Schofield, B. (2003). Re-instating the vague. *The Sociological Review*, 51(3): 321–338.

Schütz, A. (1972). *The Phenomenology of the Social World*. London: Heinemann.

Stronbach, I., Corbin, B. & McNamara, O. (2012). Towards an uncertain politics of professionalism: Teacher and nurse identities in flux. *Journal of Education Policy*, 17(1): 109–138.

Sullivan, W.M. (2005). *Work and Integrity: The Crisis and Promise of Professionalism in America*. San Francisco: Jossey-Bass.

Tawney, R.H. (1920). *The Acquisitive Society*. Harcourt, Brace & Co: New York.

Taylor, B. & Garratt, D. (2010a). The professionalisation of sports coaching: Relations of power, resistance and compliance. *Sport, Education and Society*, 15(1): 121–139.

Taylor, B. & Garratt, D. (2010b). The professionalisation of sports coaching: Definitions, challenges and critiques. In J. Lyle & C. Cushion (eds.) *Sports Coaching: Professionalism and Practice*. London: Elsevier.

Taylor, W.G., Piper, H. & Garratt, D. (2014). Sports coaches as dangerous individuals: Practice as governmentality. *Sport, Education and Society*, DOI:10.1080/13573322. 2014.899492 (1–19).

# Section II

# The coach

# Coaches' selves

## INTRODUCTION

As outlined in the introduction to this book, much coaching literature and accompanying education provision has traditionally adopted an instrumentalist view of coaches' work. Here, 'what works' has been positioned as of utmost importance in terms of the knowledge, methods and ideas presented to aspiring and developing coaches (Denison *et al.* 2013; Jones *et al.* 2011). In contrast, relatively little consideration has been given to what it is to 'be' a coach (e.g. Norman 2010, 2012; Potrac *et al.* 2013a). Indeed, there remain precious few opportunities for coaches to critically consider the interrelated issues of 'what I do' and 'why I am here' (Mockler 2011). Mockler suggested that this state of affairs might be attributed to increasingly entrenched neo-liberal discourses, which privilege narrow, technical-rational understandings of various occupations and professions, which have a tendency to fixate on aspects of practice that 'are easier to quantify, measure, and mandate'. That is, neo-liberalism prioritizes the reproduction of alleged 'gold standard' routines and procedures, rather than the development of 'reflexive, politically aware' practitioners (Mockler 2011: 525).

Taking our lead from Kelchtermans' (2009a, 2009b) work in education, as well as pertinent scholarship in coaching science (e.g. Jones *et al.* 2003; Jones *et al.* 2004; Jones *et al.* 2012), this chapter focuses on the idea that, as coaching is something that is done or enacted by someone, time should be spent considering 'who' the coach is, as well as how coaches experience and make sense of practice. This would seem especially appropriate given that an evolving body of coaching research has highlighted how coaches view themselves as crucial to the pedagogical process (e.g. Cushion & Jones, 2006; Jones *et al.* 2004; Potrac & Jones 2009a, 2009b; Purdy *et al.* 2008). The findings of such studies have also shown how a coach's self-image and self-esteem can be bound tightly to practice since, unlike some other occupations, within coaching the person cannot be easily detached from the craft (Jones *et al.* 2004; Nias 1989; Potrac *et al.* 2013a, 2013b; Thompson *et al.* 2013).

In terms of its structure, the chapter begins by considering Kelchtermans' (2009a, 2009b) concept of a 'personal interpretative framework' as a means to make sense of the ways in which coaches may variously consider themselves. Attention then shifts to analysing the popularly held view that coaches enjoy unimpeded agency in their practice. Here, we focus on the vulnerability that coaches may experience as a consequence of their exposure to, and sometimes reliance upon, other individuals (Jones *et al.* 2011; Jones *et al.* 2013; Kelchtermans 2009a, 2009b). Finally, the chapter considers the inherently emotional nature of coaches' work, and the ways in which the sometimes challenging circumstances that feature on the coaching landscape (Potrac & Jones 2009a, 2009b; Potrac *et al.* 2013b) may require coaches to possess, and display, varying degrees of emotional stamina (Hochschild 1983 [2000]).

## THE PERSONAL INTERPRETATIVE FRAMEWORK

According to Kelchtermans (2009a, 2009b), a *personal interpretative framework* comprises a set of cognitions used to make sense of particular work places or practice settings, as well as the actions within it. Rather than being fixed in nature, such a framework 'is both a condition for, and a result of, the interaction' that an individual engages in (Kelchtermans 2009a: 261). That is, while a personal interpretative framework may guide a person's actions and interactions, it can also be modified and revised as a consequence of engagements with other people and events (Kelchtermans, 2009a, 2009b). Kelchtermans likens the personal interpretative framework to a pair of reading glasses. Here, he noted that:

> [p]eople who wear glasses are most of the time not consciously aware that they do so. If the glasses provide a clear view or fit correctly one tends to forget about them. However, when one's perceptions become hazy or when the frame starts to irritate or – even more importantly – when others comment that the frame is out-dated, then one becomes aware of the glasses, of the way they 'frame' reality and thus influence what one sees and how one is 'seen' (evaluated, appreciated) by others. This awareness then triggers a response, including critical examination of the lenses (or better of one's eyes in order to adapt the lenses) or eventually going to get a new frame. All of these actions are often afterwards commented on in vivid stories, for example elicited by others' comments on how nicely the new frame sits, how 'cool one looks...'

> (Kelchtermans, 2009a: 261)

Importantly, Kelchtermans suggested that a personal interpretative framework consists of two interrelated domains; an individual's *professional self-understanding* and their respective *subjective educational theory*. Each is now considered in turn.

## Professional self-understanding

Professional self-understanding refers not only to the discernment that an individual may have of his or her 'self' at a particular moment in time, but also to the ways in which ongoing interactions and experiences impact upon that sense of self. The self then, from Kelchtermans' (2009a, 2009b) perspective, is not static in nature. Rather, it is something constructed, dynamic, and mediated. Kelchtermans' analysis of the career stories of teachers led him to suggest that an individual's professional self-understanding is made up of five components; self-image, self-esteem, job motivation, task perception and future perspective. In the context of coaching, self-image refers to an individual's typification, or image, of himself or herself as a coach. This is somewhat based on an individual's self-perception, but also on the returned messages from others. This was illustrated in Potrac *et al.*'s (2013a) work, where a coaching self-image was profoundly influenced by the treatment received from other contextual actors (e.g. the players, a head coach, and other assistant coaches). Equally, a participant in Norman's (2012: 715) investigation of the experiences of lesbian coaches noted that:

> [My governing body] regularly informed [me] that I had to be very careful about being gay around all these young girls ... I believe there is an implication that they think I would do something inappropriate or that gay women coaches could potentially be inappropriate with young female players, which I find unbelievably offensive.

Closely related to *self-image* is the notion of *self-esteem*, which is concerned with a coach's appreciation of how well he or she is performing. While the feedback of others is important here, Kelchtermans (2009a, 2009b) distinguished *self-image* from *self-esteem* through the latter's emphasis on the filtering and interpretation of feedback. Specifically, the focus is on the way in which a coach may, for example, consider feedback from some individuals or groups as being more important. An individual's efforts to obtain positive recognition from others are also understood by Kelchtermans and Ballet (2002a: 766) to be a 'politics of identity'.

In applying this idea to coaching, developing a socially recognized identity as a good or 'proper' coach is important for practitioners. This is because the failure to do so may lead to feelings of being threatened, vulnerable and uncertain. He also noted that the development of positive self-esteem was a process entailing being continuously torn between experiences of success and the threat of vulnerability. This has been alluded to in several coaching studies (e.g. Jones *et al.* 2004; Potrac *et al.* 2002; Potrac & Jones 2009a, 2009b; Potrac *et al.* 2013a). Such investigations have highlighted how, among other things, coaches attached considerable store to obtaining positive feedback and support from athletes, as well as a number of important and relevant others. Indeed, coaches' understandings of how these various individuals responded to their ideas and methods was a crucial feature in terms of how they judged their 'effectiveness' at any particular point in time. Similarly, Jones' (2006) auto-ethnography charted his fears of being stigmatized as a dysfluent coach by the players and colleagues he worked with. In reflecting on and with Kelchtermans' (1996, 2009a, 2009b) work, the coaches in these studies considered the need to obtain and maintain a positive regard to be a dynamic and on-going process. It was, in short, something that occupied their thoughts and actions on a daily basis.

Kelchtermans (2009a, 2009b) also suggested that the concept of self-esteem has an emotional component. For him, positive self-esteem was not only critical for feeling at ease in any particular job, but also for experiencing a high degree of job satisfaction and fulfilment. He also acknowledged that positive self-evaluations might be fragile in nature, fluctuate across time, and require on-going work and regular re-establishment. This is why negative public judgements, even those that might appear as trivial, can have significant impacts. This was evidenced in the work of Potrac *et al.* (2013a), who highlighted how a coach's public criticism led to feelings of shame and guilt. Similarly, Thompson *et al.*'s (2013) recent work outlined how Adam, a neophyte coach, felt totally deflated when he overheard his boss' less than positive or negative appraisal of him. Specifically:

> The Manager says, still not realising I am behind him [filling the fridge with energy drinks], 'this is so and so ... we wanted to bring him in but we could not afford him, so we brought in Adam instead'. It was then I realised how low (in the pecking order) I was; how unsafe I was.
>
> (Thompson *et al.* 2013: 9)

The third dimension of Kelchtermans' (2009a, 2009b) concept of professional self-understanding is *task perception*. This encompasses an individual's idea of what constitutes his or her professional programme, as well as the duties and tasks required to do the job well. In the context of coaching, this might represent a coach's response to the following questions:

- What must I do to be a proper coach?
- What are the essential tasks I have to perform in order to have the justified feeling that I am doing well?
- What do I consider legitimate duties to perform?
- What do I refuse to accept as part of my coaching practice?

Interestingly, Kelchtermans (2009a, 2009b) suggested that these questions reflect how an individual's engagement in pedagogical practice is not a neutral endeavour. Rather, it is one characterized by various moral and value-laden choices and considerations. From this perspective, it could be argued that a coach's *task perception* is characterized by his or her deeply held beliefs about what constitutes 'good' practice, especially in terms of one's moral duties and responsibilities. This is something that has been increasingly alluded to in the coaching literature (e.g. Cushion *et al.* 2003; Jones 2009; Jones *et al.* 2004; Jones *et al.* 2011). Importantly, Kelchtermans (2009a, 2009b) noted that when individuals' views and beliefs are challenged, they might feel they are being called into question as people. Such occurrences are likely to have strong emotional consequences for coaches, not only in terms of *self-esteem* and job satisfaction, but also to possible burnout and professional longevity (Potrac *et al.* 2013a; Lundkvist *et al.* 2012). Equally, Kelchtermans (2009a, 2009b) argued that practitioners often choose to engage in micropolitical action to obtain, preserve and advance desirable working conditions, including those related to *task perception*. This aspect of coaching is considered in more detail in Chapter 4.

The penultimate component of professional self-understanding is *job motivation*. In the context of this book, this is concerned with what makes people choose to coach, as well as to continue, or not, to coach (Kelchtermans 2009a, 2009b). Kelchtermans contended that *job motivation* is not only impacted by an individual's *task perception* and working conditions, but is also something that may change over time. For example, an individual may initially decide to coach because of a passion for a particular sport. However, through experiences of, and reflections upon, coaching, he or she may come to understand that their presence and actions are meaningful to others in a broader educational sense. Thus, a coach may find such engagements very motivational, as well as a source of job satisfaction and positive *self-esteem* (Kelchtermans 2009a, 2009b; Jones 2009).

The final dimension of Kelchtermans' (2009a, 2009b) professional self-understanding is called *future perspectives*. Future perspectives are temporal in nature and are, from a coaching perspective, primarily concerned with how someone sees themselves professionally in the years ahead, as well as the feelings that accompany these thoughts. According to Kelchtermans, *future perspectives* reflect the dynamic nature of practitioners' selves, as it is constituted by an active and on-going process of individual sense-making. Importantly then, this concept encourages us to think about how a coach's actions in the present may be influenced both by past meaningful experiences and expectations about the future (Potrac *et al.* 2013a). In illustrating this point, Potrac described how he felt unable to challenge what he considered social wrongs within a specific coaching environment. This was because he feared such actions would have a highly detrimental impact upon his coaching tenure and related reputation. His thinking was influenced by past engagements with, and understandings of, a football subculture, where individuals have to protect themselves if they wish to maintain a place in a very competitive and selfish order. Similarly, Norman's (2010) work highlighted how female coaches increasingly understood their sporting subcultures as restrictive in terms of opportunities to gain full-time or high-status coaching positions. Here, one coach explained that:

> At times, you have been frustrated because you think 'I think I've done a really good job' and yet I haven't actually been seen as the next person to step into that coaching role. That's the frustrating bit, because it doesn't matter how good a job you do sometimes … you don't get the opportunity.
>
> (Norman 2010: 97)

While we have considered the five dimensions of Kelchtermans (2009a, 2009b) professional self-understanding separately, it is, of course, important to recognize that they are inextricably intertwined. This highlights how self-understanding is 'both an encompassing (integrative) and an analytical (differentiated) concept' (Kelchtermans 2009a: 263). That is, 'it does justice to the dynamic nature and contextual embeddedness of' a practitioner's sense of self, whilst also providing 'an analytical framework that allows us to consider the ways in which the self' might pervade all aspects of coaching (Kelchtermans 2009a: 263).

## Subjective educational theory

Kelchtermans (2009a: 264) defined *subjective educational theory* as the 'personal system of knowledge and beliefs' an individual uses to guide his or her practice. In differentiating between knowledge and beliefs, he outlined how the former relates to the insights and understandings derived from formal education, continuing professional development and reading of research. The latter meanwhile was considered more idiosyncratic, person-based, and derived from various practical experiences. While he suggested that knowledge and beliefs represented two separate categories of information, he considered them better understood as two ends of a continuum (Kelchtermans, 2009a, 2009b).

Kelchtermans (2009a, 2009b) also suggested that the content of *subjective educational theory* was idiosyncratic, in that it is largely based on what an individual considers to 'work for them' or be 'true in practice'. Consequently, whether it be formal knowledge gleaned in a coach education seminar or 'rules of thumb' passed on from more experienced others, the epistemological status of *subjective educational theory* is what 'holds true' for any individual coach (Kelchtermans 2009a: 264). This, of course, has important implications for coach educators, especially in terms of critiquing 'incomplete, one-sided, or simply wrong' (even if a coach found that it 'works') understandings of practice (Kelchtermans 2009a: 264). Equally, it is important to recognize that the case made here is not for unproblematically replacing unproven beliefs with researched knowledge. Instead, the emphasis should be on encouraging practitioners to carefully frame and reframe choices and actions in the quest to enhance individual practice.

Kelchtermans (2009a, 2009b) believed that *subjective educational theory* represented an individual's response to questions such as:

- How should I deal with this particular situation? What should I do?
- Why should I act in that way? Why do I believe that this is an appropriate strategy?

Such questions require a coach to engage with an interpretative process of deliberation or judgement before embarking on what he or she regards as an appropriate course of action. While Kelchtermans (2009a, 2009b) argued that this ability to read, reflect and then act is crucial within teaching, the sentiment has been increasingly recognized within coaching (e.g. Jones *et al.* 2013; Lyle & Vergeer 2013; Purdy *et al.* 2013). Indeed, a central premise of this text is that a coach's judgement about what, when, and how 'to do' is never as simple as applying various rules or techniques (Jones *et al.* 2004). Instead, coaches, like teachers, have to make contextually appropriate judgements, which include decisions about taking exceptional action, and when to follow 'rules' (Kelchtermans 2009a, 2009b).

It is here, Kelchtermans (2009a, 2009b) suggested, that we can see the interconnections between professional self-understanding and subjective educational theory. Specifically, he argued that an individual's reading (i.e. perception, interpretation and judgement of appropriate action) of a particular encounter or event 'always implies both the self-understanding and the subjective educational theory' (Kelchtermans 2009a: 43). For example, it could be suggested that whatever action a coach takes, it is likely to reflect 'the norms of the task perception, the drives from the job motivation, and the emotional meaning in relation to self-esteem' (Kelchtermans 2009b: 43). Equally, the self of the coach is reflected in the 'specific knowledge and beliefs' that leads him or her to choose a particular action and enact it in a specific way (Kelchtermans 2009b: 43). That is, professional self-understanding encompasses personal goals and norms (i.e. what a coach wishes to achieve), while subjective educational theory specifically focuses on the knowledge required to achieve these desired outcomes (i.e. how these outcomes are to be achieved). In essence, then, they are 'two interwoven domains' (Kelchtermans 2009a: 265).

## THE SELF, AGENCY AND VULNERABLE COMMITMENT IN COACHING

It has been increasingly acknowledged that coaches do not enjoy unfettered agency in their work (Jones *et al.* 2004; Jones *et al.* 2011). Such critiques run counter to the rather functionalist, heroic and naïve conceptualizations of coaches and coaching that have dominated much traditional literature and provision. While coaches may take a stance or make a commitment towards a particular set of values and goals, the achievement of these is a frequently problematic and emotionally challenging endeavour (Purdy *et al.* 2013; Potrac *et al.* 2013a) (see also Chapter 4 and Chapter 7 for further discussion). Indeed, it could be argued that, due to its inherently relational nature, coaching is also characterized by varying degrees of passivity and vulnerability that can result from a coach's exposure to other people (e.g. athletes, parents, administrators, sponsors) and events (Jones *et al.* 2011). Like teachers then, coaches work 'in a fish bowl' (Blase 1988: 135), where actions are perceived, interpreted, and judged by a range of significant others. In echoing Kelchtermans' (2009a, 2009b, 2011) theorzing, vulnerability is not only something that might be experienced emotionally by coaches, but is also very much a structural condition of coaching (e.g. Potrac *et al.* 2013a; 2013b; Purdy *et al.* 2013).

Kelchtermans (2009a, 2009b, 2011) provides three specific elements of vulnerability that could enhance our understanding of coaching in this regard. The first relates to the fact that coaches never have full control of their respective working conditions. These include the material resources at their disposal, and the composition of the athletes or participants with whom they engage. For example, Purdy *et al.* (2013) provided an account of a coach's sense of relative powerlessness regarding the time, space and resources allocated by his employers. In particular, their work addressed how such resource distribution might not only influence a coach's ability to produce competitive achievements, but also how reputations might be subsequently eroded. This situation is perhaps exasperated in contemporary society, where the neoliberal emphasizes on individual effectiveness, efficiency, accountability and the achievement of desired outcomes is increasingly common (Kelchtermans 2009a, 2009b, 2011). This is not only true in professional sport but also in a variety of UK community coaching settings. Here, research has begun to chart some of the challenges that such coaches endure to achieve targets in the face of ever decreasing funding, staffing and resource availability (Gale 2014; Ives *et al.* in press).

The second element of Kelchtermans' (2009a, 2009b, 2011) conceptualization of vulnerability concerns the degree to which a pedagogue can directly link his or her practices to the enhanced learning and performances of those in their charge. For example, while the achievements of athletes may be partially attributed to a coach's decisions and actions, other personal (e.g. dedication, motivation, perseverance) and social factors are not easily controlled, changed or influenced. Similarly, it may be difficult, if not impossible, for a coach to accurately predict when the fruits of his or her work will manifest themselves in terms of athlete performance(s). It could further be argued that these circumstances may promote a sense of ambivalence among coaches. For example, while coaches with a high internal locus of control might experience strong feelings of satisfaction when athletes appear to learn and/or perform well, they may also blame themselves and feel very frustrated when athletes do not learn or perform to the expected level. In contrast, coaches with a high external locus of control may view athlete learning and performance as being beyond their control and could, subsequently, experience low levels of professional competence, motivation, and self-esteem (Kelchtermans 2009a, 2009b, 2011).

The final element of vulnerability described by Kelchtermans (2009a, 2009b, 2011) relates to the perception that pedagogues do not have a firm body of knowledge upon which to base their decisions. As a result, even when strong justifications for certain decisions and actions are provided, others can often challenge them. This is due to the existence of copious educational theories, as well as variously experienced practices. It could be argued then, that most people have some degree of knowledge of, and opinion about, education. This is a feature of pedagogical practice from which coaches are certainly not immune. It is, according to Kelchtermans (2009a: 266), the fundamental condition that a pedagogue 'finds himself/herself in', and is a position that clearly resonates with our increasing understanding of the complex, power dominated, and ambiguous nature of coaching (e.g. Potrac & Jones 2009a, 2009b; Potrac *et al.* 2013a).

## THE SELF AND EMOTION IN COACHING

Denzin (1984:1) asserted that 'people are their emotions'. Hence, 'it is necessary to understand emotion' as part of any attempt to 'understand who a person is'. As such, an individual's engagement in pedagogical work could be understood to be an emotional, as well as a cognitive, activity (Day & Gu 2009). It has been suggested that the emotions a practitioner experiences are a reflection of his or her moral commitment and care for others over whom they feel a sense of responsibility (Kelchtermans 2009a, 2009b, 2011). However, coaches' emotions have been afforded little attention, being viewed as a reflection of an individual's personality or coaching style (Potrac *et al.* 2013b). Indeed, the existing literature has largely represented coaches (and athletes) as dispassionate and rational beings, free from emotionality (Potrac & Marshall 2011; Potrac *et al.* 2013b). This is unfortunate because coaches undoubtedly experience a variety of strong emotions as they navigate the challenges and opportunities of their dynamic sporting worlds (Potrac & Marshall 2011; Potrac *et al.* 2013a, 2013b). Indeed, the tensions and dilemmas that coaches face are not only cognitive in nature, but are also inherently emotional (Potrac & Marshall 2011; Potrac *et al.* 2013a, 2013b). This is because coaching requires 'intensive personal interactions and an investment of the self in practice' (Potrac & Marshall 2011: 62). Consequently, it is very difficult, if not impossible, for coaches to separate 'feeling from perception' and 'affectivity from judgement' (Nias 1996: 294; Potrac & Marshall 2011; Potrac *et al.* 2013b). Emotions then, are an inherent part of coaches' decision-making, especially in terms of narrowing down the range of potential actions to a realistic and manageable number (Damasio 1994; Hargreaves 2005; Potrac & Marshall 2011). Simply put, 'you can't judge if you can't feel' (Hargreaves 2005: 280).

This outlook on the emotional aspects of practice has been illustrated in coaching research (e.g. Jones 2006, 2009; Nelson *et al.* 2014; Potrac *et al.* 2013a). For example, Nelson *et al.*'s (2014) study of semi-professional football revealed how the participant coach understood his efforts to be positively regarded within the club as an inherently emotional activity. This was especially in terms of having to express, or suppress, certain emotions at particular times depending on the 'audience'. Such efforts led him to experience strong feelings of anxiety, frustration and misgiving. In his own words:

> I'm thinking that you go into coaching with your principles. You look at all the coaches that you've had and think that you're not going to do anything like that because you have to treat people how you want to be treated ... So, I'm on the way home texting him really apologising, saying that I was out of order and that I didn't mean to do it ... The lad knew he cost us the game, the other players knew that, I came in and made it 50-60 times worse ... That will probably live with me, and that's a massive learning experience for me, and I will never go down that road and down to that level again.
> (Nelson *et al.* 2014: 481)

In addition to the micropolitical nature of coaching outlined in Chapter 4 the personal investment and vulnerability experienced by coaches suggest that they need a degree of *emotional stamina* to cope with the job (Hochschild 1983 [2000]). Indeed, perhaps a central feature of coaching is the requirement to sustain 'a particular controlled feeling for an extended period of time' (Turner & Stets 2005: 39). Of course, acting in this way can place a strain on coaches, who may, at various times, feel alienated, inauthentic, and self-estranged (Hochschild 1983, 2000; Potrac & Marshall 2011; Potrac *et al.* 2013a). At other times, however, coaches may find such emotional challenges to be rewarding and exciting aspects of the job, especially if they assist in improving athlete performances (Potrac & Marshall 2011). What is not in doubt, however, is the emotional demand that coaching makes of coaches.

## CONCLUDING THOUGHTS

In primarily drawing upon the work of Kelchtermans (2009a, 2009b), the purpose of this chapter was to provide some insights into the ways coaching selves might be understood as matters both 'of the social and the individual' (Clarke 2009: 189). Specifically, we sought to raise awareness of how an individual's coaching self is something not only bound up in his or her experiences of practice, but also constructed and reconstructed through on-going contextual interactions (Alsup 2006; Jones *et al.* 2004; Jones 2006). Doing so further challenges the representation of coaching as a depersonalized and technical activity, while assisting in the recognition of the intensive emotional investment that coaching demands (Jones *et al.* 2011; Potrac *et al.* 2013b).

## END-OF-CHAPTER TASKS

1 What do you consider to be good coaching? What are the critical incidents, people, and phases of time that have contributed to you thinking in this way? How have these critical moments influenced how you think and feel about your coaching practices and beliefs?
2 How do you react to others' opinions on good coaching that are different to yours? How do you react if someone criticizes your coaching practices? Why do you react in the ways that you do? How do you seek to cope with different stances on this matter?
3 What do you do when athletes are not learning as you think they should? How do you feel? Why do you feel this way?

## REFERENCES

Alsup, J. (2006). *Teacher Identity Discourses: Negotiating Personal and Professional Spaces.* London: Routledge.

Blase, J. (1988). The everyday political perspectives of teachers: Vulnerability and conservatism. *International Journal of Qualitative Studies in Education,* 1(2): 125–142.

Clarke, M. (2009). The ethico-politics of teacher identity. *Educational Philosophy and Theory,* 41(2): 185–200.

Cushion, C. & Jones, R. (2006). Power, discourse and symbolic violence in professional youth soccer: The case of Albion FC. *Sociology of Sport Journal,* 23(2): 142–161.

Cushion, C., Armour, K. & Jones, R. (2003). Coach education and continuing professional development: Experience and learning to coach. *Quest,* 55, 215–230.

Damasio, A. (1994). *Descartes' Error: Emotion, Reason, and the Human Brain.* London: Putnam Publishers.

Day, C. & Gu, Q. (2009). Veteran teachers: Commitment, resilience and quality retention. *Teachers and Teaching: Theory and Practice.* 15(4): 441–457.

Denison, J., Mills, J.P. & Jones, L. (2013). Effective coaching as a modernist formation: A Foucauldian critique. In P. Potrac, W. Gilbert & J. Dennison (eds.) *Routledge Handbook of Sports Coaching.* London: Routledge.

Denzin, N. (1984). *On Understanding Emotion.* San Francisco: Jossey-Bass.

Gale, L. (2014). The everyday realities of community sports coaching, unpublished PhD thesis, University of Hull, United Kingdom.

Hargreaves, A. (2005). The emotions of teaching and educational change. In A. Hargreaves (ed.) *Extending Educational Change.* Netherlands: Springer.

Hochschild, A. (1983 [2000]). *The Managed Heart. Commercialisation of Human Feeling.* Berkeley, CA: University of California Press.

Ives, B., Gale, L., Nelson, L. & Potrac, P. (in press). Enacting youth sport policy: Towards a micro-political and emotional understanding of community sports coaching work. In A. Smith & K. Green (eds.) *The Routledge Handbook of Youth Sport.* London: Routledge.

Jones, R. (2006). Dilemmas, maintaining 'face' and paranoia: An average coaching life. *Qualitative Inquiry*, 12(5): 1012–1021.

Jones, R. (2009). Coaching as caring (The smiling gallery): Accessing hidden knowledge. *Physical Education and Sport Pedagogy*, 14(4): 377–390.

Jones, R., Armour, K. & Potrac, P. (2003). Constructing expert knowledge: A case study of a top-level professional soccer coach. *Sport, Education, and Society*, 8(2): 213–229.

Jones, R., Armour, K. & Potrac, P. (2004). *Sports Coaching Cultures: From Practice to Theory.* London: Routledge.

Jones, R., Bailey, J., Santos, S. & Edwards, C. (2012). Who is coaching? Developing the person of the coach. In D. Day (ed.) *Sports and Coaching: Pasts and Futures.* Crewe: MMU Press.

Jones, R.L., Bailey, J. & Thompson, A. (2013). Ambiguity, noticing and orchestration: Further thoughts on managing the complex coaching context. In P. Potrac, W. Gilbert & J. Dennison (eds.) *Routledge Handbook of Sports Coaching.* London: Routledge.

Jones, R., Potrac, P., Cushion, C. & Ronglan, L.T. (2011). *The Sociology of Sports Coaching.* London: Routledge.

Kelchtermans, G. (1996). Teacher vulnerability: Understanding its moral and political roots. *Cambridge Journal of Education*. 26(3): 307–323.

Kelchtermans, G. (2009a). Who I am in how I teach is the message: Self-understanding, vulnerability and reflection. *Teachers and Teaching: Theory and Practice*, 15(2): 257–272.

Kelchtermans, G. (2009b). Career stories as gateway to understanding teacher development. In M. Bayer, U. Brinkkjær, H. Plauborg & S. Rolls (eds.) *Teachers' Career Trajectories and Work Lives.* The Netherlands: Springer.

Kelchtermans, G. (2011). Vulnerability in teaching: The moral and political roots of a structural condition. In C. Day & J. Lee (eds.) *New Understandings of Teacher's Work.* The Netherlands: Springer.

Kelchtermans, G. & Ballet, K. (2002a). Micropolitical literacy: Reconstructing a neglected dimension in teacher development. *International Journal of Educational Research*, 37, 755–767.

Lundkvist, E., Gustafsson, H., Hjälm, S. & Hassmén, P. (2012). An interpretative phenomenological analysis of burnout and recovery in elite soccer coaches. *Qualitative Research in Sport, Exercise and Health*, 4(3): 400–419.

Lyle, J. & Vergeer, I. (2013). Recommendations on the methods used to investigate coaches' decision making. In P. Potrac, W. Gilbert & J. Denison (eds.) *Routledge Handbook of Sports Coaching.* London: Routledge.

Mockler, N. (2011). Beyond 'what works': Understanding teacher identity as a practical and political tool. *Teachers and Teaching*, 17(5): 517–528.

Nelson, L., Potrac, P., Gilbourne, D., Allanson, A., Gale, L. & Marshall, P. (2014). Thinking, feeling, acting: The case of a semi-professional soccer coach. *Sociology of Sport Journal*, 19(1): 19–40.

Nias, J. (1989). Subjectively speaking: English primary teachers' careers. *International Journal of Educational Research*, 13(4): 391–402.

Nias, J. (1996). Thinking about feeling: The emotions in teaching. *Cambridge Journal of Education*, 26(3): 293–306.

Norman, L. (2010). Feeling second best: Elite women coaches' experiences. *Sociology of Sport Journal*, 27(1): 89–104.

Norman, L. (2012). Gendered homophobia in sport and coaching: Understanding the everyday experiences of lesbian coaches. *International Review for the Sociology of Sport*, 47(6): 705–723.

Potrac, P. & Jones, R. (2009a). Micro-political workings in semi-professional football coaching. *Sociology of Sport Journal*, 26, 557–577.

Potrac, P. & Jones, R. (2009b). Power, conflict and co-operation: Towards a micro-politics of coaching. *Quest*, 61, 223–236.

Potrac, P. & Marshall, P. (2011). Arlie Russell Hochschild: The managed heart, feeling rules, and emotional labour: Coaching as an emotional endeavour. In R. Jones, P. Potrac, C. Cushion, & L.T. Ronglan (eds.) *The Sociology of Sports Coaching*. London: Routledge.

Potrac, P., Jones, R. & Armour, K. (2002). 'It's all about getting respect': The coaching behaviors of a top-level English football coach. *Sport, Education and Society*, 7(2): 183–202.

Potrac, P., Jones, R., Gilbourne, D. & Nelson, L. (2013a). Handshakes, BBQs, and bullets: A tale of self-interest and regret in football coaching. *Sports Coaching Review*, 1(2): 79–92.

Potrac, P., Jones, R., Purdy, L., Nelson, J. & Marshall, P. (2013b). Coaches, coaching, and emotion: A suggested research agenda. In P. Potrac, W. Gilbert & J. Denison (eds.) *The Routledge Handbook of Sports Coaching*. London: Routledge.

Purdy, L., Potrac, P. & Jones, R. (2008). Power, consent and resistance: An autoethnography of competitive rowing. *Sport, Education, and Society*, 13(3): 319–336.

Purdy, L., Potrac, P. & Nelson, L. (2013). Trust, distrust and coaching practice. In P. Potrac, W. Gilbert & J. Denison (eds.) *The Routledge Handbook of Sports Coaching*. London: Routledge.

Thompson, A., Potrac, P. & Jones, R. (2013). 'I found out the hard way': Micro-political workings in professional football. *Sport, Education and Society*, 1–19.

Turner, J. & Stets, J. (2005). *The Sociology of Emotion*. Cambridge: Cambridge University Press.

## CHAPTER 7

# The coach as a pedagogical performer

## INTRODUCTION

> Unless people are willing to listen to you, unless you're prepared to listen to them and understand them as people, the best coaching book in the world isn't going to help you. It all comes down to how well they really want to do for you. It all comes back to the relationships that you have with players and the trust that exists between you ... That's just life.
>
> (Graham Taylor in Jones *et al.* 2004: 28)

> Sometimes you just have to get on with it, and give the players the impression that you are in control of it. Just get on with it, without missing a beat, as if it's part of the plan. You've got to be bullet proof, or you've got to portray that you are.
>
> (Steve Harrison in Jones *et al.* 2004: 139)

The above quotations, taken from a wider examination of elite level sport, illustrate the importance of working relationships to coaching. Indeed, it is the interaction that occurs between a coach and various contextual others that not only influences athlete learning but also how a coach connects, bonds, and generally gets on with these individuals and groups (e.g. Huggan *et al.* 2015; Jones *et al.* 2003; Jones *et al.* 2004; Purdy & Jones 2011; Thompson *et al.* 2013). As evidenced in Chapters 4 and 6, the perceptions and judgements of different organizational stakeholders are important features of the coaching landscape. This is because they invariably have a significant impact on the time and resources afforded to coaches, as well as the context in which they work.

Rather than being unproblematically obtained and advanced, or a fixed quality that an individual has or doesn't have, the 'buy-in' a coach receives from others is largely dependent upon how these people experience, make sense of, and evaluate that coach's choices and actions. What perhaps matters most then, is not exactly what the coach does, but how others perceive the impression given by the coach (Jones *et al.* 2011; Thompson *et al.* 2013). Indeed, it could be argued that coaching is somewhat akin to a theatrical (dramaturgical) performance. This is because it requires one to perform the coaching role to a scrutinizing audience, who review in terms of the qualities and attributes the coach claims to possess (Jones *et al.* 2004). Importantly, the audience evaluation, in turn, influences the nature and quality of future engagement, and the on-going treatment of the coach (Edgley 2013; Jones *et al.* 2011; Purdy *et al.* 2008). Similarly, the responses of others can also have a significant influence on how a coach feels about, and views, him or her self in the role.

In adopting a dramaturgical perspective, this chapter seeks to consider ways in which coaching can be considered a social performance. In doing so, it advances the earlier developed notion that if coaching is an act, it is invariably enacted. Hence, it is important to consider what this performance entails, and why it appears as it does (Jones *et al.* 2012). In this respect, we not only argue that coaching work requires careful consideration and reflection upon engagements and interactions, but also the managing of various emotions, especially those a coach chooses to show (or not) to others within the working environment (Jones *et al.* 2011; Potrac *et al.* 2013). The chapter begins by introducing the pivotal dramaturgical writings of Erving Goffman and Arlie Russell Hochschild. It is important to note that we do not seek to provide an exhaustive coverage of these authors' works or, indeed, their associated critiques (see Jones *et al.* 2011). Rather, our intention is to illuminate various concepts and ideas that might facilitate a reflection upon the dramaturgical features of coaching. The focus then shifts to exploring how coaches engage in various acts of impression management and emotional labour to achieve their goals. Finally, the chapter concludes by considering the potential merits of viewing and examining coaching as a social performance.

## DRAMATURGY, IMPRESSION MANAGEMENT AND EMOTIONAL LABOUR

A principal theoretical backdrop used to underpin the chapter is provided by the writings of Erving Goffman (1959, 1969a, 1969b), and his thesis addressing *The Presentation of the Self in Everyday Life*. Goffman (1959) was the leading exponent of the dramaturgical metaphor as a means to understand social life. This was particularly in terms of how and why people behave as they do during face-to-face interaction. Here, Goffman (1959) examined how, in order to fulfil societal expectations of acceptable behaviour, individuals frequently 'play roles, negotiate situations, and to a larger extent are forced to be actors' (Marsh *et al.* 1996: 73). Goffman's (1959) sociology then, was primarily concerned with how individuals and groups seek to present themselves to others; how they attempt to control the impressions they give off, and the kinds of actions that they may or may not engage in to protect and advance the version of the self exhibited (Jones *et al.* 2002; Jones *et al.* 2004; Jones *et al.* 2011).

Central to Goffman's writings was the belief that individuals are not totally free to choose the images of self that they would have others accept. Instead, people are 'constrained to define themselves in congruence with the statuses, roles, and relationships that they are accorded by the social order' (Branaman 2000: xlvii). Equally, he believed that the thoughts, choices, and behaviours of individuals are not entirely determined by society, as people are able to strategically manipulate social situations, including others' impression of themselves; something he termed 'self work' (Goffman 1959; Jones *et al.* 2004; Jones *et al.* 2011). In this regard, he believed that:

> an individual does not ... merely go about his [sic] business. He goes about constrained to sustain a viable image of himself in the eyes of others. Some local circumstances always reflect upon him, and since these experiences will reflect upon him, and since these circumstances will vary unexpectedly and constantly, footwork or rather self-work, will be continuously necessary.
>
> (Goffman 1971: 185)

Face-to-face interaction then, occupied a special place in Goffman's theorizing on the dynamics of social life. This was because of his belief that through expressive performance (e.g. appearance, manner and style), an individual can influence an audience's perception of his or her intent and competency.

In unfolding his dramaturgical metaphor, Goffman (1959) introduced the notions of performance, front, impression management, team and region (i.e. front and back stage). He defined performance as 'all the activity of an individual that occurs during a period marked by his continuous presence before a particular set of observers and which has some influence on the observers' (Goffman 1959: 32). More simply put, the purpose of a performance is to allow an individual to give a certain impression of self to others in order to achieve desired goals. Interestingly, Goffman (1959) emphasized that his notion of performance not only dealt with how individuals presented themselves to others, but also how teams or groups staged such performances. A performance team in this respect, referred to 'any set of individuals who co-operate in staging a single routine'; a concept that reflects the realities of social life where we invariably live and work with others (e.g. family and work life) (Goffman 1959: 85).

Related to the notion of performance is that of front. Front refers to 'that part of the individual's performance which regularly functions in a general and fixed fashion to define the social situation for those who observe performance' (Goffman 1959: 22). In constructing and managing a particular front, an individual may be required to instantaneously and consistently exhibit the qualities that he or she claims for the front during interaction with others in order to maintain it (Jones *et al.* 2004; Jones *et al.* 2011). In illustrating this point, Goffman (1959: 30) gave the example of a baseball umpire:

> [i]f a baseball umpire is to give the impression that he [sic] is sure of his judgement, he must forgo the moment of thought which might make him sure of his judgement. He must give an instantaneous decision so that the audience will be sure that he is sure of his judgement.

Dramatic realization relates to a person's use of dramatic signs to ensure that the audience understands the points that are difficult to see (Jones *et al.* 2011). This requires an engagement in the process of impression management, as individuals seek to protect the credibility of the front presented from being discredited. Such action entails managing individual appearance, manner, and utilizing a variety of contextually relevant props (Jones *et al.* 2004). Goffman's (1959) work also highlighted how individual performances are not only dramatically realized, but are also idealized. In this regard, he described how individuals seek to present themselves in the best possible manner in terms of their compatibility with cultural norms and values (Jones *et al.* 2011). For example,

> [t]he self, then, as a performed character is not an organic thing that has a specific location, whose fundamental purpose is to be born, mature, and to die; it is a dramatic effect rising from a scene that is presented, and the characteristic issue, the crucial concern, is whether it will be credited or discredited.
>
> (Goffman 1959: 252–253)

Finally, Goffman's dramaturgical framework also included two regions where social performances were informed by different behavioural principles and guidelines; the front (front stage) and back regions (back stage). The front region refers to the place where performance is given. Here, an individual or team seek to present an idealized image whilst simultaneously concealing aspects that might discredit the impression they are trying to create (Goffman 1959; Jones *et al.* 2011). In contrast, the back region is where the performer can, to some degree, relax, drop the front, and step out of character. It is also the place where performances can be planned, practiced and reflected upon (Jones *et al.* 2011). Despite this distinction between the regions, Goffman (1959) did not consider the back region to be a place where any real or authentic self could emerge. Rather, he noted how people could still provide performances to varying degrees 'backstage' (Jones *et al.* 2011).

Inspired by the work of Goffman, Hochschild's (1983, 1997, 2000, 2003) thinking addressed the interrelationship between social interaction, impression management and emotion. Her classic text, *The Managed Heart* (1983, 2000), provided fascinating and rich insights into the relationship between the emotions an individual feels in the workplace, and those that are acted out for the benefit of others (Potrac & Marshall 2011). Her work is widely acknowledged as 'not only providing a significant foundation for the rise of the sociology of emotions as a bona-fide area of inquiry', but also for underpinning and influencing 'contemporary explorations of the emotional nature of [professional] practice' (Potrac & Marshall 2011: 55).

Hochschild's (1983, 2000) dramaturgical theorizing is based around the concepts of emotional labour and emotion management, feeling and display rules, and surface and deep acting. According to Hochschild (2000: 7), emotion management focuses on the 'management of feeling to create a publicly observable facial and bodily display'. In the context of everyday life, Hochschild argued that, through the process of socialization, we learn what emotions are appropriate and expected in particular situations. Similar to Goffman's (1959) notion of front and back regions, Hochschild distinguished between the emotional work that takes place (a) in the home and (b) in the work place. Specifically, she outlined that emotion work occurs in private lives, while emotional labour takes place in occupational and professional settings. Hence, she defined the latter as:

> [l]abour that requires one to induce or suppress feeling in order to sustain the outward countenance that produces the proper state of mind in others [such as] the sense of being cared for in a convivial and safe place. This kind of labour calls for communication of mind and feeling, and it sometimes draws on a source of self that we honour as deep and integral to our individuality ... Emotional labour is sold for a wage and, therefore, has exchange value.
>
> (Hochschild 1983: 7)

While the clear-cut distinction between our private (back stage) and work (front stage) lives proffered by Hochschild has been challenged (e.g. Theodosius 2008; Wouters 1991), the key point to consider is that 'the distinction is really one of difference of self, between what individuals consider to belong to them, representing their "real" selves, and what is socially acceptable for public consumption' (Theodosius 2008: 15).

Hochschild's (1983, 2000) work highlighted how an individual's engagement in emotion work or emotional labour is frequently framed by socially constructed feeling rules and display rules. Feeling rules not only refer to the specific emotions that an individual should experience in a particular situation (e.g. grief at a funeral, happiness at a birthday party), but also their duration (i.e. fleeting to long lasting). Here, she noted that:

> [a]cts of emotion management are not only simply private acts; they are used in exchanges under the guidance of feeling rules. Feeling rules are standards used in emotional conversations to determine what is rightly owed in the currency of feeling. Through them, we tell what is 'due' in each relation, each role. We pay tribute to each other in the currency of managing the act. In interaction, we pay, overpay, underpay, play with paying, acknowledge our due, pretend to pay, or acknowledge what is emotionally due to another person.
>
> (Hochschild 2000: 180)

In contrast, display rules focus on when and how particular overt expressions of emotion should occur. For example, an individual may put on a 'happy face' to sustain a social encounter where display rules and/or occupational norms require that they should feel happy (Turner & Stets 2005).

Like Goffman (1959), Hochschild (1983, 2000) suggested that, in our social encounters with others, we engage in a certain amount of acting. She categorized these into deep and surface acting. Surface acting refers to a desire to deceive others in terms of how a person really feels without attempting to deceive him or her self about their true feelings. This primarily relates to how an individual manages body language to others, and includes 'the put on sneer, the posed shrug, [and] the controlled sigh' (Hochschild 2000: 35). Deep acting occurs when an individual works on his or her feelings through 'conscious mental work' to the extent that he or she believes in the emotions they express (Hochschild 2000: 36; Potrac & Marshall 2011). For example, in applying the work of the method actor and theatre director Constantin Stanislavski, Hochschild (2000: 35) suggested that an individual's public display of emotion 'is a natural result of working on the feeling; the actor does not try to seem happy or sad but rather expresses spontaneously a real feeling that is self-induced'. When engaging in deep acting, an individual can draw upon two principal supportive strategies. The first is exhortations, which primarily refer to the efforts made to feel particular emotions. For example, an individual might describe how 'I psyched myself up' or 'I mustered up some gratitude' (Hochschild 2000: 39). In addition to exhortations, deep acting also involves training memories or imaginations to believe the feelings being experienced. For example, an individual may transfer memories of emotions from a past situation to a current one. In these circumstances, Hochschild (1983, 2000) argued that it was possible to forget the extent of the work required to create such feelings.

## DRAMATURGY, IMPRESSION MANAGEMENT AND EMOTIONAL LABOUR IN COACHING

While Goffman never wrote directly about sport, his theorizing has been increasingly utilized to explore the social dynamics of coaching (Jones *et al.* 2011). In particular, it has helped to better understand how coaches present themselves to others inclusive of the impression management strategies used. Such work has provided insights into the dramaturgical nature of coaching work; and, in particular, the ways in which top-level coaches preserve and advance the image or front presented (e.g. Jones *et al.* 2004; Jones *et al.* 2011; Partington & Cushion 2012; Potrac *et al.* 2002; Ronglan & Aggerholm 2014; Thompson *et al.* 2013). Significantly, at the core of individual practices has been found a desire to avoid performance disruptions that might negatively influence personal credibility and, hence, the levels of trust and respect afforded. A primary practice utilized in this regard is 'dramaturgical discipline' (Goffman 1959), which refers to an individual's conscious immersion and engrossment in (the coaching) role (Jones *et al.* 2004). Consequently, while coaches are often emotionally and intellectually committed to their working role, they also continuously seek to avoid 'unmeant gestures when performing it' (Goffman 1959: 217). In one coach's words:

> [y]ou've got to think on your feet. Whereas if you start bawling or saying, 'Where is so and so?' [using a panicky voice], you're not being professional. You can make a joke about it and throw your notes down, 'Come on let's piss off to the pub'. You make light of it, but you try to and show that you're not bothered; you're in control and know what you are going to do. You've got to adapt, think on your feet and have things in your mind, first reserve, second reserve type of thing, which isn't easy but has to be done.
>
> (Steve Harrison in Jones *et al.* 2004: 144)

In echoing the comments above, another coach emphasized the need to appear knowledgeable when interacting with athletes:

> [f]ootball players will test you. I find that when you go to a new club ... they will test you to see if you know. They usually pump you with questions. They'll say they've

never done that before, and if I can't say why I want it done that way, if I can't give a good reason, then I've got trouble. You can't afford to lose players. If they have no respect for your coaching ability then you've had it, you've lost respect and coaching sessions become very difficult. So, you've got to know your subject; it is the most important thing. You can get away with being a bit quiet or a bit noisy, but if you don't know your subject then you have real problems.

(Potrac *et al.* 2002: 192)

Jones (2006) shared similar anxieties regarding the front projected to players and assistants in the context of semi-professional football. In this regard, he provided a visceral account of being a dysfluent coach, and the efforts engaged in to manage the 'stigma' within the club setting. In particular, he charted fears regarding how others might judge his coaching persona and abilities. After a problematic experience of giving a pre-game team talk he documented:

[m]aybe nobody noticed, maybe it wasn't that bad of a stumble? Of course it was, what an idiot I must have looked. Why me? And, why just then? I could come clean about it, maybe the players would respect that? ... Thoughts about 'coming out' continue to pervade my mind. It's the struggle between who I am and who I want to be. Politically, maybe I should forsake attempts to 'cover' up, yet the fear of social ridicule and rejection is too strong. Sensitivity to difference is not easily found in football dressing rooms.

(Jones 2006: 1016)

A second strategy used by coaches to protect their constructed fronts has been that of dramaturgical circumspection (Goffman 1959). This relates to the sincerity of the performances engaged in. In this regard, coaches described how they did not think of themselves as participating in cynical performances aimed at deluding audiences for the purposes of private gain (Jones *et al.* 2004; Potrac *et al.* 2002). Instead, they considered how such performances were engaged in for the good of the team and/or others. A particular tactic here was that of telling 'white lies' (Goffman 1959; Jones *et al.* 2004; Potrac *et al.* 2002), which were used to gloss over poor performances, or not tell athletes how good they were. Such acts were justified in terms of protecting or deflating egos as necessary. Rather than considering such untruths to be misleading or insincere, they were perceived to be undertaken with others, in this case athletes', best interests in mind (Jones *et al.* 2004; Partington & Cushion 2012; Potrac *et al.* 2002). For example, Ian McGeechan, an elite level rugby union coach noted that 'sometimes I won't tell players how good they are. I need to keep their feet on the ground, so I'll just tell them how to get better' (Jones *et al.* 2004: 145). Similarly, a top-level football coach recounted how he built up the self-confidence of players. In his own words:

[p]layers by and large want to be praised. Most people see them as spoilt overpaid whatevers. I see them every day, most of them are insecure, and most of them are frightened to death 5 minutes before they go out for a game. So you've really got to be encouraging them Monday to Friday. You've got to tell them that they are good

players, try and bring out the good points … make them feel good about themselves … I'm trying to boost the players' egos a little bit. I think it's all part of coaching.

(Potrac *et al.* 2002: 195–196)

A third strategy related to detailed, advanced planning by coaches, and the consideration of 'all possible expressive contingencies' (Goffman 1959: 227). This entailed meticulous planning and preparation as an everyday part of working practice. Interestingly, the coaches' planning not only focused on the techniques and tactics to be learned or practiced, but also on the role specifications and responsibilities of those in the performance (e.g. athletes, assistant coaches). In their own words:

> I don't compromise in the sense that I work hard at the preparation. I think you have to be right in your own mind and put that to the players, you've got to be well prepared.
>
> (Ian McGeechan in Jones *et al.* 2004: 146)

I have to show how tiny movements give clues to the man in possession. You see, a difference of only 3 inches can be significant, as it's that much closer or further away from the defender, and I have to make sure that the players know how much difference that really makes to the execution of a move. I also have to know how exactly I'm going to present that [to the players].

(Bob Dwyer in Jones *et al.* 2004: 146)

Interestingly, Potrac and Jones (2009a) illustrated how one coach gave considerable attention to planning his interactions and training session content when managing conflict with one player, David, who was resistant to the coach's programme and methods. In this respect, the coach feared how David's derogatory comments about him might influence others' perceptions, especially that of his employer, the club Chairman. In his own words:

> I knew David was pretty close to the Chairman, so I had to be careful in terms of how I dealt with him … I started setting things up in training so that he'd fail. He just didn't have the technical ability or the speed to play in the position that he wanted, so I decided to exploit that. We'd set up some patterns of play and the players would be working hard and every time he'd be in the wrong place, make a bad pass or have a crap touch. After a couple of sessions, I began to hear complaints from the players about him. His status within the group changed and he became more and more isolated.
>
> (Potrac and Jones 2009a: 569)

The coach also outlined how he also took time to meet with a small group of senior players, whom he had recruited to the club, to discuss the problems that David had presented. In his own words:

> I [also] spoke [privately] to the [senior] boys about what was happening. I suggested that maybe the players should get together and tell David they weren't happy with his attitude and performance, which might be more meaningful than if I did it. So,

they started letting David know they weren't happy with him and soon the other players began to join in. In the end, I think that played a large part in why David left the club … It also looked better for me because I wasn't seen [by the Chairman] as the person who was throwing out an established player.

(Potrac & Jones 2009a: 570)

Finally, literature has highlighted how some coaches utilize strategies related to being seen to visibly care about athlete learning through the provision of additional sessions and learning resources, advice, as well as taking an interest in athletes' lives outside of the sporting environment (Jones *et al.* 2004; Jones 2009; Potrac & Jones 2009a, 2009b). In this respect, Graham Taylor, a former elite level football coach, noted: 'you're actually showing them that you care, and whilst you show them that you think about them and the other side of life, you stand to gain a great deal in terms of your working relationship with them' (Jones *et al.* 2004: 158).

While coaches take various actions to build and protect their respective fronts, inevitably there are occasions when things don't go to plan. One way to handle such disruptions has been through the use of self-deprecating humour (Jones *et al.* 2004). Specifically, such humour can be used proactively (see Jones *et al.* 2003; Jones *et al.* 2011; Ronglan & Aggerholm 2014) to build working consensuses with others or as a reactive strategy to dampen the implications of potentially discrediting events. In this regard, some coaches believe that humour can limit the 'fall-out' from performance disruptions by lessening the expectation of leader infallibility, thus locating such faux pas within the range of normative behaviour. Humour was also considered to help display the 'human side of the coach', which can further foster the development of functional relationships. For example, a top-level Norwegian coach noted that:

I use self-irony; reveal weaknesses and show 'human traits', in a way. The players chuckle when I ask for help to handle the technical gadgets that the players know everything about. It's important to be able to laugh at oneself and to be relaxed regarding one's own limitations. Self- importance really doesn't work in the Norwegian culture.

(Ronglan and Aggerholm 2014: 41)

Like Goffman, Hochschild didn't write directly about coaching. However, in recent years, her work has found some traction in terms of helping to further develop knowledge of coaching's dramaturgical nature (e.g. Nelson *et al.* 2014; Potrac & Marshall, 2011; Potrac *et al.* 2013a, 2013b). While embryonic, the literature has illustrated the emotional demands and challenges that coaches face in practice. For example, Nelson *et al.*'s (2014) study of emotional labour in semi-professional football highlighted how the participant coach engaged in regular bouts of surface acting. In his own words: 'last night I didn't feel too good, going to a training session … So you're thinking, "I don't fancy this tonight". However, I can't show that to the players … I have to put an act on' (Nelson *et al.* 2014: 475).

Interestingly, the coach also highlighted how he tried to manage the outward projections of his emotions according to the display rules dominant within the sporting subculture. He described how he disliked having to interact with certain supporters in the clubhouse after matches. However, he knew that he was not only expected to attend such gatherings by the club Chairman, but also to present himself to the supporters as a polite and 'up beat' coach, genuinely interested in their views and thoughts.

> It's just a nightmare. You get frustrated and you also get angry. You want to turn round to them and say, 'What have you done? What level have you played at? What qualifications have you got?' But you know you can't.
>
> (Nelson *et al.* 2014: 477)

For this coach, his long-term engagement in emotional labour was not an easy task. He described how he ultimately chose to take a break from coaching, as he became fatigued and demotivated by consistently feeling obliged to engage in inauthentic behaviours and emotional displays. The decline in his ability to sustain required emotional displays, which Hochschild (1983, 2000) considered a reduction in his emotional stamina, led to a situation where both his sincerity and credibility were questioned. In his own words: 'I think, especially with adults, you gradually get found out, and there is only so much acting you can do before players start realizing ...' (Nelson *et al.* 2014: 478).

Similarly, Potrac *et al.'s* (unpublished manuscript) auto-ethnographic study addressed the lead author's experiences of emotional labour. Particularly, the paper explores his increasing estrangement and alienation from coaching, especially in terms of his frustration with others' contradictory beliefs.

> Several of the parents offered to buy me a drink. I accepted with thanks, returned their smiles, and laughed at their jokes, but ultimately my heart wasn't in it. I just couldn't make myself feel happy. Eric [the team sponsor] came over. 'We've not won a game for a long time. It's great that the girls get to feel that for a change' he grinned. I agreed as I opened another can of coke. But, as I looked around the room, my shoulders tightened and that familiar but uncomfortable feeling grew stronger. The clammy hands. The constant butterflies. My head began to ache. I wondered what Eric would say if he knew how I truly felt. Hardly the actions of a competent or so called effective coach. Not a particularly manly thing to do either. I doubt they'd be interested anyway. I was paid to provide a service, after all. Eric continued his monologue on the merits of the 4-3-3 playing system. I glanced down at my watch. It had been a long and tiring day. Fuck me, Eric! You just don't get it do you! If only it were that simple. I'd heard enough. Time to use the emergency exit. 'Sorry Eric, I'm just going to nip up to the bar for another coke and some crisps' I smiled. I always had to smile.

Of course, it is important to recognize that engaging in emotional labour is not always a negative activity. Indeed, it has been suggested that through engagement in such work individuals often experience a sense of excitement, fun and satisfaction. This may be especially so when they contribute to improving the performances, experiences and lives of others (Isenbarger& Zembylas 2006; Potrac & Marshall 2011). In illustrating this point, one track and field athletics coach noted:

> [o]verall, I feel that the emotional labour I invest in my coaching offers many positives. I coach through choice, because I enjoy it. While coaching does come with an

emotional cost, it is also hugely rewarding. By engaging in emotional labour, I am able to support athletes more effectively, to help them achieve their goals and competitive ambitions. The reward is seeing this happen, in watching those you work with enjoy their training, growing in confidence and ability. For many of the athletes I work with, they desperately want to succeed. This brings with it a high emotional cost to me as a coach, in managing their emotions and expectations. However, it also brings with it a huge feeling of satisfaction in a job well done when they do achieve.

(Potrac & Marshall 2011: 66)

## CONCLUDING THOUGHTS

The purpose of this chapter was to stimulate reflection on some of the dramaturgical features of coaching work. Through considering selected concepts from Goffman (1959) and Hochschild (1983, 2000), the chapter hopefully contributes to a greater understanding of the personal, emotionally laden, and interactive challenges that remain an inherent feature of the coaching landscape (Potrac *et al.* 2013a). In keeping with the wider mission of the book, the intention here was to 'see through some of the mystification and common sense superficiality' that has plagued coaching both theoretically and practically (Jones *et al.* 2011: 26). Indeed, it is important to recognize coaching as 'an obligation driven social activity' (Jones *et al.* 2011: 26) that requires coaches to consciously consider how they present themselves, their choices, and their actions to others. Seeking to exhibit and maintain an idealized image in the eyes of others is certainly not an easy or, indeed, an unemotional undertaking. Rather, coaching is an embodied and dynamic activity requiring us to consider how we feel and make others feels, with any achievements linked to the quality of our social engagements (Jones *et al.* 2011). As such, we would strongly encourage coaches and coach educators to not underestimate the importance of their respective social performances.

### END-OF-CHAPTER TASKS

Consider the following questions within a sporting setting of your choice (e.g. amateur netball, high performance track and field athletics):

1 What do you consider to be the expectations of coaches' behaviours and interactions in your sporting setting? How do people respond when they perceive these expectations to be met, exceeded or unfulfilled? How might their reactions impact the coach's on-going relationship with them?

2 In seeking to provide a credible coaching front, what strategies and behaviours do you use? When? How? Why? What do you avoid doing? Why?

3 What emotions would you show in the coaching environment? To whom and to what extent? When? Why? What emotions would you avoid showing? To whom? When? Why?

# REFERENCES

Branaman, A. (2000). Goffman's social theory. In C. Lemert & A. Branaman (eds.) *The Goffman Reader*. Oxford: Blackwell Publishers.

Edgley, C. (2013). Introduction. In C. Edgley (ed.) *The Drama of Social Life: A Dramaturgical Handbook*. Burlington, VT: Ashgate Publishing Limited.

Goffman, E. (1959). *The Presentation of Self in Everyday Life*. London: Penguin.

Goffman, E. (1969a). *Strategic Interaction*. Philadelphia: University of Pennsylvannia Press.

Goffman, E. (1969b). *Where the Action Is*. London: Penguin.

Goffman, E. (1971). *Relations in Public: Microstudies of the Public Order*. New York, NY: Basic Books.

Hochschild, A. (1983, 2000). *The Managed Heart. Commercialisation of Human Feeling*. Berkeley, CA: University of California Press.

Hochschild, A. (1997). *The Time Bind: When Work Becomes Home and Home Becomes Work*. New York, NY: Metropolitan Holt.

Hochschild, A. & Machung, A. (2003). *The Second Shift: Working Parents and the Revolution at Home*. London: Penguin.

Huggan, R., Nelson, L. & Potrac, P. (2015). Developing micropolitical literacy in professional soccer: A performance analyst's tale. *Qualitative Research in Sport, Exercise and Health*, 7(4): 504–520.

Isenbarger, L. & Zembylas, M. (2006). The emotional labour of caring in teaching. *Teaching and Teacher Education*, 22: 120–134.

Jones, R. (2006). Dilemmas, maintaining 'face' and paranoia: An average coaching life. *Qualitative Inquiry*, 12(5): 1012–1021.

Jones, R., Armour, K. & Potrac, P. (2002). Understanding coaching practice: A suggested framework for social analysis. *Quest*, 54(1): 34–48.

Jones, R., Armour, K. & Potrac, P. (2003). Constructing expert knowledge: A case study of a top-level professional soccer coach. *Sport, Education, and Society*, 8(2): 213–229.

Jones, R., Armour, K. & Potrac, P. (2004). *Sports Coaching Cultures: From Practice to Theory*. London: Routledge.

Jones, R., Bailey, J., Santos, S. & Edwards, C. (2012). Who is coaching? Developing the person of the coach. In D. Day (ed.) *Sports and Coaching: Pasts and Futures*. Crewe: MMU Press.

Jones, R., Potrac, P., Cushion, C. & Ronglan, L.T. (2011). Erving Goffman: Interaction and impression management: Playing the coaching role. In R. Jones, P. Potrac, C. Cushion, & L. Ronglan (eds.) *The Sociology of Sports Coaching*. London: Routledge.

Marsh, I., Keating, M., Eyre, A., Campbell, R. & McKenzie, J. (1996). *Making Sense of Society: An Introduction to Sociology*. London: Longman.

Nelson, L., Potrac, P., Gilbourne, D., Allanson, A., Gale, L. & Marshall, P. (2014). Thinking, feeling, acting: The case of a semi-professional soccer coach. *Sociology of Sport Journal*, 19(1): 19–40.

Partington, M. & Cushion, C.J. (2012). Performance during performance: Using Goffman to understand the behaviours of elite youth football coaches during games. *Sports Coaching Review*, 1(2): 93–105.

Potrac, P. & Jones, R. (2009a). Micro-political workings in semi-professional football coaching. *Sociology of Sport Journal*, 26: 557–577.

Potrac, P. & Jones, R. (2009b). Power, conflict and co-operation: Towards a micro-politics of coaching. *Quest*, 61: 223–236.

Potrac, P. & Marshall, P. (2011). Arlie Russell Hochschild: The managed heart, feeling rules, and emotional labour: Coaching as an emotional endeavour. In R. Jones, P. Potrac, C. Cushion, & L. T. Ronglan (eds.) *The Sociology of Sports Coaching*. London: Routledge.

Potrac, P., Jones, R. & Armour, K. (2002). It's all about getting respect: The coaching behaviours of a top-level English football coach. *Sport, Education and Society*, 7(2): 183–202.

Potrac, P., Jones, R., Gilbourne, D. & Nelson, L. (2013a). Handshakes, BBQs, and bullets: A tale of self-interest and regret in football coaching. *Sports Coaching Review*, 1(2): 79–92.

Potrac, P., Jones, R., Purdy, L., Nelson, J. & Marshall, P. (2013b). Coaches, coaching, and emotion: A suggested research agenda. In P. Potrac, W. Gilbert & J. Denison (eds.) *The Routledge Handbook of Sports Coaching*. London: Routledge.

Potrac, P., Mallett, C., Jones, R. & Nelson, L. Emotional labour in sports coaching: One coach's tale. Unpublished manuscript.

Purdy, L. & Jones, R. (2011). Choppy waters: Elite rowers perceptions of coaching. *Sociology of Sport Journal*, 28(3): 329–346.

Purdy, L., Potrac, P. & Jones, R. (2008). Power, consent and resistance: An autoethnography of competitive rowing. *Sport, Education, and Society*, 13(3): 319–336.

Ronglan, L.T. & Aggerholm, K. (2014). 'Humour helps': Elite sports coaching as a balancing act. *Sports Coaching Review*, 3(1): 33–45.

Theodosius, C. (2008). *Emotional Labour in Health Care: The Unmanaged Heart of Nursing*. London: Routledge.

Thompson, A., Potrac, P. & Jones, R. (2013). 'I found out the hard way': Micro-political workings in professional football. *Sport, Education and Society*, (ahead-of-print), 1–19.

Turner, J. & Stets, J. (2005). *The Sociology of Emotions*. Cambridge: Cambridge University Press.

Wouters, C. (1991). On status competition and emotion management. *Journal of Social History*, 24(4): 99–717.

## Section III

# The athletes

# Athlete learning

## INTRODUCTION

In 2010, Sports Coach UK released a review of literature on coach learning and development (Cushion *et al.* 2010). The review was structured around 'learning sources' (informal, non-formal and formal), which reflected a constructivist view of learning, and focused on specific strategies to support it, e.g. reflection, mentoring and problem-based learning. The authors, however, did say that if we are to increase coaches' knowledge, it is 'essential' to better understand 'different conceptions of learning ... the theories supporting them, and the assumptions that underpin them' (Cushion *et al.* 2010: 7). Yet, developing such an understanding is not a straightforward exercise. This is because learning is a complex and broad concept that is perceived (and, therefore categorized) in varied and contested ways (Armour 2010; Cushion *et al.* 2010). For example, Cushion *et al.* (2010) categorized perspectives of learning under the headings of behaviourism, cognitivism and constructivism, while others have subdivided constructivism into psychological constructivism and social constructivism (Phillips 2000). The content of this chapter is organized into two broad categories, behaviourism and constructivism, with the latter being further divided into psychological and social constructivism. A psychological constructivist orientation views learners as active constructors of meaning or understanding and perceives knowledge as being '*made*, not *acquired*' (Phillips 2000: 7). Those who hold a social constructivist orientation consider that over time, 'public bodies of knowledge' are socially constructed and are influenced by, amongst other things, 'politics, ideologies, values, the exertion of power and the preservation of status, religious beliefs, and economic self-interest' (2000: 6).

Not all the theories discussed in this chapter have a sociocultural orientation. This may appear to be inconsistent with the subtitle of this text. However, organizing the discussion under the above headings provides an opportunity to highlight how our views on how we learn are not 'natural' or 'common sense' but, in fact, reflect particular theories of learning. Armour (2010) pointed out that one problem associated with not being explicitly aware of theories of learning is that practices are limited and limiting. This is because they are grounded in 'personal experience and strong (often unchallenged) beliefs about … best ways to learn and, by default, coach' (2010: 155). If coaches and coach educators do not reflect on their practices and philosophies, it is likely they will fail to realize that: (i) many beliefs about learning are rooted in Western culture; (ii) what is considered to be 'best' for the learner is informed, often implicitly, by a particular theory of learning and; (iii) the power personal experience has on our understanding of learning (Armour 2010; Light 2008; Lyle 2007; Rink 2001). Given these possible pitfalls, we agree with others (e.g. Light 2008; Roberts & Potrac 2014) that coaches would benefit from having a greater understanding of the philosophical and epistemological assumptions about learning. This would enable coaches to better make informed 'decisions about the strategies they adopt and to negotiate the range of challenges and problems that typically arise' (Light 2008: 35).

In 2002, Gilbert annotated a bibliography of coaching science, in which no articles were specifically identified as focusing on the learning process, or the athlete as a learner. Since, scholars of coaching science have begun to pay 'attention to how various learning theories and concepts could be used to inform coaching practice and subsequently enhance player learning' (Roberts & Potrac 2014: 180). Despite increased attention, in the recently published *Handbook of Sports Coaching* (Potrac *et al.* 2013), only two of the 39 chapters explicitly focused on learning, primarily coach learning, while another two discussed learning in the context of developing coaching competency. No chapter addressed issues related to athlete learning. Obviously, therefore, work is needed to recognize athlete learning as an important aspect of the coaching process.

The aim of this chapter is to describe some prominent theories of learning and make links to coaching practice, sporting culture and sport coaching literature. Having knowledge of the assumptions and characteristics that underpin such theories can provide coaches with a conceptual framework and vocabulary for interpreting practices that facilitate learning, whilst encouraging them to reflect on how they go about solving problems (Merriam *et al.* 2007). Similarly, a related critical discussion can support coaches and coach educators to reflect on 'previously unconsidered theoretical notions, thus giving them the options to think in different ways about their practice and their consequences' (Jones 2006: 4).

# BEHAVIOURISM

Unlikely as it may seem, a Russian Nobel Prize winner (in 1904) for his work on digestion became an instrumental figure in how we understand learning from a behaviourist orientation. Ivan Pavlov's experiments on dogs' salivation patterns had widespread implications for how behaviour and learning were initially understood. Pavlov's findings were the catalyst for work that became known as classical conditioning. Several decades later, Americans Watson and Raynor conducted another famous study with a child called Albert, which demonstrated how fears could be learned via classical conditioning (Eggen & Kauchak 2004). In the first half of the twentieth century, Thorndike defined and established educational psychology as a field of study (Lefrançois 2000), which emphasized the 'association between stimulus and response as the basis of learning' (Schunk 2004: 30). Here, it was viewed that 'responses resulting in satisfying (rewarding) consequences are learned; [while] responses producing annoying (punishing) consequences are not learned' (2004: 31). Thorndike later recognized that rewards and punishments are not opposites, but are comparable.

Behaviourist views of learning still prevail in many Western institutions with the practices of rewarding good and punishing undesirable behaviour being considered a 'natural' way to encourage learning. That this is still the case should come as no surprise because, as Tinning and Rossi (2013) pointed out, there is a 'degree of practical wisdom' associated with the view that the 'best predictor ... of future behavior continues to be past behavior' (2013: 203). While there are many interpretations of behaviourism (see Ward 2006), in this section we focus on only one, known as operant conditioning.

## Operant conditioning

The work of B.F. Skinner has become most associated with behavioural thought through his research on operant conditioning (Carlson & Buskist 1997). The basic assumption of operant conditioning is that '*an observable response changes in frequency or duration as the result of a consequence*' (i.e. response-consequence). A consequence has been described as being any outcome that '*occurs after the behavior and influences future behaviors*' (Eggen & Kauchak 2004: 200). Some of the basic processes or characteristics, of operant conditioning include: reinforcement, punishment, extinction and scheduling. Behaviour modification is the term used to describe the practices of anyone (e.g. a coach) who systematically uses reinforcement and punishment to modify another's (e.g. an athlete's) behaviour.

An assumption of the reinforcement process, which can be positive or negative, is that reinforcement increases the chances of a particular behaviour reoccurring (Schunk 2004; Siegelman & Rider 2006). In this respect, positive reinforcement is viewed as '*the process of increasing the frequency or duration of a behavior as the result of presenting a reinforcer*'; in other words, 'receiving something that increases behavior' (Eggen & Kauchak 2004: 201). Negative reinforcement, on the other hand, is '*the process of removing or avoiding a stimulus to increase behaviour*' (2004: 201). It is important to stress that negative reinforcement is not a form of punishment. A key characteristic of reinforcement is the 'reinforcer', which can also be positive or negative. A positive reinforcer will strengthen a behaviour if the learner desires the reinforcer (Vialle *et al.* 2005). A negative reinforcer also aims to increase behaviour, but does so by removing something that the learner views as unpleasant (Vialle *et al.* 2005). However, a coach needs to know what an athlete desires, and/or their motivations, if reinforcers are to be effective.

Recognizing that athletes' motivations and desires are variable, reinforcers have been categorized as: natural reinforcers (e.g. being placed in a group with a friend); social reinforcers (e.g. spending time with the coach); activity reinforcers (getting to participate in a favoured activity); tangible reinforcers (e.g. medals and certificates) and, sometimes in the case of younger athletes, edible reinforcers (e.g. chocolate bars) (Vialle *et al.* 2005). It is worth emphasizing that if a coach wants to increase a behaviour, it is not enough to indiscriminately hand out reinforcers, such as a smile or praise. This is because reinforcers are both 'situationally specific' and individually specific (Schunk 2004: 51). This specificity was reflected in a study carried out nearly 50 years ago by Rushall and Pettinger (1969) who explored the outcomes different reinforcers (money, candy/chocolate bars, coach's attention and nothing) had on swimmers' productivity in training. They found that the older and more experienced swimmers worked harder in training when the reinforcer was the coach's attention rather than a chocolate bar. While the authors did not elaborate on what was meant by the coach's attention, the findings of the study did highlight how reinforcers are individually specific.

For reinforcement to be effective, its scheduling, or timing, is important. Here, it is assumed that when a new skill or habit is being learned, it is desirable to 'provide continuous positive reinforcement … reinforcing every occurrence' (Siegelman & Rider 2006: 37). However, as time goes by, and in an effort to maintain the behaviour, it is recommended that it is not reinforced on every occasion. Instead, the behaviour should be reinforced intermittently and unpredictably. When this type of scheduling occurs the 'learner is likely to continue performing even if the reinforcement stops' (2006: 37).

Receiving a punisher 'immediately after an action' is assumed to reduce the 'frequency of that action' (Vialle *et al.* 2005: 13). Punishers can come in two forms; removal and presentation. Removal punishment is what happens when learners have something they value removed with the aim of decreasing undesired behaviour, for example, when the coach 'drops' an athlete from the starting team line for having an unexplained absence from training the hope is that the athlete will no longer have unexplained absences. Presentation punishment occurs when a learner receives (or is presented with) a punisher with the aim of decreasing undesirable behaviour (Eggen & Kauchak 2004), for example, when a coach tells an athlete to perform 10 press-ups as a consequence of fumbling the ball in a drill. The aim here is the athlete will not want to do the press-ups so will concentrate on catching the ball. Yet, if a coach wants to use a punisher, then it is useful for them to remember that, just like reinforcers, punishers cannot be used indiscriminately. For example, one punisher will not have the same effect on all players. Athletes who do not enjoy publicly performing press-ups may view having to do them as a form of punishment, so to avoid this they may decrease the undesirable behavior. In contrast athletes who desire to become physically stronger may not view having to publicly perform press-ups to be a punishment so the threat of having to do them does not decrease the undesirable behavior.

The final basic process (or characteristics) of operant conditioning is extinction, which has been described as '*the disappearance of a conditional response as a result of nonreinforcement*'

(Eggen & Kauchak 2004: 204 ). A common example of extinction is when a coach ignores the behaviour of an athlete who is off-task. The assumption behind this action is that the athlete is behaving off-task because he or she desires the coach's attention. If the coach supplies the attention, then the athlete is rewarded for being off-task.

# CONSTRUCTIVISM

The range of perspectives classified as constructivist is considerable, a situation which has caused confusion whilst potentially decreasing the effectiveness of the term. Despite this, there appears to be some general consensus around the following points: (i) the works of Dewey, Piaget and Vygotsky have been very influential in informing discussions (Light & Wallian 2008; Roberts & Potrac 2014); (ii) learning is a complex, on-going process of change and adaption, which is shaped by experience; (iii) cognition is a social process; (iv) learning involves interpretation and that we can only know the world through experience (Davis and Sumara 2003); (v) constructivism is an umbrella term to categorize theories based on the assumption that learners are 'active seekers and processors of information' (Schunk 2004: 443); and (vi) learning is a relational process, which is constantly in flux (Ovens & Godber 2013). Others have suggested that constructivism is more of an epistemology than a theory and, therefore, can be used to describe a 'philosophical explanation about the nature of learning' (Schunk 2004: 286). Despite the complexities associated with constructivism, Armour (2010) suggested that constructivist theories are appropriate for understanding and studying coaching and coach development.

## Psychological constructivism

### Cognitive learning theory

Cognitive constructivist theorists contend that learning occurs through interactions between personal and environmental factors. One such theory is Bandura's (1971) social cognitive theory[1]. Not surprisingly given the widespread influence of Skinner, the early work of Bandura was informed by operant conditioning (Schunk 2004). However, over time, Bandura's work became more 'socially orientated', focusing on 'how people influence each other' (Lefrançois 2000: 305); hence the interest in observational learning. What is more, Bandura's work demonstrated that 'reinforcement was not necessary for learning to occur' (Schunk 2004: 83). Instead, he posited that people could learn by watching others perform the actions.

A key assumption of social cognitive theory is that learning is social and occurs either '*enactively* through actual doing or *vicariously* by observing models perform' (Schunk 2004: 86). Enactive learning is the learning which occurs from the 'consequences of one's actions' (2004: 86), whereas vicarious learning occurs 'by observing the consequences of others' actions' (Eggen & Kauchak 2004: 217). It is accepted that the models in question do not have to be physically present in the environment. Rather, learning can occur from symbolic models who are represented in the environment; for example in books, movies and TV, or a combination of previously observed acts (Eggen & Kauchak 2004).

Historically, it was considered that observing the performance of others, and then modelling that practice, was nothing more than imitation. However, it is now recognized that observing models can promote cognitive, behavioural and affective changes (Schunk 2004). For example, Bandura (1971) contended that models who have power, prestige, intelligence, and are viewed as competent, are copied to a greater extent than models who are considered subordinate. Nearly three decades later, Roberts *et al.* (1999) suggested that: modelling correct behaviour is more beneficial for learning than modelling incorrect behaviour; a high-status model will be more beneficial than a low-status model; and observing a model that is similar to the self is more helpful than observing a model that is dissimilar. Building on this work, Eggen and Kauchak (2004) proposed that a model's effectiveness was dependent upon perceived similarity, competence and status.

Another key assumption of social cognitive theory is that learning is a cognitive process. This is because learners are required to pay 'attention, construct and remember mental representations...of what they saw, retrieve these representations from memory later and use them to guide behavior' (Siegelman & Rider 2006: 39). This cognitive process reflects four interrelated sub-processes associated with modelling, namely – attention, retention, production and motivation. Attention is important since simply being exposed to a model is no guarantee that learning will occur. Instead, learners need to be discriminatory as to where to place attention as well as to 'recognize, and differentiate the distinctive features of the model's responses' (Bandura 1971: 16). Retention requires observers to be 'active agents who transform, classify, and organize modelling stimuli into easily remembered schemes' (1971: 21), while production requires observers to translate modelled events into overt behaviours (Schunk 2004). Finally, motivation is important if the learned behaviour is to be enacted into an explicit performance.

Some of the suggestions regarding who makes the best models appear contradictory. For example, how does a coach working with junior athletes with limited skills make sense of the recommendation that a high-status model (e.g. an elite athlete) is more beneficial than a low-status one? Similarly, in the same context, how can observing a model similar to oneself be better than observing a model that bears no resemblance? To overcome such obstacles Eggen and Kauchak (2004: 221) suggested that 'several models are more effective than a single model, or even a few, because the likelihood of finding a model perceived as similar increases as the number of models increases'. However, they also pointed out that 'people are more likely to imitate models perceived as competent than those perceived as less competent, regardless of similarity' (2004: 221).

Often, when the effectiveness of models and modelling is discussed, little recognition is given to the importance of the affective domain. Tensions can occur with modelling when models are chosen because they are physically skilful, but have limited ability to relate, especially emotionally, to those for whom they are being the model. This was highlighted in a news item, which documented the relationship between Hamish Bond and Eric Murray[2]. When Hamish Bond was 19 years old, he was selected to be in a New Zealand rowing crew with the older Eric Murray. This could have been viewed as an opportunity for Bond to use Murray as his model. But as Bond recalls:

[t]o be honest in the first year ... when we were in the four straight off ... he [Murray] blamed everything on me. I was the new guy and I thought he was a complete arse, I didn't like him – I didn't like him at all. He was a complete prick.

(Available at http://www.3news.co.nz/Murray-Bond-share-Olympic- secrets/ tabid/1771/articleID/290132/Default.aspx#ixzz2mXuV0s8P)

The interview highlighted how the affective domain can influence the effectiveness of a model, especially if the model is expected to have a long-standing relationship with the learner. The quote also illustrates the power relations that can exist between members of a crew or team and others in the coaching community, and highlights the importance of recognizing social and power relations when choosing models.

## A Piagetian inspired view of learning

In his discussions of lifelong learning, Jarvis (2006, 2007, 2009) contended that learning occurs as a consequence of 'disjuncture' (Jarvis 2006: 16) or what Trudel *et al.* (2013: 376) call 'intellectual disharmony'. This comes about when 'our biographical repertoire is no longer sufficient to cope automatically with our situation' (2013: 376). In making links between the work of Jarvis and how coaches learn to work, Trudel *et al.* (2013) observed that while the learning processes appear to be similar for all coaches, the situations (i.e. informal, non-formal and formal) in which the coaches learn differ. Drawing on the work of Coombs and Ahmed, Cushion *et al.* (2010) defined the three (aforementioned) learning situations in the following way. A formal learning situation is one that occurs in an 'institutionalized, chronologically graded and hierarchically structured educational system' (2010: 45). A non-formal learning situation occurs in 'any organized, systematic, educational activity carried on outside the framework of the formal system to provide select types of learning to particular subgroups in the population' (2010: 37). Finally, an informal learning situation is a 'lifelong process by which every person acquires and accumulates knowledge, skills, attitudes and insights from daily experiences and exposure to the environment' (2010: 27). Many discussions of coach learning and development have been framed using one or more of these three learning situations (e.g. Bloom *et al.* 1998; Cassidy *et al.* 2006a; Culver & Trudel 2006; Cushion *et al.* 2010; Mallett *et al.* 2009; Nelson & Cushion 2006; Schempp 1998).

The metaphor of a network has been used to explain how learning occurs in various ways, with diverse groups and individuals (Moon 1999, 2001, 2004). It reflects the view that learning is participatory and not 'just an accumulation of knowledge' (Werthner & Trudel 2006: 201). Moon (2001), like Piaget, foregrounded the twin terms of assimilation and accommodation, and made links between these two concepts and the forms of learning categorized as 'surface' or 'deep' learning (Trudel *et al.* 2013). Moon's conceptual framework illustrated the links between learning situations (which she described as being mediated, unmediated and internal[3]) and stages of learning (Trudel *et al.* 2013, Werthner & Trudel 2006). Central to the framework is the cognitive structure of the learner who, in turn, engages in 'cognitive housekeeping' resulting in 'deep' learning.

## Social constructivism

### A social theory of learning

The social theory of learning (Wenger 1998) emerged from Etienne Wenger's work with Jean Lave (Lave & Wenger 1991). Their writings promoted learning as a social enterprise influenced by participation in daily life. Lave and Wenger (1991) explored the meaning of situated learning in a range of different contexts, and proposed that learning was a process that required involvement in a 'community of practice' (CoP). CoPs have been variously described as 'groups of people who share a concern, a set of problems, or a passion about a topic, and who deepen their knowledge and expertise in this area by interacting on an ongoing basis' (Wenger *et al.* 2002: 4). Another key concept in Lave and Wenger's understanding of situated learning, and associated with CoP, is legitimate peripheral participation (LPP). LPP helps us to understand the learning process by explaining how newcomers become part of a CoP, thus becoming participants in a sociocultural practice. Lave and Wenger (1991) proposed that when people join a CoP they often do so as 'newcomers' at the periphery of the community. As they become more competent, they become fuller participants with some eventually becoming 'old-timers'; a process that has been described as moving from the periphery towards the 'centre' of the community. Lave and Wenger went on to say that learning, via LPP, occurs regardless of the context or even if there is no explicit intention that learning will occur. Over the past decade, numerous coaching-related studies and commentaries have appeared which have utilized, discussed and debated the merits of Lave and Wenger's (1991) interpretation of situated learning (see Cassidy & Rossi 2006; Cassidy *et al.* 2006a; Culver & Trudel 2006, 2008; Cushion & Denstone 2011; Galipeau & Trudel 2006; Owen-Pugh 2008; Rynne *et al.* 2006).

Lave and Wenger (1991) openly acknowledged that the concept of CoP had been under-theorized. Subsequently, Wenger (1998) proposed his social theory of learning. An assumption here was that participants of a community *mutually engage* in a *joint enterprise* in which they have a *shared repertoire*. Thus, for Wenger, learning was not so much the acquisition of knowledge, rather it was a process of social participation. More recently, Wenger-Trayner and Wenger-Trayner (2015) have acknowledged that previous conceptualizations of CoPs as discrete communities constricts the ability of the concept to adequately explain the complexities associated with a learning environment. To overcome this limitation, and to explicitly recognize that people build relationships across multiple sites, Wenger-Trayner and Wenger-Trayner (2015) developed the concept of Landscape of Practice (LoP), which they describe as 'a complex system of Communities of Practice *and the boundaries between them*' (2015: 13, *emphasis added*). Wenger (1998) claimed that the process of learning in a community was a 'vehicle for the evolution of practices and the inclusion of newcomers while also (and through the same process) the vehicle for the development and transformation of identities' (1998: 13). Wenger's social theory of learning uses four metaphors to describe learning: namely, 'learning as belonging', 'learning as becoming', 'learning as experience', and 'learning as doing' (1998: 5).

A project that investigated the processes of 'becoming' an elite netball player highlighted that developing a sense of 'belonging' to a team is complicated (Cassidy *et al.* 2006b). For example, one player had been a member of the national team for 11 years. In that time, she had never been dropped except when injured. She had played under three coaches, and for most of the time, had been either the captain or vice-captain. Yet, she never really felt as if she belonged (unless she was on court). Nonetheless, she still felt comfortable to lead the team and make contributions to technical and tactical practices. In contrast, another member of the same team said that after only one year she felt a strong sense of belonging. This was evident by her statement that 'I could trust everyone of them to cover my back if I was in a life threatening position … [I] would blimmin' bleed for them'. The sense of belonging had an impact on the learning processes of both players. This was most obvious in the second player, whose sense of belonging enabled her to feel comfortable in giving feedback to coaches, trying new things and participating in tactical decision-making. In short, it provided her with increased confidence and self-belief.

Given the above, coaches need to recognize that team members will have, and need, different degrees of belonging and that this will influence how and what they learn. However, Fitzclarence (2004) highlighted an alternative, 'shadowy' side of belonging. He argued that emphasizing belonging has the potential to establish what he called 'group think'; when members of a group 'learn to create a "them and us" mentality by isolating the "other" in order to assert the authority of the dominant' (Hickey & Fitzclarence 1997: 19). Hickey and Fitzclarence (1997) go onto say that when individuals are in the dominant group, it is often easier for them to 'express a sense of entitlement with regard to the person on the "outside" who is deemed to be in a vulnerable, marginal, position' (1997: 19). Coaches need to be cognizant of the development of 'group think', because it is often 'forged in traditions, customs, routines and habits' and, therefore, can be difficult to subvert; a situation which has implications for those who wish to change culture and practice. Also 'group think' can support anti-social behaviour by explaining it away as 'boys will be boys', 's/he deserved it', thereby distancing the 'aggressor from taking responsibility for their actions' (1997: 20).

### Learning culturally: a theory of learning cultures and a cultural theory of learning

Hodkinson *et al.* (2008: 30) developed 'a theoretical framework that builds the individual learner squarely within a cultural theory of learning'. The framework was informed by their view that (i) learning should be understood from an individual as well as a situational perspective; (ii) the histories of an individual and the situation will influence learning; (iii) that learning is also influenced by 'wider social, economic and political factors'; and (iv) that all these factors are interrelated (2008: 28). To keep both the social and individual foregrounded, Hodkinson *et al.* (2008) proposed the 'integration of a cultural theory of learning within a theory of learning cultures' (2008: 39). A theory of learning culture can be viewed as a framework to 'explain how and why situation influences learning' (2008: 28), while a cultural theory of learning 'sets out to explain how and why people learn' (2008: 28).

Hodkinson *et al.* (2008: 30) acknowledge that a focus on individual learning within a 'broadly situated or socio-cultural perspective' is not new (e.g. Beach 1995, 1999; Billett 2001; Billett & Somerville 2004; Hodkinson & Hodkinson 2003). Some of this work has been utilized in the sports coaching literature when discussing high performance coaching (e.g. Mallett *et al.* 2014; Rynne *et al.* 2006, 2010; Rynne & Mallett 2012), workplace learning (Rynne *et al.* 2006, 2010), communities of practice (Rynne 2008), formal and informal coach education (Mallett *et al.* 2009), culture change (Rynne *et al.* 2010; Rynne 2013), and coaches' social capital (Rynne 2014).

We interpret the following incident, which appeared in the Australian media in March 2015, using a theory of learning cultures and a cultural theory of learning (Hodkinson *et al.* 2008). On 22 March 2015, *The Australian* reported on the Super 15 rugby union match between the ACT[4] Brumbies and NSW[5] Waratahs under the headline 'David Pocock accuses Waratahs players of homophobic slurs', with an accompanying image of Pocock implicitly referencing 'muscular Christianity'[6]. The report noted that late in the match David Pocock (a Brumbies and Wallabies[7] player) twice approached the referee to accuse a Waratah player of making homophobic slurs against his teammate. The referee later described the slurs as 'pretty aggressive comments'. After the game the Brumbies captain (not Pocock) said that he

> didn't consider any of the "banter" to be out of the ordinary in the niggly encounter … I think it was all in the spirit of the game, and that's the way it goes out there and I didn't see it as an issue.

A day later, the accused Waratah player was fined A$20,000 for 'uttering a homophobic slur'. The Chief Executive of the Australian Rugby Union said 'we take the issue of homophobia in sport seriously and want to provide a positive environment for everyone involved in rugby. Comments of this nature cannot be tolerated' (Guinness 2015). Later the Waratah player, who was identified as coming from South Africa, issued a statement in which he said 'I'm very sorry for any offence caused by what I said on the field during a heated encounter' (Guinness 2015). In the ensuing media commentary, an Australian Rugby League player, Bradley Clyde said that Pocock's action had 'changed the Australian sporting landscape' (Polkinghome 2015). After praising Pocock's courage, Clyde said the actions that resulted as a consequence of Pocock's complaint to the referee is 'a bit of a milestone case, things like this happen every now and then that move the goal posts and you've got to adapt and learn from them and implement policy accordingly. Most sporting organisations will learn from it and educate their players around diversity' (Polkinghome 2015). That there is a need for this learning to occur is undeniable. A recent international study, which surveyed nearly 9,500 people from six countries, found that 82 per cent of lesbian, gay and bisexual participants reported witnessing or experiencing homophobia in sport (Gregory 2015).

The above incident can be understood using a theory of learning cultures (used to 'explain how and why situation influences learning'), and a cultural theory of learning (used to 'explain how and why people learn') (Hodkinson *et al.* 2008: 28). Bourdieu's notion of a field is particularly useful for analyzing the constitution of a learning culture, particularly as it occurs on an individual, local and institutional scale. Many analogies have been used to describe Bourdieu's notion of field, one of which is that it mirrors a market because it is a social space. In a field, like a market, there is inequality as well as mutual dependency, and people have different degrees of purchasing power as a consequence of their various backgrounds, tastes and circumstances. Finally, it is important to recognize that the dynamics of fields are such that similar fields can differ from site to site while 'some struggles that are highly important in one site [are] hardly present in another' (Hodkinson *et al.* 2008: 36).

Using the notion of field in the example supplied above, it is evident that within the Brumbies' team there were different interpretations of the comments made. Pocock viewed them as objectionable, whereas his captain said they were not 'out of the ordinary'. Arguably, Pocock's reputation as a member of the Wallabies gave him the power to challenge the homophobic slurs, which would not have been available to a rookie player in the same situation. That the media identified the accused as coming from South Africa suggests that they were trying to point out differences between how Australian and South African rugby players behave. Insight into the institutional scale of the learning culture was provided by the referee (who is also South African but interestingly was not identified as such), who was reported as saying the homophobic comments were 'pretty aggressive', and the Chief Executive of Australian Rugby Union stating that there was 'no place for homophobia' in rugby (Guinness 2015).

Using the cultural theory of learning to understand how and why players learn gives credence to the fact that players are socially positioned within a learning culture and that every player will contribute to the 'reconstruction' of that culture (Hodkinson *et al.* 2008). Drawing on the work of Bourdieu, Hodkinson *et al.* (2008) explained that the impact any individual has on a learning culture will be dependent upon 'a combination of their position within that culture, their dispositions towards that culture and the various types of capital that they possess' (2008: 13). They also contended that the Bourdieusian concept of habitus provides a way to understand both the social and individual aspects of learning. This is because it is viewed as a collection of durable, but also changeable, dispositions to 'all aspects of life that are often sub-conscious or tacit ... [as well as] social structures operating within and through individuals, rather than something outside of us' (2008: 14).

The notions of capital, habitus and field can be used to analyze the learning culture of the Super 15 rugby union competition. Here, the referee and Chief Executive of the Australian Rugby Union used their social and cultural capital, as did David Pocock in addition to his physical capital, to challenge the use of homophobic slurs, which according to some exist as an 'ordinary' part of the game. The challenge, instigated by Pocock, provided opportunities for coaches, administrators and other players to change their dispositions towards homophobia and potentially other discriminatory behaviour, as well as facilitate a learning process. Hodkinson *et al.* (2008) used a metaphor of 'learning as becoming'[8] to conceptualize the 'ways in which an individual learner learns through participation in many different situations, both simultaneously and successively' and is based on the assumption that 'in any situation there are opportunities to learn' (2008: 16). Yet the opportunities, and the ease in which they facilitate the learning process, is dependent upon 'the nature of the learning culture and of the position, habitus and capitals of the individuals, in interaction with each other' (2008: 16).

### *Experiential learning*

When learning is viewed via a participation metaphor (Sfrad 1998), the individual is positioned as 'someone who is interested in participating in certain kinds of activities rather than accumulating private possessions' (Trudel & Gilbert 2006: 516). This is consistent with those who view learning as a situated process occurring through experience. Experience is key to experiential learning models (e.g. Kolb 1984; Lewin 1951), and can be thought of as relating to an individual's engagement with 'specific events' as well as with how they participate more globally (Trudel & Gilbert 2006). Here, experiential learning is not considered the same as learning from experience. However, in the sports coaching literature a lack of clarity exists around experiential learning, which has resulted in the terms 'learning from experience' and 'experiential learning' being used interchangeably (Cushion *et al.* 2010).

Learning from experience can be thought of as the learning that occurs in everyday contexts (Usher & Solomon 1999) and is informal and unmediated. While no universal definition of experiential learning exists, commonalities between various definitions can be found: (i) it is cyclical; (ii) occurs via observation of and reflection on practice; and (iii) the practitioner tests out new constructs that subsequently emerged from the observations and reflections. What is more, experiential learning often occurs in mediated and formal and/or non-formal situations (Cushion *et al.* 2010). A common and influential interpretation of experiential learning is the Kolb (1984) cycle. Yet, the Kolb cycle has been criticized for being too simplistic and formulaic, and for not taking into account social power relations. Over the past 15 years, reflection has increasingly become a topic in many coach development initiatives, with links being made between reflection and experiential learning. When such connections are made, an opportunity is provided for the experiential cycle to become an iterative spiral (see Carr & Kemmis 1986). Similarly, Gilbert and Trudel's (2001) six-stage model of experiential learning provided opportunities for coaches to have a reflective conversation with themselves and others (Gilbert & Trudel 2005, 2006). They proposed that while initially the model mediates and formalizes opportunities to reflect, once coaches begin to do so, the experiential learning process can become unmediated and occur in informal situations. This outcome provides a possible explanation for why the terms 'learning from experience' and 'experiential learning' are used interchangeably.

## CONCLUDING THOUGHTS

As we stated in the introduction, the aim of this chapter was to describe some prominent theories of learning and make links to coaching practice, sporting culture and sport coaching literature. We hope that by doing so the chapter goes some way to assist coaches to recognize, as well as systematically examine, the theoretical assumptions that inform their practices that purport to facilitate learning. We recognize is not easy to understand the complexities associated with the various interpretations of learning, but not to try to understand is not an option if the coaching community genuinely wishes to assist athletes to learn. Coach and athlete learning is now on the radar of many national sporting organizations (Cushion *et al.* 2010) yet more work is needed by scholars of coaching science to translate the theories in a way that coaches, who desire to improve their practices and enhance athlete's learning opportunities, can engage with the ideas.

## END-OF-CHAPTER TASKS

1 Drawing on your experiences of being a coach or of being coached, identify and describe examples of reinforcement (positive and negative) and punishment (removal and presentation). Discuss some of the consequences for the athlete of receiving these reinforcers and punishers.
2 Reflect on a time when a coach required you to watch a model with the aim of improving performance. Describe how the coach encouraged, or could have encouraged, involvement of the cognitive process in your learning.
3 Describe a community of practice in which you are involved where you do not operate on the periphery. Explain the process you went through to become a more legitimate member of this community and what you learned in the process. Remember what you learned may not have been explicitly intended.
4 Drawing on a sport with which you are familiar, provide an example of where the habitus and capital of an individual(s) facilitated the learning culture in that sport.

## NOTES

1 Formerly called social learning theory (Siegelman & Rider 2006).
2 In August 2014, Bond and Murray set a new mark of dominance in world rowing. Up to that point, they had won 18 consecutive titles at Olympic, World Championship and World Cup level. Bond and Murray had not lost since teaming up in the men's pair in 2009.
3 A mediated learning situation is 'an episodic learning experience where the learner does not select the material to be taught' (Trudel *et al.* 2013: 380). An unmediated learning situation is where the learner makes their own decisions as to what information they need and what sources to utilize. An internal learning situation is where the learners 'reorganize what they already know' (2013: 383).
4 ACT is an acronym for Australian Capital Territory.
5 NSW is an acronym for the state of New South Wales.
6 A nineteenth-century cultural movement that made links between physical strength and religious certainty (Hall 1994).
7 The name of the Australian men's rugby team
8 Hodkinson *et al.* (2008) acknowledge that the 'learning as becoming' metaphor is extensively influenced by Sfard's (1998) metaphor of 'learning as participation' and Dewey's (1963) view that learning is embodied. They proposed the value of the 'learning as becoming' metaphor was that it enabled a more 'holistic' understanding of learning and a recognition that 'a person is constantly learning through becoming, and becoming through learning' (Hodkinson *et al.* 2008: 41). They are not the only learning theorists to use 'becoming' as a metaphor to understand the learning process (see Wenger 1998).

# REFERENCES

Armour, K. (2010). The learning coach, the learning approach: Professional development for sport coach professionals. In J. Lyle & C. Cushion (eds.) *Sports Coaching Professionalization and Practice*. London: Elsevier: 153–164.

Bandura, A. (1971). *Psychological modeling: Conflicting theories*. Chicago: Aldine-Atherton.

Beach, K. (1995). Activity as a mediator of sociocultural change and individual development: The case of school-work transition in Nepal. *Mind, Culture and Activity*, 2: 285–302.

Beach, K. (1999). Consequential transitions: A socio-cultural expedition beyond transfer in education. *Review of Research in Education*, 28: 46–69.

Billett, S. (2001). Learning through working life: Interdependencies at work. *Studies in Continuing Education*, 23(1): 19–35.

Billett, S. & Somerville, M. (2004). Transformations at work: Identity and learning. *Studies in Continuing Education*, 26(2): 309–326.

Bloom, G., Durand-Bush, N., Schinke, R. & Salmela, J. (1998). The importance of mentoring in the development of coaches and athletes. *International Journal of Sport Psychology*, 29: 267–281.

Carlson, N. & Buskist, W. (1997). *Psychology: The Science of Behavior*. London: Allyn and Bacon.

Carr, W. & Kemmis, S. (1986). *Becoming Critical: Education, Knowledge and Action Research*. London: Falmer Press.

Cassidy, T. & Rossi, T. (2006). Situating learning: (Re)examining the notion of apprentice-ship in coach education. *International Journal of Sports Science and Coaching*, 1(3): 235–246.

Cassidy, T., Merrilees, J. & Shaw, S. (2015). National governing bodies: Sport policy, practice and mentoring. In F. Chambers (ed.) *Mentoring in Physical Education and Sports Coaching*. London: Routledge.

Cassidy, T., Potrac, P. & McKenzie, A. (2006a). Evaluating and reflecting upon a coach education initiative: The CoDe of rugby. *The Sports Psychologist*, 20(2): 145–161.

Cassidy, T., Potrac, P. & Allen, J. (2006b). Examining the developmental experiences of elite athletes using a social theory of learning. Paper presented at the Association Internationale des Éscoles Superieures d'Education Physique (AIESEP) conference Jyväskylä, Finland, July.

Culver, D. & Trudel, P. (2006). Cultivating coaches' communities of practice: Developing the potential for learning through interactions. In R. Jones (ed.) *The Sports Coach as Educator. Re-conceptualising Sports Coaching*. London: Routledge.

Culver, D. & Trudel, P. (2008). Clarifying the concept of communities of practice in sport. *International Journal of Sports Science and Coaching*, 3(1): 1–10.

Culver, D., Trudel, P. & Werthner, P. (2009). A sport leader's attempt to foster a coaches' community of practice. *International Journal of Sports Science and Coaching*, 4(4): 365–383.

Cushion C. & Denstone G. (2011). Etienne Wenger: Coaching and communities of practice. In R. Jones, P. Potrac, C. Cushion & L. Ronglan (eds.) *The Sociology of Sports Coaching*. London: Routledge.

Cushion, C., Nelson, L., Armour, K., Lyle, J., Jones, R., Sandford, R. & O'Callaghan, C. (2010). *Coach Learning and Development: A Review of Literature*. London: Sports Coach UK.

Davis, B. & Sumara, D. (2003). Why aren't they getting this? Working through the regressive myths of constructivist pedagogy. *Teaching Education*, 14: 123–140.

Dewey, J. (1963). *Experience and Education*. New York: Collier.

Eggen, P. & Kauchak, D. (2004). *Educational Psychology. Windows on Classrooms*, 6th edn. New Jersey: Pearson.

Fitzclarence, L. (2004). Boys, balls and bad behaviour. Available at Monash.edu/news/releases/show/85. [Accessed on 30 April 2015].

Galipeau, J. & Trudel, P. (2006). Athlete learning in a community of practice: Is there a role for the coach? In R. Jones (ed.) *The Sports Coach as Educator. Re-conceptualising Sports Coaching*. London: Routledge.

Gilbert, W. (2002). An annotated bibliography and analysis of coaching science. Unpublished report sponsored by the Research Consortium of the American Alliance for Health, Physical Education, Recreation and Dance.

Gilbert, W. & Trudel, P. (2001). Learning to coach through experience: Reflection in model youth sport coaches. *Journal of Teaching in Physical Education*, 21(1): 16–34.

Gilbert, W. & Trudel, P. (2005). Learning to coach through experience: Conditions that influence reflection. *Physical Educator*, 62(1): 32–43.

Gilbert, W. & Trudel, P. (2006). The coach as reflective practitioner. In R. Jones (ed.) *The Sports Coach as Educator: Re-conceptualising Sports Coaching*. London: Routledge.

Gregory, S. (2015). U.S. ranks worst in sports homophobia study. Available at http://www.time.com/3852611/sports-homophobia-study. [Accessed on 10 May 2015].

Guinness, R. (2015). NSW Waratahs forward Jacques Potgieter fined $20,000 for homophobic slurs against ACT Brumbies. Available at http://www.smh.com.au/rugby-union/union-news/nsw-waratahs-forward-jacques-potgieter-fined-20000-for-homophobic-slurs-against-act-brumbies-20150323-lm5wau.html. [Accessed on 30 April 2015].

Hall, D. (1994). *Muscular Christianity: Embodying the Victorian Age*. Cambridge: Cambridge University Press.

Hickey, C. & Fitzclarence, L. (1997). Masculinity, violence and football. *Changing Education*, 4(2/3): 18–21.

Hodkinson, P. & Hodkinson, H. (2003). Individuals, communities of practice and the policy context: School-teachers learning in their workplace. *Studies in Continuing Education*, 25(1): 3–21.

Hodkinson, P., Biesta, G. & James, D. (2008). Understanding learning culturally: Overcoming the dualism between social and individual views of learning. *Vocations and Learning*, 1(1): 27–47.

Jarvis, P. (2006). *Towards a Comprehensive Theory of Human Learning*. London: Routledge.

Jarvis, P. (2007). *Globalisation, Lifelong Learning and the Learning Society: Sociological Perspectives*. London: Routledge.

Jarvis, P. (2009). Learning to be a person in society: Learning to be me. In K. Illeris (ed.) *Contemporary Learning Theories of Learning. Learning Theorists, In Their Own Words*. London: Routledge.

Jones, R. (2006). How can educational concepts inform sports coaching? In R. Jones (ed.) *The Sports Coach as Educator. Re-conceptualising Sports Coaching*. London: Routledge.

Kolb, D. (1984). *Experiential Learning as the Science of Learning and Development*. Englewood Cliffs, NJ: Prentice Hall.

Lave, J. & Wenger, E. (1991). *Situated Learning: Legitimate Peripheral Participation*. Cambridge: Cambridge University Press.

Lefrançois, G. (2000). *Theories of Learning*, 4th edn. Belmont, CA: Wadsworth/Thomson Learning.

Lewin, K. (1951). *Field Theory in Social Science*. Tavistock Publications, London.

Light, R. (2008). Complex learning theory – its epistemology and its assumptions about learning: Implications for Physical Education. *Journal of Teaching in Physical Education*, 27(1): 21–37.

Light, R. & Wallian, N. (2008). A constructivist-informed approach to teaching swimming. *Quest*, 60: 387–404.

Lyle, J. (2007). A review of the research evidence for the impact of coach education. *International Journal of Coaching Science*, 1(1): 17–34.

Mallett, C., Rossi, T. & Tinning, R. (2009). Relational interdependence between individual agency and affordances in how high performance coaches learn. In T. Rossi, P. Hay, L. McCuaig, R. Tinning & D. Macdonald (eds.) *Sport Pedagogy Research, Policy and Practice: International Perspectives in Physical Education and Sports Coaching. North meets South; East meets West*. AIESEP World Congress.

Mallett, C., Rynne, S. & Billett, S. (2014). Valued learning experiences of early career and experienced high-performance coaches. *Physical Education and Sport Pedagogy*. 1–16. DOI:10.1080/17408989.2014.892062.

Mallett, C., Trudel, P., Lyle, J. & Rynne, S. (2009). Formal vs informal coach education. *International Journal of Sports Science and Coaching*, 4(3): 325–334.

Merriam, S., Caffarella, R. & Baumgartner, L. (2007). *Learning in Adulthood. A Comprehensive Guide*, 3rd edn. San Francisco: John Wiley.

Merrilees, J. (2014). Women's experiences of becoming elite track and field coaches in New Zealand. Unpublished MPhEd, University of Otago, Dunedin, New Zealand.

Moon, J. (1999). *Reflection in Learning and Professional Development: Theory and Practice*. London: Routledge.

Moon, J. (2001). *Short Courses and Workshops: Improving the Impact of Learning and Professional Development*. London: Kogan Page.

Moon, J. (2004). *A Handbook of Reflective and Experiential Learning. Theory and Practice*. London: Routledge.

Nelson, L. & Cushion, C. (2006). Reflection in coach education. *The Sports Psychologist*, 20(2): 174–184.

Occhino, J., Mallett, C. & Rynne, S. (2013). Dynamic social networks in high performance football coaching. *Physical Education and Sport Pedagogy*, 18 (1): 90–102.

Ovens, A. & Godber, K. (2013). Affordance networks and the complexity of learning. In A. Ovens, T. Hopper & J. Butler (eds.) *Complexity Thinking in Physical Education: Reframing Curriculum, Pedagogy and Research*. London: Routledge.

Owen-Pugh, V. (2008). Clarifying the concept of communities of practice in sport: A commentary. *International Journal of Sports Science and Coaching*, 3(1): 23–27.

Phillips, D. (2000). *Constructivism in Education: Opinions and Second Opinions on Controversial Issues. Ninety-ninth Yearbook of the National Society for the Study of Education*. Chicago: The University of Chicago Press.

Polkinghome, D. (2015). Former Wallaby Richard Harry says David Pocock could be World Cup star. Available at http://www.smh.com.au/rugby-union/union-news/nsw-waratahs-forward-jacques-potgieter-fined-20000-for-homophobic-slurs-against-act-brumbies-20150323-1m5wau.html. [Accessed on 30 April 2015].

Potrac, P., Gilbert, W. & Denison, J. (eds.) (2013). *Routledge Handbook of Sports Coaching*. London: Routledge.

Rink, J. (2001). Investigating the assumptions of pedagogy. *Journal of Teaching in Physical Education*, 20(2): 112–128.

Roberts, G., Spink, K. & Pemberton, C. (1999). *Learning Experiences in Sport Psychology*, 2nd edn. Champaign, IL: Human Kinetics.

Roberts, S. & Potrac, P. (2014). Behaviourism, constructivism and sports coaching pedagogy: A conversational narrative in the facilitation of player learning. *International Sport Coaching Journal*, 1: 180–187.

Rushall, B. & Pettinger, J. (1969). An evaluation of the effect of various reinforcers used as motivators in swimming. *Research Quarterly*, 40: 540–545.

Rynne, S. (2008). Clarifying the concept of communities of practice in sport: A commentary. *International Journal of Sports Science and Coaching*, 3(1): 11–14.

Rynne, S. (2013). Culture change in a professional sports team: Shaping environmental contexts and regulating power. *International Journal of Sports Science and Coaching*, 8(2): 301–304.

Rynne, S. (2014). 'Fast track' and 'traditional path' coaches: Affordances, agency and social capital. *Sport, Education and Society*, 19(3): 299–313.

Rynne, S. & Mallett, C. (2012). Understanding the work and learning of high performance coaches. *Physical Education and Sport Pedagogy*, 17(5): 507–523.

Rynne, S., Mallett, C. & Tinning, R. (2006). High performance sport coaching: Institutes of sport as sites for learning. *International Journal of Sports Science and Coaching*, 1(3): 223–234.

Rynne, S. Mallett, C. & Tinning, R. (2010). Workplace learning of high performance sports coaches. *Sport, Education and Society*, 15(3): 315–330.

Schempp, P. (1998). The dynamics of human diversity in sport pedagogy scholarship. *Sociology of Sport On Line*, 1(1): Available at http://physed.otago.ac.nz/sosol/v1i1/v1i1.htm.

Schunk, D. (2004). *Learning Theories. An Educational Perspective*, 4th edn. New Jersey: Pearson.

Sfard, A. (1998). On two metaphors for learning and the danger of choosing just one. *Educational Researcher*, 27: 4–13.

Shilling, C. (1991). Educating the body: Physical capital and the production of social inequalities. *Sociology*, 25(4): 653–672.

Siegelman, C. & Rider, E. (2006). *Life-Span Human Development*, 5th edn. Melbourne: Thomson.

Tinning, R. & Rossi, A. (2013). Thinking about complexity thinking for physical education. In A. Ovens, T. Hopper & J. Butler (eds.) *Complexity Thinking in Physical Education: Reframing Curriculum, Pedagogy and Research*. London: Routledge.

Trudel, P. & Gilbert, W. (2006). Coaching and Coach Education, in D. Kirk, D. Macdonald & M. O'Sullivan (eds.) *The Handbook of Physical Education*. London: Sage.

Trudel, P., Culver, D. & Werthner, P. (2013). Looking at coach development from the coach-learner's perspective: Considerations for coach development administrators. In P. Potrac, W. Gilbert & J. Denison (eds.) *Routledge Handbook of Sports Coaching*. London: Routledge.

Usher, R. & Solomon, N. (1999). Experiential learning and the shaping of subjectivity in the workplace. *Studies in the Education of Adults*, 31(2): 155–163.

Vialle, W., Lysaght, P. & Verenikina, I. (2005). *Psychology for Educators*. Melbourne: Thomson.

Ward, P. (2006). The philosophy, science and application of behavior analysis in physical education. In D. Kirk, D. Macdonald & M. O'Sullivan (eds.) *The Handbook of Physical Education*. London: Sage.

Wenger, E. (1998). *Communities of Practice. Learning, Meaning and Identity*. Cambridge: Cambridge University Press.

Wenger, E., McDermott, R. & Snyder, W. (2002). *Cultivating Communities of Practice: A Guide to Managing Knowledge*. Boston: Harvard University Press.

Wenger-Trayner, E. & Wenger-Trayner, B. (2015). Learning in a landscape of practice. A framework. In E. Wenger-Trayner, M. Fenton-O'Creevy, S. Hutchinson, C. Kubiak & B. Wenger-Trayner (eds.) *Learning in Landscapes of Practice. Boundaries, Identity, and Knowledgeability in Practice-based Learning*. London: Routledge.

Werthner, P. & Trudel, P. (2006). A new theoretical perspective for understanding how coaches learn to coach. *The Sport Psychologist*, 20: 198–212.

Wright, T., Trudel, P. & Culver, D. (2007). Learning how to coach: The different learning situations reported by youth ice hockey coaches. *Physical Education and Sport*, 12 (2): 127-144.

## CHAPTER 9

# 'Developing' athletes (with Lisette Burrows)

## INTRODUCTION

In November 2013, Lydia Ko, the then top-ranked women's amateur golfer in the world, turned professional. What made this event 'newsworthy' was the fact that she was 16 years old. In the golfing world Lydia was considered a prodigy. When she was 12, she made the cut in her first professional event, and then never missed one as an amateur in her subsequent 12 professional tournaments. At the age of 14 years (and nine months) she won the 2012 New South Wales Open in Australia, making her the youngest ever winner of a professional event worldwide. We marvel at Lydia's achievements, because we do not expect this from a teenage girl. We expect teenagers to be experimenting, searching for an identity, and rebelling against parents or caregivers. Similarly, when coaching a team of five year olds in football we do not expect them to be executing finely honed passing, dribbling and kicking skills, positioning themselves strategically on the field or engaging in complex tactical play. We expect such players to cluster around the ball because 'that's the stage they're at'. Both of these expectations arise from developmental assumptions.

It is not only the actions of the young that are subject to developmental assumptions. In October 2013, 78-year-old Harriet Anderson completed the World Ironman Championships[1] in Kailua-Kona, Hawaii. Harriet began racing in Ironman competitions when she was in her 50s, and since then has completed the Kona Ironman more than

20 times, including in 2010 when she broke her clavicle mid-race after another cyclist bumped into her. In 2013, she was the only woman competing in the 75 to 79 age group. Harriet's story has become newsworthy because her actions do not fit the expectations we have of 78-year-old women. In this chapter, we highlight the pervasiveness of developmental assumptions, and demonstrate how they are reflected in some of the practices of sports coaches and in the academic accounts of how people develop. Additionally, in the final section of the chapter we introduce and discuss the notion of developmentalism and how it implicitly informs many things that are done in the name of sports coaching.

## DEVELOPMENTAL ASSUMPTIONS

Developmental assumptions can be readily found within the everyday 'common sense' beliefs about human change throughout a lifespan. These assumptions shape our view of what people can and cannot do at particular ages and life stages. They can often be witnessed by such statements as 'he's too old for that', 'she's acting like a baby', 'she's a terrible two', and 'grow up, Johnny'. We hear these types of developmental statements every day in homes, schools and on sports fields.

One assumption underpinning developmental language is that people think and act in particular ways depending on their age and/or stage. We also assume that those ages and stages are universally recognizable; that is, if we say, 'Tom's a terrible teen', others will know what we mean. Chances are, in Western society at least, people *will* know what a 'teen' means. Indeed, decades of experimental research in developmental psychology has 'proved' that teenagers exist, that they behave in particular ways (e.g. they take risks, they are egocentric), and that all of this is very different from the world of 'grown-ups'. But are teenagers really like that? Do all teenagers, feel, act and think in similar ways? Is it necessarily the case that a 13 year old thinks more about himself or herself than others? Are all teenagers clumsy? Do they all eat lots of junk food? Are they all concerned with image? What happens to our views on how people develop when something, or someone like Lydia Ko, challenges them? Another assumption underpinning the use of developmental language is that what happens to us when we are young will influence how we 'turn out' when we are older. Movement is accorded a primary role in 'setting a child up for life'. Similarly, links are often forged in public and professional discourse between playing sport and becoming a better person; someone with capacities to work in teams, cooperate with others, set and achieve goals, and so on.

The prevalence of developmental language in the sport sector is evident in phrases associated with youth sports such as 'catch them quick', 'mastering the basics', and 'fundamental motor skills'. The notion that children learn to walk before they run, creep before they crawl, and float before they swim, is an understanding shared by many coaches. It is also instantiated as 'fact' in motor-development literature, and reflects the assumption that there is 'developmentally appropriate practice' and that learning occurs sequentially. When it is assumed that early experiences determine what happens later in life, it is not uncommon to find children as young as two years old learning to throw, kick or bat a ball 'in preparation' for their subsequent participation in sport. Increasingly, young children are being encouraged to participate in sport not only for the recreational benefits it affords, but also to decrease the likelihood that those children will grow up to be obese and unhealthy adults (Burrows & Wright 2003). A consequence of this assumption is the belief that children need to be taught fundamental motor skills *before* they can incorporate these into more complex motor scripts (like a game). Coaches whose practices are informed by initiatives such as *Teaching Games for Understanding* and *Games Sense* challenge such assumptions. These coaches see playing games as opportunities to teach and learn.

## PROMINENT PERSPECTIVES ON DEVELOPMENT

The work and writings of Jean Piaget and Lev Vygotsky, which originated in the twentieth century, have been influential in the literature that has focused on the development of young people. In the middle of the twentieth century, many researchers began to expand upon Piaget's ideas, whilst remaining loyal to his interpretation of cognitive development. They became known as neo-Piagetians. One neo-Piagetian was Fischer who adopted a 'dynamic systems approach' to skill development (Morra *et al.* 2007); ideas that have subsequently been utilized by some working in the area of sports skill acquisition (see Davids *et al.* 2008; McMorris 2004). Such work reflects and reaffirms Piaget's view that development precedes learning (Siegelman & Rider 2006: 196). Other neo-Piagetians like Suizzo (2000) explored the socio-emotional context and cultural meanings of cognitive development. The importance of contexts in a young person's development was key to Vygotsky's view of development (Vialle *et al.* 2005). In the West, there has been less application of Vygotsky's ideas, in part due to his work not being easily accessible until relatively recently. Nevertheless, in the context of sports coaching, a Vygotskian approach has been used to discuss coach development (Mallett 2010; Potrac & Cassidy 2006) and enhance the acquisition of physical skills (Veraksa & Gorovaya 2013). However, discussions of Vygotsky's work have been more focused on learning than development as was highlighted in the previous chapter. One possible reason for this is that Vygotsky, unlike Piaget, perceived learning as setting 'developmental process in motion' (Driscoll 2005: 255).

Many have discussed the work of Piaget and Vygotsky in terms of their differences and, as a consequence, their work has often been seen in terms of dualisms e.g. biological/social or locational/contextual. But, in a detailed analysis of Vygotsky and pedagogy, Daniels (2001) pointed out that the work of Biddell (1992: 37) 'moves the Vygotsky versus Piaget debate beyond the somewhat sterile opposition'. Daniels illustrates this point by quoting Biddell's thesis at length:

> Piaget's constructivism implicitly supports a contextualist approach to knowledge development and stands in contradiction to the individualism and interactionism of his stage theory ... Vygotsky presents a dialectical conception of the relations between personal and social that differs diametrically from reductionist views ...[Vygotsky goes on to say] dimensions of reality such as the social and the personal are not separate and self-contained but have a shared existence as differing tendencies united within real developing systems ... replaces the reductionist metaphor of separation and interaction with the dialectical metaphor of participation.
>
> (Daniels 2001: 37)

Having analyzed the writings of Piaget and Vygotsky, Daniels (2001) makes a persuasive case as to the 'poverty' of taking up an 'either-or' position. We acknowledge this, and do not do so in our discussion of learning in Chapter 7. However, in this chapter, we do discuss how some of the assumptions of Piaget's stage theory, which is acknowledged as being individualist and interactionist, are reflected in prominent perspectives of development, and how this differs from the work of Vygotsky.

## A stage perspective of development

Jean Piaget was a Swiss scholar born in 1896, whose work continues to influence how we understand cognitive development. He was interested in studying 'how humans acquire knowledge and use it to adapt to their world' (Siegelman & Rider 2006: 41). Possibly, due to his background in zoology and philosophy, his theories reflect the assumptions of constructivism and structuralism. These assumptions are grounded in the view that cognitive development 'depends on four factors: biological maturation, experience with the physical environment, experience with the social environment and equilibration' (Schunk 2004: 447). The first three factors are self-explanatory, but it is the 'concept of equilibrium and the need to achieve it' that is the focus of this section (Eggen & Kauchak 2004: 37). Equilibrium has been described as '*a state of cognitive balance between individuals' understanding of the world and their experiences*' (2004: 37). To understand the concept of equilibrium, it is useful to be familiar with its associated processes; namely, organization, adaptation, assimilation and accommodation.

A sense of balance or equilibrium is considered to be important to our development and can be understood when we reflect on how we can interpret new experiences. For example, if we are unable to understand new experiences, a state of disequilibrium occurs. This can cause some discomfort, hence the saying 'I'm out of my comfort zone'. According to this perspective of development, disequilibrium is considered to be 'a major energizing force'. This is because it requires the employment of two separate but linked processes to restore a sense of equilibrium (or balance): specifically, organization and adaptation (Eggen & Kauchak 2004: 37). As the name suggests, organization relates to arranging and structuring the vast number of experiences we have everyday to make sure we are not swamped. In our effort to achieve equilibrium, we organize these experiences into some form of systems or mental patterns that Piaget called schemes. It is the process of forming and using schemes that helps us to understand our world (Eggen & Kauchak 2004). However, when acquiring new experiences, existing schemes can become inadequate, which then requires us to adapt.

The process of adaptation takes place when schemes and experiences are adjusted in an effort to maintain equilibrium (Eggen & Kauchak 2004). Adaptation occurs via 'two equally important and complementary processes: assimilation and accommodation' (Vialle *et al.* 2005: 26). Assimilation is the initial process we use upon meeting a new situation, and occurs when we attempt to fit (or assimilate) the new information into existing schemes (Vialle *et al.* 2005). For example, when a non-Australian coach saw her first game of Australian Rules Football she initially relied on her existing schemes; that is, her knowledge of other forms of football (rugby union and rugby league) to understand the game. Similarly, when she saw her first game of handball, she judged it against her existing schemes; knowledge of sports she considered to be similar, such as basketball, netball and water polo. When the sports could not be *assimilated* into her existing schemes, the second process came into play as the new information needed to be *accommodated*. This resulted in changes being made to her schemes (Vialle *et al.* 2005). As we interpret new experiences, assimilation and accommodation are in 'constant flow', with equilibrium occurring when a balance is found between the two (Vialle *et al.* 2005). Equilibrium was one of the mechanisms Piaget suggested was responsible for progression from one developmental 'stage' to the next (Driscoll 2005). The view that development is 'stage-like' has had, and continues to have, considerable purchase in the coaching community, especially in relation to coaching youth sport and developing young people.

Even those who critique the growing pressure on young people to begin their formal sporting experiences early, still organize the developing athletes into stages. For example, Fraser-Thomas *et al.* (2005: 27) observed that elite athletes generally transitioned through three stages of development, 'the sampling years (age 6–12), the specializing years (age 13–15), and the investment years (age 16+)'. In the studies that informed the Developmental Model of Sports Participation (DMSP), from where the above stages emerged, it was found that elite athletes had participated in a variety of different sports during sampling years. The number of sports decreased over time until the athlete made a commitment to one in his or her investment years. While the stages were identified, Côté *et al.* (2014) did state that the DMSP was only a general guideline and, as such, must be adapted to suit specific individuals.

## A social, cultural-historical perspective of development

Lev Vygotsky was a Russian educational psychologist, whose work in the early twentieth century was revolutionary in that he viewed 'learning and development as culturally, socially and historically mediated' (Vialle *et al.* 2005: 48). Vygotsky's social, cultural-historical theory of development is complex, consequently we only briefly touch on two features here; knowledge co-construction, and the zone of proximal development (ZPD).

We acknowledge that there are limitations of only focusing on one or two concepts and not the whole theory. Vialle *et al.* (2005) pointed out that ZPD 'should be understood in the context of the theory as a whole … otherwise the zone of proximal development can be interpreted as being a "restricted view of learning processes and reduces the learner's role to one of passivity and dependence upon the adult"' (Vialle *et al.* 2005: 61). Similarly, Schunk (2004: 296) observed that the 'emphasis it [ZPD] has received in Western cultures has served to distort its meaning and downplay the complexity of Vygotsky's theory' (for comprehensive overviews of Vygotsky's work see Daniels 2001; Kozulin *et al.* 2003, Moll 1990; Wink & Putney 2002). Despite recognizing these limitations we consider it beneficial for coaches and students of coaching to be introduced to Vygotsky's work so they can begin to understand how his ideas are, or are not, reflected in the prominent perspectives on development

Underpinning Vygotsky's work was his belief in the importance of surrounding a child (and we would suggest any learner) with support people or significant others in an effort to support and enhance their development. For Vygotsky, development occurred in 'interactions between people', a process he called 'co-construction'. Co-construction reflected his belief that 'knowledge creation' is 'a dynamic process' (Drewery & Bird 2004: 21). However, Vygotsky's focus was not just on the child, or the learner, but also on the effect of the interactions that occur between the learner and their supporters, whether they are adults or older peers.

Linked to co-construction is the concept of the zone of proximal development where Vygotsky believed our 'higher mental functions' take place. He described the zone of proximal development as:

> [t]he distance between the actual developmental level as determined by independent problem solving and the level of potential development as determined through problem solving under adult guidance or in collaboration with more capable peers.
>
> (Vygotsky 1978: 86)

A useful metaphor for understanding Vygotsky's perspective on the zone of proximal development is a staircase. Here, the zone of proximal development can be viewed as the vertical distance (the riser) between the tread of the stair on which the learner is standing and the next tread. To reach the higher stair, the learner collaborates with others, and/or receives assistance by others, to perform. Over time, the collaboration/assistance is reduced as the learners internalize what is required to perform the activity. Once the internalization has occurred, and the learner no longer needs assistance to perform the activity, it can be said that he or she has reached the tread of the next stair. When this occurs, the zone of proximal development becomes the vertical distance to the next stair, and so on (Royal Tangaere 1997). Another metaphor linked to the zone of proximal development is scaffolding. Despite scaffolding being widely used to operationalize the concept of the zone of proximal development, Vygotsky did not use this metaphor (Daniels 2001). Rather it has been suggested that Wood *et al.* (1976) defined scaffolding, while Cazden (1979) linked the term scaffolding to the work of Vygotsky (Daniels 2001). While the staircase metaphor can be useful to operationalize the zone of proximal development, it also has limitations. This is because it suggests that development occurs uninterrupted, albeit with rises and plateaus, from point A to point B. Vygotsky certainly did not view development as being linear. Instead, he saw it as being inclusive of 'periodic crises and revolutions' (McMillan 1991: 33).

Urie Bronfenbrenner, a Russian emigrant to the US, is attributed as being one of the key people who brought Vygotsky's work to the attention of the English-speaking world. Although his ecological theory of development is not as comprehensive as the others previously discussed, his work is beneficial because he 'provides a useful extension of Vygotsky's ideas on cultural context' (Drewery & Bird 2004: 23). Bronfenbrenner's ecological model of development can be described as the 'influences surrounding the developing individual' (Drewery & Bird 2004: 24). These influences go from *microsystems* (immediate environment e.g. family, teammates), through *mesosystems* ('connections that link microsystems'), and *exosystems* (larger social systems e.g. communities), to *macrosystems* (cultural patterns). The interconnectedness of the systems, going from micro to macro can be explained by considering them as a set of nested Russian dolls.[2]

The ideas expressed in Bronfenbrenner's model are beginning to gain some momentum within the coaching community. For example, the Developmental Model of Sport Participation (DMSP) begins to recognize that sport programmes need to be designed in ways that acknowledge young people's social, physical, psychological and intellectual development. The interviews that informed the DMSP highlighted the 'relative age effect', which can be afforded to those young people whose birth date occurs just after the cut-off date for age group sport. They also identified the 'birth place effect', which favours those young people born in mid-sized cities due to their ability to access facilities, as well as have opportunities to play informally in their local community. Additionally, the importance of family influences on young people's development in sport was underlined. It is not surprising then, that the DMSP supports young people becoming, and staying, involved in 'a diverse number of activities during early childhood', thereby favouring diversification rather than specialization. It also recommends a shift 'from deliberate play to deliberate practice (as the child moves from) childhood to adolescence' (Fraser-Thomas *et al.* 2005: 31).

## WHAT IS DEVELOPMENTALISM AND WHAT DOES IT DO?

Piaget's ideas on development being 'stage-like' have become so influential that they are now often considered 'common-sense'. So much so, that an assumed understanding is that children grow larger and taller, are more coordinated over time, exhibit progressively complex motor skills, and become more capable of abstract thought as they age. The fact that most children *do* seem to be able to run faster, jump further, wield bigger cricket bats and understand game plans better at 12 than 6 years of age confers a truth status upon these developmental claims. We regard the processes of change that children go through en route to maturity as both natural and to some extent, predictable. We 'look' for these kinds of changes in children, and worry if we cannot see them. Developmentalism is an umbrella term used by some critical psychologists (for example, Baker 2001; Morss 1996) to refer to these assumptions, and the subsequent practices informed by them.

An important question that critical psychologists have asked is: who is marginalized or misses out when we adopt a particular view of development? As Walkerdine (1984, 1993), Burrows (2002), and Stainton Rogers and Stainton Rogers (1992) suggested, the developmental 'story' of human change is just that – *one* amongst many possible tales. The fact that some stories have more currency than others means that some ways of thinking about and practising human development are privileged, while others are marginalized. Furthermore, as Walkerdine (1993) has suggested, developmentalism can actually work to construct the ways in which people recognize themselves and others. In other words, developmentalism produces the 'development' we think we observe.

Since the 1960s, critical psychologists have been questioning the implied naturalness and universality of developmental 'norms' (Baker 2001; Broughton 1987; Burman 1994; Morss 1996; Walkerdine 1993). What most of this work shares is an understanding that developmental milestones are cultural constructions rather than scientific truths. In other words, 'normal' is what a particular group of people with the power to define what 'counts' says is 'normal'. Commenting on the developmental accounts prevailing in American textbooks, Parker and Shotter (1990: 50) attest that 'what we have here are features of white middle class US society mapped onto models of development which are then treated as universal'.

The trouble with developmental 'norms', is that they tend to universalize tendencies and traits that relate to a particular sort of child – a masculine, European one – and stigmatize any child who fails to measure up to that idealized vision (Burman 1991, 1994; Walkerdine 1993). Once standards of 'normal' motor development, for example, are established, those deviating from the 'norm' are inevitably construed as in need of remedial assistance. Burrows (2012) highlighted this in her discussion of Suzy who, at five years old, was referred to a movement development clinic because of her 'condition'. This condition (according to her mother), was that Suzy was 'plump' and 'doesn't seem to *want* to "play" like her friends … she's shy and withdrawn, and not that physical' (2012: 38).

Another problem associated with universalizing developmental norms was identified by Wright's (1997) critique of fundamental motor-skills programmes. She drew attention to the specificity of the skills included in Fundamental Motor Skills (FMS) assessment batteries widely used in Australia and New Zealand. Here, she highlighted how skills like the overhand throw, catch and kick were intimately related to performance in competitive sports played predominantly by men. According to Wright, the lack of emphasis in FMS tests on motor skills, which link to activities such as dance or gymnastics, contributes 'to the (re) production of gender differences which construct girls and women as deficient, as lacking in comparison to a male standard' (Wright 1997: 20). Nearly two decades on, children's fundamental skills are still being tested and the findings are still showing that 'boys are more proficient with object control (OC) skills, such as throwing, catching, and kicking' (Spessato *et al.* 2013). The standards and norms informing motor-skill measurement marginalize not only girls, but also all children whose interests and proclivities lie with skills requiring balance, flexibility or fine motor coordination.

Human development is often represented as a linear process, thus people are assumed to be *progressing* and getting *better* at something when they improve in an upward and onwards sort of fashion. But what happens when development does not work like this? What happens when little Johnny stays short instead of growing into the towering 6 foot 5 inch frame that was expected? What happens if Mary never learns to 'run'? What happens when 'grown-ups' behave 'like children'? What generally happens is they are labelled as 'developmentally delayed' or 'immature'. This highlights an issue with developmental claims, namely their evaluative tone. These labels only acquire their pejorative quality because a norm or 'ideal' exists, yet as we have suggested, those norms themselves may rest on shaky foundations. Coaches often feel the impact of these developmental claims, as highlighted in the three following examples. First, a coach who fields a team of athletes, some of whom have difficulty playing by the rules or respecting the referee, will feel the disapproval of peers, parents and administrators. A parent whose five-year-old child cannot throw the ball as far as the others in the team, will worry. A coach whose teenage athlete fails to develop his/her 'full potential' under their tutelage will feel like they could have done more. When competency is linked with age, as it is in developmental claims, judgements are inevitable. Second, we all go through many biological transitional periods from birth to death, and during these periods, performance can become unstable. This is particularly noticeable in youth sports when an athlete has a growth spurt, which changes the length of the individual's limbs. As a consequence, the young person will be required to learn new motor patterns (Cassidy *et al.* 2014), which may cause performance to decline, even if only for a short period. The ability of the coach and athlete to cope with these unstable periods is key to the athlete's successful long-term development (Davids *et al.* 2000). Third, a coach can perceive an athlete reaching a plateau in their training as a problem. This, however, is only problematic because of the developmental norms held by the coach. If the coach didn't hold these normative assumptions, it is possible that he or she may view the athlete's performance plateau as evidence of reaching a consistent state of performance (Denison & Avner 2011).

Many of these developmental claims focus on the individual, or the problem(s) of the individual. But development also occurs in a context and is influenced by access to resources. In reviewing some of the 'prominent resource-related factors affecting skill development', Hodge and Baker (2011: 32) concluded that many of these were not controllable by the individual. Even if one has difficulty thinking of development as social rather than 'natural', questions about the inevitability of normative ages and stages are raised when athletes do surprising things that are out of step with expectations (see the examples of Harriet Anderson or Lydia Ko described at the beginning of this chapter). It is not only the 'exceptional' that alerts us to the problems of assuming age-related competency, though. Precise claims about what people of particular ages can and cannot do, simply cannot hold true for all people all of the time.

## CONCLUDING THOUGHTS

Prominent perspectives of development are very persuasive, that is why they have become dominant and considered by many as 'common-sense' and 'natural'. Consequently, it can be difficult to envisage development done differently. At one level, doing development differently might simply mean asking ourselves why we categorize athletes the way we do. For example, a starting question might be, is it 'fair' or 'pedagogically correct' to have nine year olds of widely variable strength and size playing together in competitive sports? In New Zealand, some junior rugby competitions use weight (e.g. under 38 kgs) as an organizing framework for allocating athletes to teams. Wrestling and weightlifting clubs adopt a similar practice. In most other sports, however, chronological age (e.g. under 11) continues to function as the means for characterizing children as members of a team or coaching group. Rethinking this mode of classification would be one step towards disrupting the restrictive (e.g. short nine year olds still have to get the ball in the standard hoop) and often discriminatory connotations (e.g. featherweight Johnny being squashed by heavy Karl) of age-related groupings.

A second strategy to disrupt developmental effects is to adopt a reflective stance towards our own pedagogical choices, in terms of both content and delivery. Why do we always do the drills first and then play the game? Why do we presume athletes need to master the basics before moving on to the more complex task of using those fundamentals in a 'real' context? Why do coaches think they are the only ones with insights about what might make the team work more collaboratively? Similarly, given what we know about the historical and cultural variability of childhood, why do we continue to use chronological age as a marker to shape our expectations of what children can achieve, think about and do? As Baker (2001) suggests, a grand narrative of child development as progressive, linear and gradual has been entrenched in the thinking and practice of Western peoples for centuries. The idea that children develop through a sequentially organized series of steps towards an ideal, is so firmly embedded in both professional and everyday understandings, it seems impossible at times to imagine child development differently. Just because we have always thought about development this way does not mean it is the best or only framework available for organizing human endeavour.

## END-OF-CHAPTER TASKS

It is the first day of training for a group of ten 'little nippers' (novice surf life-savers). An assortment of children expectantly hover in the clubhouse. All they have in common is a desire to learn surf skills and their age – they are either 10 or 11 years old.

1  What will you do with this group on their first day?
2  What assumptions about their capacity might you make?
3  How will you tailor the first session to take into account of what possibly is a widely divergent set of strengths, experience levels and dispositions?
4  What factors other than age will influence what and how you design this first 'little nippers' session?
5  From where will you get your information about the group?

## NOTES

1    An Ironman consists of a 2.4 mile (3.8 km) swim, 112 mile (180 km) bike ride and a full 26.2 mile (42 km) marathon.
2    Other names for a set of nested Russian dolls are Matryoshka doll, a stacking doll, or a Babushka doll, and comprises a set of dolls of decreasing sizes placed one inside the other.

## REFERENCES

Baker, B. (2001). Moving on (part 2): Power and the child in curriculum history. *Journal of Curriculum Studies*, 33: 277–302.

Biddell, T. (1992). Beyond interactionism in contextualist models of development. *Human Development*, 35(5): 306–15.

Broughton, J. (ed.) (1987). *Critical Theories of Psychological Development*. New York: Plenum.

Burman, E. (1991). Power, gender and developmental psychology. *Feminism & Psychology*, 1: 141–153.

Burman, E. (1994). *Deconstructing Developmental Psychology*. London: Routledge.

Burrows, L. (2002). Constructing the child: Developmental discourses in school physical education. *New Zealand Journal of Educational Studies*, 37(2): 127–140.

Burrows, L. (2012). Developing Suzy. In M. Miyahara (ed.) *Learning from Individual Movement Development*, 2nd edn. Dunedin, NZ: University of Otago.

Burrows, L. & Wright, J. (2003). The discursive production of childhood, identity and health. In J. Evans, B. Davies & J. Wright (eds.) *Body, Knowledge and Control: Studies in the Sociology of Education and Physical Culture*. London: Routledge.

Cassidy, T., Jackson, A.M., Miyahara, M. & Shemmell, J. (2014). Greta: Weaving strands to allow Greta to flourish as Greta. In K. Armour (ed.) *Pedagogical Cases in Sport, Exercise and Physical Activity. Volume 1: Physical Education and Youth Sport*. London: Routledge.

Cazden, B. (1979). Peekaboo as an instructional model: Discourse development at home and a school. In papers and reports on child language development, 17. Palo Alto, CA: Stanford University.

Côté, J., Hancock, D., Fischer, S. & Gurd, B. (2014). Rob. Talent in ice hockey: Age, neighbourhood, and training. In K. Armour (ed.) *Pedagogical Cases in Sport, Exercise and Physical Activity. Volume 1: Physical Education and Youth Sport*. London: Routledge.

Daniels, H. (2001). *Vygotsky and Pedagogy*. London: Routledge-Falmer.

Davids, K., Button, C. & Bennett, S. (2008). *Dynamics of Skill Acquisition*. Champaign, Il: Human Kinetics.

Davids, K., Lees, A. & Burwitz, L. (2000). Understanding and measuring coordination and control in soccer skills: Implications for talent identification and skill acquisition. *Journal of Sports Sciences*, 18: 703–714.

Denison, J. & Avner, Z. (2011). Positive coaching: Ethical practices for athlete development. *Quest*, 63: 209–227.

Drewery, W. & Bird, L. (2004). *Human Development in Aotearoa. A Journey Through Life*, 2nd edn. Sydney: McGraw Hill.

Driscoll, M. (2005). *Psychology of Learning for Instruction*, 3rd edn. London: Pearson.

Eggen, P. & Kauchak, D. (2004). *Educational Psychology. Windows on Classrooms*, 6th edn. New Jersey: Pearson.

Fraser-Thomas, J., Côté, J. & Deakin, J. (2005). Youth sport programs: An avenue to foster positive youth development. *Physical Education and Sport Pedagogy*, 10(1): 19–40.

Hodge, N. & Baker, J. (2011). Expertise: The goal of performance development. In D. Collins, A. Button, & H. Richards (eds.) *Performance Psychology. A Practitioner's Guide*. Edinburgh: Elsevier.

Kozulin, A., Gindis, B., Ageyev, V. & Miller, S. (2003). *Vygotsky's Educational Theory in a Cultural Context*. Cambridge: Cambridge University Press.

Mallett, C. (2010). Becoming a high-performance coach: Pathways and communities. In J. Lyle & C. Cushion (eds.) *Sports Coaching: Professionalism and Practice*. Edinburgh: Churchill Livingstone.

McMillan, B. (1991). All in the mind: Human learning and development from an ecological perspective. In J. Morss & T. Linzey (eds.) *Growing up: The Politics of Human Learning*. Auckland: Longman Paul.

McMorris, T. (2004). *Acquisition and Performance of Sports Skills*. Hoboken, NJ: Wiley.

Moll, L. (1990). *Vygotsky and Education: Instructional Implications and Applications of Socio-historical Psychology*. Cambridge: Cambridge University Press.

Morra, S., Gobbo, C., Marini, Z. & Sheese, R. (2007). *Cognitive Development: Neo-Piagetian Perspectives*. New York: Lawrence Erlbaum Associates.

Morss, J. (1996). *Growing Critical: Alternatives to Developmental Psychology*. London: Routledge.

Parker, I. & Shotter, J. (eds.) (1990). *Deconstructing Social Psychology*. London: Routledge.

Potrac, P. & Cassidy, T. (2006). The coach as a 'more capable other'. In R. Jones (ed.) *The Sports Coach as Educator: Re-conceptualising Sports Coaching*. London: Routledge.

Royal Tangaere, A. (1997). Māori human development learning theory. In P. Te Whāiti, M. McCarthy & A. Durie (eds.) *Mai I Rangiātea: Māori Wellbeing and Development*. Auckland: Auckland University Press.

Schunk, D. (2004). *Learning Theories. An Educational Perspective*, 4th edn. New Jersey: Pearson.

Siegelman, C. & Rider, E. (2006). *Life-Span Human Development*, 5th edn. Melbourne: Thomson.

Spessato, C., Gabbard, C., Valentini, N. & Rudisill, M. (2013). Gender differences in Brazilian children's fundamental movement skill performance. *Early Child Development and Care*, 183(7): 916–923.

Stainton Rogers, R. & Stainton Rogers, W. (1992). *Stories of Childhood: Shifting Agendas of Child Concern*. Buffalo, NY: University of Toronto Press.

Suizzo, M.A. (2000). The Social-emotional and cultural contexts of cognitive development: Neo-Piagetian perspectives. *Child Development*, 71(4): 846–849.

Veraksa, A. & Gorovaya, A. (2013). The possibility of using sign and symbolic tools in the development of motor skills by beginning soccer players. *Procedia-Social and Behavioral Sciences*, 78: 285–289.

Vialle, W., Lysaght, P. & Verenikina, I. (2005). *Psychology for Educators*, Melbourne: Thomson.

Vygotsky, L. (1978). *Mind in Society: The Development of Higher Psychological Processes* (M. Cole, V. John-Steiner, S. Scribner & E. Souberman, transl.). Cambridge, MA: Harvard University Press.

Walkerdine, V. (1984). Development psychology and the child-centred pedagogy: The insertion of Piaget into early education. In W. Henriques, C. Hollway, C. Urwin, C. Venn & V. Walkerdine (eds.) *Changing the Subject: Psychology, Social Regulation and Subjectivity*. London: Methuen.

Walkerdine, V. (1993). Beyond developmentalism? *Theory and Psychology*, 3: 451–469.

Wink, J. & Putney, L. (2002). *A Vision of Vygotsky*. London: Allyn and Bacon.

Wood, D., Bruner, J. & Ross, G. (1976). The role of tutoring in problem solving. *Journal of Child Psychology and Psychiatry*, 17: 89–100.

Wright, J. (1997). Fundamental motor skills testing as problematic practice: A feminist analysis. *ACHPER Healthy Lifestyles Journal*, 44(4): 18–29.

## CHAPTER 10

# Talent identification and development

## INTRODUCTION

> Superstar lawyers and math whizzes and software entrepreneurs appear at first blush to lie outside ordinary experience. But they don't. They are the products of history and community, of opportunity and legacy. Their success is not exceptional or mysterious. It is grounded in a web of advantages and inheritances, some deserved, some not, some earned, some just plain lucky – but critical to making them who they are. The outlier, in the end, is not an outlier at all.
>
> (Gladwell 2008: 285)

In *Outliers*, Gladwell (2008) described the exploits of people considered to be out of the ordinary, and argued the need to critically examine how such people come to be viewed as talented and successful. Gladwell's view of talent development is multi-dimensional and dynamic. Although not traditionally always the case, researchers from a range of disciplinary backgrounds are increasingly recognizing the dynamic nature of (talent) development (see Farrow *et al.* 2008; Baker & Farrow 2015; Hollings *et al.* 2014; Lidor *et al.* 2009). This has led to the adoption of a multi-disciplinary perspective to examine the dynamic nature of talent development of young athletes (see Barker *et al.* 2014; Cassidy *et al.* 2014; Côté *et al.* 2014; Harvey *et al.* 2014; van Vuuren-Cassar *et al.* 2014).

Two acknowledged challenges exist in the discussion of talent development and identification; (i) a lack of agreement regarding what constitutes talent and, (ii) the absence of an agreed upon conceptual framework to guide research and practice related to talent identification or development (Tranckle & Cushion 2006; Vaeyens *et al.* 2008; Wiseman *et al.* 2014). Vaeyens *et al.* (2008) explicitly draw on Russell (1989) and Williams and Reilly's (2000) definitions of talent identification and development to develop a collective understanding of the terms. They defined talent identification as 'the process of recognizing current participants with the potential to excel in a particular sport', and talent development as 'providing the most appropriate learning environment to realize this potential' (Vaeyens *et al.* 2008: 703). Yet, a precursor to understanding talent identification and development is an appreciation of what constitutes talent. In making a case that talent is socially constructed, Tranckle and Cushion (2006) quoted Csikszentmihalyi and colleagues, who argued that talent is a 'label of approval we place on traits that have positive value in the particular context in which we live' (2006: 266). Another who recognized that talent was socially constructed was Gagné (1993), who proposed that it was complex and multifaceted. In his 'Differentiated Model of Giftedness and Talent' (DMGT) Gagné (2000) considered *giftedness* to be the *use of natural abilities or aptitudes* in one of four domains: the intellectual, creative, socio-affective or sensorimotor that enabled an individual to be ranked in the top 10 per cent of peers. Talent, on the other hand, was viewed as the mastery of competencies, or abilities, systematically developed resulting in an individual being ranked in the top 10 per cent in that field. Tranckle and Cushion (2006: 273) described the development process as the 'transformation of gifts into talent'.

A notable absence in the debates on developing and identifying talent is a robust and sustained contribution from sport sociologists. This is surprising, given that the process is considered a social and relational one and sociology has been described as '*the study of social worlds that people create, organize, maintain and change through their relationship with each other*' (Coakley *et al.* 2011: 4). To somewhat address this neglect, in this chapter we use C. Wright Mills' (1959) concept of the sociological imagination (SI) to guide our discussion of developing and identifying talent. In this chapter we follow the lead of Willis (1993) and Molnar and Kelly (2013) and organize the discussion of talent identification and development around the four sensibilities embedded in SI; specifically, historical, cultural, structural and critical. It is to these that we now turn.

## SOCIOLOGICAL IMAGINATION

The value of C. Wright Mills' concept of the sociological imagination (SI) lies in its encouragement of critical reflection, and highlighting the interplay between social structures and individual agency. Many have adopted, and at times adapted, Mills's concept. For example, Loy and Booth (2004) deduced SI as being focused on three interconnected components; craft, commitment and consciousness. In his discussion of what constitutes 'good sociology' Giddens (1982: 16), meanwhile, argued that 'the sociological imagination involve an *historical*, an *anthropological* and *critical* sensitivity' (*italics in the original*). Some years later, Willis (1993) expanded the discussion by suggesting that SI comprises four sensibilities: historical, cultural, structural and critical.

A decade on, Loy and Booth (2004) added a fifth sensibility – corporeality. Inherent within the concept of SI lies the view that a sociological awareness requires acknowledgement of a 'relationship between biography and history' (Scott & Nilsen 2013: xvi), or as Mills described it as 'personal troubles of milieu' and 'the public issues of social structure' (in Loy & Booth 2004: 69).

## Historical

'The problems of our time ... cannot be stated adequately without consistent practice of the view that history is the shank of social study' (Mills 1959: 143). Taken as such, if we are to understand the practices associated with the development and identification of talented athletes, then we need to recognize that practices 'change as social, economic and political forces change' (Coakley *et al.* 2011: 63). In contemporary times, sport organizations are under increasing pressure to generate a 'product' (read a winning team or individual) desirable for sponsors and funders. With rising costs associated with the operationalization of formal sports, and the often reduced financial support from governments and other bodies, sport organizations are increasingly turning their attention to identifying and developing talent in the hope of picking 'winners' early to enable the sport organization to promote their sport to potential funders and sponsors.

General explanations of talent are often implicitly informed by Sir Francis Galton's 1874 proposal that nature (biology) and nurture (environment) are involved in an individual's development. Thus, many researchers have adopted a dualist (either genes or environment) approach (Phillips *et al.* 2010), as witnessed in anthropometric research. This has resulted in the suggestion that a 'close relationship between physical characteristics and [success in] specific Olympic events' exists (2010: 271). In turn, the relationship between physical characteristics and specific sports has been 'over-interpreted' with the 'questionable practice of anthropometric profiling of adolescents to identify potential for early specialization in a sport' (2010: 271) becoming widespread. Increasingly, however, this dualist approach has been questioned for failing to recognize the 'complementary' relationship between nature and nurture (Phillips *et al.* 2010).

Another dualism has also influenced the practices of developing and identifying talented athletes. During the Renaissance[1] René Descartes (1596–1650) philosophized the relationship between the mind and body (which became known as the Cartesian dualism). In recent times, the Cartesian dualism has been reflected in the dominance of performance-based models of talent identification, which privilege physiological determinants of performance. In an attempt to challenge the primacy of physiological determinism, some researchers have developed and promoted the use of psycho-behavioural models to assist in the development and identification of talented athletes. These models highlight the role cognitive processes play in development, and problematize the view that athlete development is a linear progression (Button 2011).

## Cultural

Cultural sensibility was described by Willis (1993) as having two key characteristics: '[o]ne is to push back what is frequently the conventionally held notion of the boundary between the natural and the social world, and the other is to challenge notions that some cultures are superior to others' (1993: 47). When a cultural sensibility is used in a sports coaching context questions can be raised such as: (i) why is ability still viewed as largely inherited? And (ii) why are performance and/or anthropometric models of talent identification still privileged?

To understand the 'push back' from such critical questioning it is useful to know a little of the history of athlete development orthodoxy. The Cold War (post World War II) between the then communist bloc countries and the West was, amongst many things, a battle for cultural supremacy, of which sport was one aspect. Inevitably, then, it had an influence on how we identified (and continue to identify) and develop sporting talent. At the height of the Cold War, sport was used as a vehicle to demonstrate cultural supremacy. The dominance of Soviet and Eastern bloc athletes in the Olympic Games during this period caused concern amongst many politicians in the West. Upon the fall of the Berlin wall in 1989, many East European sports coaches and administrators, and their ideas, were in demand by Western sporting organizations. One example was Istvan Balyi, a Hungarian, whose Long Term Athlete Development (LTAD) model continues, albeit in various guises, to be recommended by many national sporting organizations as a guide for developing sporting talent. Balyi's LTAD model 'combines the training ethos employed within East European countries alongside a scientific basis of biological maturation' (Bailey *et al.* 2011: 45). Despite considerable criticisms of its shortcomings, LTAD has become so ingrained in many sport governing organizations that Day (2011: 181) went as far as saying that it has become viewed by some as a 'global law that must be adhered to for athletes to be internationally competitive'.

Due to the absence of sport sociologists discussing the issues associated with identifying and developing talent, much of the current associated thinking has been influenced by psychology. This, according to Phillips *et al.* (2010: 280), has 'significant implications for understanding processes of expertise and talent development'. Some social psychologists have challenged the LTAD orthodoxy described above, giving greater credence to the way social factors influence the development process. For example, Côté (1999) focused on the influence of the family on the development of sporting talent, while Côté *et al.* (2006) and later Fraser-Thomas *et al.* (2010) explored the impact of birthplace on athlete development. Recently, two studies examined practices within rural communities in New Zealand and Canada to explain why young people within them were overrepresented in high-level sports and national teams (Balish & Côté 2013; Pennell 2014). Despite mixed support for the findings of the research on birthplace (see Baker *et al.* 2009), work that focuses on how social factors influence the development process has challenged the LTAD orthodoxy and influenced some national sporting organizations to recognize that an athlete's development pathway is not linear or unproblematic (e.g. Sport New Zealand's Sport and Recreation Participant and Athlete Pathway [Sport New Zealand 2012]).

Cultural sensibility in the sports coaching world has also been influenced by Bronfenbrenner's (1979) ecological approach to development. It is a perspective that challenges the mind/body dualism, and is another multidimensional framework beginning to be used to understand the development of sporting talent (see Araújo *et al.* 2010; Henriksen *et al.* 2011; Hewetson 2014; Hollings *et al.* 2014; Larsen *et al.* 2012, Pennell

2014). In later work, Bronfenbrenner (2005) expanded his initial proposal to highlight the importance of recognizing that, 'over the life course, human development takes place through the process of progressively more complex reciprocal interaction between an active, evolving biopsychological human organism and the persons, objects, and symbols in its immediate external environment' (2005: 5). (For further description of Bronfenbrenner's ideas see Chapter 9).

## Structural

A structural sensibility refers to a desire to examine the relationship between society (structure) and the individual (agency). In doing so, it encourages questions to be asked regarding why and how events happen in the ways that they do. For example, the question '[w]hat is it about the way our society is organized as a whole that would explain this phenomenon?' (Willis 1993: 61) could be asked about the phenomenon that is the Junior World Golf Championship, which has competitions for under sixes to a 15–17-year-old division (see http://www.juniorworldgolf.com). What were the circumstances that resulted in the creation of the tournament? What conditions keep it viable? Who attends this tournament and for what purposes? Where are the winners of this tournament 10 years after they have held the winner's trophy aloft? Why do parents support their children to play in this event?

Many social changes have occurred in Western society since the 1950s, one of which has been the growth in organized youth sports. Coakley *et al.* (2011) proposed five reasons for this growth: (i) an increase in both parents working outside the home has created a demand for formally structured, adult supervised after school programmes; (ii) a cultural shift as to what constitutes a 'good parent'; (iii) a cultural change which views child-controlled, informal activities, as being opportunities for children to get into trouble; (iv) a growing fear among parents that the outside world is dangerous for children, which has resulted in them regarding organized sport as a 'safe' space; and (v) an increased visibility of elite and professional sports which has raised an awareness of, and the value placed on organized competitive sports. Not surprisingly, such societal changes, and the ensuing modifications in youth sports practice have influenced talent identification and development practices at the youth level. For example, if parents are investing considerable resources into their children's sport participation, then many will want evidence that their children are developing to the best of their ability.

It could be argued that Kelly and Hickey (2008) adopted a structural sensibility when examining talent identification within the Australian Football League (AFL). In a study funded by the AFL, Kelly and Hickey (2008: 14) interviewed 21 club officials from three clubs (e.g. coaching staff, recruiting and player development managers, general managers) about, among other things, 'talent identification processes and practices'. Kelly and Hickey's analysis and discussion was informed by the view that 'the individuals who want to play football at the elite level, who want to develop an identity as a professional footballer, need to be understood, developed and coached as a complete package, as young men who are more than the sum of the parts of their body, their mind and their soul' (2008: 17). One of Kelly and Hickey's findings was that:

> [a]t a club level there is an increasing emphasis put on minimizing the risk of recruiting players who might cause trouble in the club. In talent identification and recruiting processes clubs and their officials are interested in much more than football ability. At this level, there is greater emphasis on identifying, measuring and quantifying the intangible elements of *character*.
>
> (Kelly & Hickey 2008: 36)

According to club officials, managing the risk to the club played a big part in the talent identification, recruitment and development of players. This, Kelly and Hickey (2008: 77) contended, may have been because of the 'mass mediated, brand driven, celebrity elements of the AFL'. Consequently, club officials undertook risk assessments related to the players' character *as well as* their physical skills. Some of the risk assessment practices adopted here consisted of interviewing the players, while others were more comprehensive, and arguably, intrusive. For example, officials said that they had been observing players for two or three years. In that time, they had not only interviewed the potential recruit, but also their teachers, principals, previous employers and coaches, as well as current coaches. A more invasive practice still was unearthed when one coach said that he 'got a really good sense of a player's character when he visited his family and got to have a look at the player's bedroom' (2008: 75). For many of the potential recruits, these risk assessment practices did not come as a surprise. In fact, the recruitment managers said that an increasing number of the potential recruits were becoming accomplished in the recruitment process. Notably, the potential recruits were 'highly skilled' in both interviewing and completing the psychological tests (2008: 77).

However, not all recruits were viewed as equal in the risk assessment and, therefore, the recruitment processes. In this respect, some players were considered a 'certain type'; a type that was considered more of a 'recruitment risk' (Kelly & Hickey 2008: 79). The 'certain types' were often indigenous players and those who came from lower socio-economic groups. Here, references were made to the 'suburbs/areas from where the players came, [the] schools that potential draftees attended and/or family status (good, bad, broken, close)' (2008: 82). One late career player even commented that 'the way things are going we'll only recruit private school boys in the future' (2008: 82). Yet the risk assessments weren't restricted to concrete categories such as indigeneity and socio-economics, as illustrated by one club official who said,

> I'll be interested to see how one young kid goes this year. Everyone knows he can play football but to be honest once you've met the old man you just don't want to go there. It's a shame, but the reality is that you don't want to bring people in that have the potential to stuff up your club.
>
> (Kelly & Hickey 2008: 83)

## Critical

Having a critical sensibility does not mean viewing every social issue negatively. Nor does it mean adopting a classical critical position like that advocated by members of the Frankfurt School (e.g. Adorno, Marcuse or Horkheimer). Instead, it requires an acknowledgement that 'any social endeavor or practice has consequences for those engaged within or by that endeavor, and that these consequences are disproportionate in their effects' (Hay & Penney 2013: 4). This means that it is 'important to consider what these effects might be, how the effects are distributed and what factors may contribute to these effects' (2013: 4). Molnar and Kelly (2013) hold a similar position to Hay and Penney (2013: 28), illustrated in their claim that 'to be critical, you have to become sceptical'. Similarly, Willis (1993: 72) stated that '[a]pplying a critical sensibility means engaging in "systematic doubt" about the accounts of the social world'.

When a critical sensibility is used to examine the pyramid view[2] of talent development, numerous questions and discussion points are raised. For example:

- Why is the measurement of 'talent' often confined to physiological characteristics and motor skills and not, for example, to tactical skills, to the potential to perform, or the rate of learning? (Abbott & Collins 2004; Burgess & Naughton 2010; Côté *et al.* 2009; Lidor *et al.* 2009; Tranckle & Cushion 2006).
- Why does the measurement of 'talent' occur at a young age, often prior to puberty, when there is limited evidence to suggest that successful performance at a young age is a reliable predictor of future elite performance? (Abbott & Collins 2004; Abbott *et al.* 2005; Bailey *et al.* 2010; Bailey & Collins 2013; Burgess & Naughton 2010; Côté *et al.* 2009; Lidor *et al.* 2009).
- What are the consequences of early identification/selection for those athletes who are late developers, or those born at an unfavourable time in the selection year? (Bailey *et al.* 2011; Farrow 2012; MacNamara 2011; Meylan *et al.* 2010; Renshaw *et al.* 2012).
- What are the consequences of using the pyramid model, which is based on meritocratic claims of ability and effort, to guide talent development? (Bailey *et al.* 2010; Bailey *et al.* 2011; Collins 2011).
- What are the consequences for athlete development if no consideration is given to family resources needed to participate in organized sport?
- What are the upshots of the increasing emphasis of a performance ethic in youth sports, the emergence of specialist youth training centres, and the availability and quality of coaching? (Bloom 1985; Coakley *et al.* 2011; Bailey *et al.* 2011).
- What are the implications for athlete development and talent identification if development is assumed as being linear and chronological? (Ford *et al.* 2011; Gulbin *et al.* 2013; Gulbin & Weissensteiner 2013).

Kelly and Hickey (2008) used Foucault's extensive work, specifically around care of the self when adopting a critical sensibility to interpret talent identification processes of three AFL clubs. They expressed concern about the practices that occurred once the 'more rationalized, more scientific ways to identify and recruit the talent' had reached their limits (Kelly & Hickey 2008: 93). They argued that '[w]hen these limits are reached intuition, preconceptions, stereotypes, generalisations, experiences, gut instincts enter the picture to drive the processes of talent identification and recruitment' (Kelly & Hickey 2008: 93). Whilst not degrading the value of rich experiences, they considered it important to 'ask questions about the consequences – intended or otherwise' – for the way practices associated with talent identified are 'governed and regulated' (Kelly & Hickey 2008: 93). One such question is:

[w]ill the trend towards psychological profiling, and character assessment and judgement as a major element of talent identification and the management of risks associated with these processes, work against the participation of certain groups or communities?'

(Kelly & Hickey 2008: 84)

## CONCLUDING THOUGHTS

Increasingly talent identification and development is being recognized as dynamic, multidimensional and socially constructed. Yet within the sports community there is little agreement regarding what constitutes talent, how to identify it, the appropriateness of implementing a talent identification programme – and if it is deemed appropriate – what such a programme would look like. A notable absence in the discussion and debates on developing and identifying sporting talent is a robust and sustained contribution from sport sociologists. In this chapter, we used C. Wright Mills' (1959) concept of the sociological imagination (SI) to guide our discussion in an attempt to begin addressing this neglect. Mills' SI framework provides opportunities to focus on historical, cultural, structural and critical issues, and provides guidance for those interested in sociological ideas and issues to make a contribution to the debates and discussion surrounding talent identification and development generally, and sports coaching more specifically. Time will tell if sociologists take up the challenge and begin contributing to our understanding of talent identification and development.

## END-OF-CHAPTER TASKS

Using a critical sensibility, examine the talent identification and development practices that occur in your sport by answering the following questions.

1 What is the focus of the current practices used in your sport to identify talented athletes in the under-13 age group? Why is this the focus? Who benefits, and who is disadvantaged, by having this as the focus? What consideration is given to the familial and financial resources needed to participate in organized sport when identifying and developing young athletes?
2 What is the purpose of identifying so-called talented athletes at the under-13 age group? If identification is viewed as necessary, how could the focus of identification process be adapted so fewer athletes are disadvantaged? What considerations are given to identifying talents in the intellectual, creative, socio-affective and sensorimotor domains?
3 Reflect upon, and discuss the pros and cons of the increasing emphasis being placed on specialist youth training centres in some sports.

## NOTES

1   The Renaissance period was from the fourteenth to seventeenth centuries.
2   The base of the pyramid is where mass participation in sport occurs and fundamental motor skills are learnt. The peak of the pyramid is elite competition. A common assumption is that progression towards the peak of the pyramid is based on ability and effort alone.

## REFERENCES

Abbott, A. & Collins, D. (2004). Eliminating the dichotomy between theory and practice in talent identification and development: Considering the role of psychology. *Journal of Sports Sciences*, 22: 395–408.

Abbott, A., Button, C., Pepping, G. & Collins, D. (2005). Unnatural selection: Talent identification and development in sport. *Nonlinear Dynamics, Psychology, and Life Sciences*, 9(1): 61–88.

Araújo, D., Rocha, L. & Davids, K. (2010). The ecological dynamics of decision-making in sailing. In I. Renshaw, K. Davids & G. Savelsbergh (eds.) *Motor Learning in Practice: A Constraints-Led Approach*. London: Routledge.

Bailey, R. & Collins, D. (2013). The standard model of talent development and its discontents. *Kinesiology Review*, 2: 248–259.

Bailey, R., Collins, D., Ford, P., MacNamara, A., Toms, M. & Pearce, G. (2010). *Participant Development in Sport: An Academic Review*. Sports Coach UK.

Bailey, R., Toms, M., Collins, D., Ford, P., MacNamara, A. & Pearce, G. (2011). Models of young player development in sport. In I. Stafford (ed.) *Coaching Children in Sport*. London: Routledge.

Baker, J. & Farrow, D. (2015). *The Routledge Handbook of Sport Expertise*. London: Routledge.

Baker, J., Schorer, J., Cobley, S., Schimmer, G. & Wattie, N. (2009). Circumstantial development and athletic excellence: The role of date of birth and birthplace. *European Journal of Sport Science*, 9: 329–339.

Balish, S. & Côté, J. (2013). The influence of community on athletic development: An integrated case study. *Qualitative Research in Sport, Exercise and Health* 6(1): 98–120.

Barker, D., Barker-Ruchti, N., Gerber, M. & Pühse, U. (2014). Maria: Italian, female, and pursuing dreams of elite soccer success in Switzerland. In K. Armour (ed.) *Pedagogical Cases in Sport, Exercise and Physical Activity. Volume 1: Physical Education and Youth Sport*. London: Routledge.

Bloom, B. (1985). *Developing Talent in Young People*. New York: Ballantines.

Bronfenbrenner, U. (1979). *The Ecology of Human Development*. Boston: Harvard University Press.

Bronfenbrenner, U. (2005). *Making Human Beings Human*. London: Sage Publications.

Burgess, D. & Naughton, G. (2010). Talent development in adolescent team sports: A review. *International Journal of Sports Physiology and Performance*, 5: 103–116.

Button, A. (2011). Aims, principles, and methodologies in talent identification and development. In D. Collins, A. Button & H. Richards (eds.) *Performance Psychology: A Practitioner's Guide*. Edinburgh: Elsevier.

Cassidy, T., Jackson, A-M., Miyahara, M. & Shemmell, J. (2014). Greta. Weaving strands to allow Greta to flourish as Greta. In K. Armour (ed.) *Pedagogical Cases in Sport, Exercise and Physical Activity. Volume 1: Physical Education and Youth Sport*. London: Routledge.

Coakley, J., Hallinan, C. & McDonald, B. (2011). *Sports in Society: Sociological Issues and Controversies*. Sydney: McGraw-Hill.

Collins, D. (2011). Introduction: Getting ready to perform. In D. Collins, A. Button & H. Richards (eds.) *Performance Psychology: A Practitioner's Guide*. Edinburgh: Elsevier.

Côté, J. (1999). The influence of the family in the development of talent in sport. *The Sport Psychologist*, 13: 395–417.

Côté, J., Hancock, D., Fischer, S. & Gurd, B. (2014). Rob. Talent in ice hockey: age, neighborhood, and training. In K. Armour (ed.) *Pedagogical Cases in Sport, Exercise and Physical Activity. Volume 1: Physical Education and Youth Sport*. London: Routledge.

Côté, J., Lidor, R. & Hackfort, D. (2009). ISSP position stand: To sample or specialize? Seven postulates about youth sport activities that lead to continued participation and elite performance. *International Journal of Sport and Exercise Psychology*, 9: 7–17.

Côté, J., MacDonald, D., Baker, J. & Abernethy, B. (2006). When 'where' is more important than 'when': Birthplace and birthdate effects on the achievement of sporting expertise. *Journal of Sports Sciences*, 24(10): 1065–1073.

Day, D. (2011). Craft coaching and the 'discerning eye' of the coach. *International Journal of Sport Science and Coaching*, 6(1): 179–195.

Farrow, D. (2012). What skill acquisition and expertise research tells us about talent identification and development. In J. Baker, S. Cobley & J. Schorer (eds.) *Talent Identification and Development in Sport: International Perspectives*. London: Routledge.

Farrow, D., Baker, J. & MacMahon, C. (2008). *Developing Sports Expertise: Researchers and Coaches put Theory into Practice*. London: Routledge.

Ford, P., De Ste Croix, M., Lloyd, R., Meyers, R., Moosavi, M., Oliver, J., Till, K. & Williams, C. (2011). The Long-Term Athlete Development Model: Physiological evidence and application. *Journal of Sports Sciences*, 29(4): 389–402.

Fraser-Thomas, J., Côté, J. & MacDonald, D. (2010). Community size in youth sport settings: Examining developmental assets and sport withdrawal. *Physical and Health Education Academic Journal*, 2: 1–9.

Gagné, F. (1993). Constructs and models pertaining to exceptional human abilities. In K. Heller, F. Mönks & A. Passow (eds.) *International Handbook of Research and Development of Giftedness and Talent*. Oxford: Pergamon Press.

Gagné, F. (2000). Understanding the complex choreography of talent development through DMGT-based analysis. In K. Heller, F. Mönks, R. Sternberg & R. Subotnik (eds.) *International Handbook for Research on Giftedness and Talent*, 2nd edn. Oxford: Pergamon Press.

Giddens, A. (1982). *Profiles and Critiques in Social Theory*. London: Macmillan.

Gladwell, M. (2008). *Outliers: The Story of Success*. London: Allen Lane.

Gulbin, J. & Weissensteiner, J. (2013). Functional sport expertise systems. In D. Farrow, J. Baker & C. MacMahon (eds.) *Developing Sport Expertise: Researchers and Coaches put Theory into Practice*, 2nd edn. London: Routledge.

Gulbin, J., Croser, M., Morley, E. & Weissensteiner, J. (2013). An integrated framework for the optimisation of sport and athlete development: A practitioner approach. *Journal of Sports Sciences*, 31(12): 1319–1331.

Harvey, S., Pope, S., Fletcher, I. & Kerner, C. (2014). Jenny. Specialist needs for the specializing phase. In K. Armour (ed.) *Pedagogical Cases in Sport, Exercise and Physical Activity. Volume 1: Physical Education and Youth Sport*. London: Routledge.

Hay, P. & Penney, D. (2013). *Assessment in Physical Education. A Sociocultural Perspective*. London: Routledge.

Henriksen, K., Stambulova, N. & Roessler, K. (2011). Riding the wave of an expert: A successful talent development environment in kayaking. *The Sport Psychologist*, 25: 341–362.

Hewetson, A. (2014). Talent identification and development: An investigation into the policies, systems and practices of one New Zealand rugby provincial union. Unpublished manuscript, University of Otago.

Hollings, S., Mallett, C. & Hume, P. (2014). The transition from elite junior track-and-field athlete to successful senior athlete: Why some do, why others don't. *International Journal of Sports Science and Coaching*, 9(3): 457–471.

Kelly, P. & Hickey, C. (2008). *The Struggle for the Body, Mind and Soul of AFL Footballers*. Melbourne: Australian Scholarly Publishing.

Larsen, C., Alfermann, D. & Christensen, M. (2012). Psychosocial skills in a youth soccer academy: A holistic ecological perspective. *Sport Science Review*, XXI, 3–4: 51–74.

Lidor, R., Côté, J. & Hackfort, D. (2009). To test or not to test? – The use of physical skill tests in talent detection and in early phases of sport development. *International Journal of Sport and Exercise Psychology*, 7: 131–146.

Loy, J. & Booth, D. (2004). Social structure and social theory: The intellectual insights of Robert K. Merton. In R. Giulianotti (ed.) *Sport and Modern Social Theorists*. London: Palgrave Macmillan.

MacNamara, A. (2011). Psychological characteristics of developing excellence. In D. Collins, A. Button & H. Richards (eds.) *Performance Psychology. A Practitioner's Guide*. Edinburgh: Elsevier.

Meylan, C., Cronin, J., Oliver, J. & Hughes, M. (2010). Talent identification in soccer: The role of maturity status on physical, physiological and technical characteristics. *International Journal of Sports Science and Coaching*, 5 (4): 571–592.

Mills, C.W. (1959). *The Sociological Imagination*. Oxford: Oxford University Press.

Molnar, G. & Kelly, J. (2013). *Sport, Exercise and Social Theory: An Introduction*. London: Routledge.

Pennell, K. (2014). A 'Touch' of class: Investigating rural talent development. Unpublished honours dissertation, University of Otago.

Phillips, E., Davids, K., Renshaw, I. & Portus, M. (2010). Expert performance and the dynamics of talent development. *Sports Medicine*, 40: 271–283.

Renshaw, I., Davids, K., Phillips, E. & Kerhervé, H. (2012). Developing talent in athletes as complex neurobiological systems. In J. Baker, S. Cobley & J. Schorer (eds.) *Talent Identification and Development in Sport: International Perspectives*. London: Routledge.

Russell, K. (1989). Athletic talent: From detection to perfection. *Science Periodical on Research and Technology in Sport*, 9(1): 1–6.

Scott, J. & Nilsen, A. (2013). C. *Wright Mills and the Sociological Imagination: Contemporary Perspectives*. Cheltenham, UK: Edward Elgar Publishing.

Sport New Zealand (2012). New Zealand Community Sport Coaching Plan, 2012–2020. Sport New Zealand. Available at http://www.sportnz.org.nz/assets/Uploads/attachments/managing-sport/coaching/New-Zealand-Community-Sport-Coaching-Plan-20122020.pdf [Accessed on 17 September 2015].

Tranckle, P. & Cushion, C. (2006). Rethinking giftedness and talent in sport. *Quest*, 58: 265–282.

Vaeyens, R., Lenoir, M., Williams, A. & Philippaerts, R. (2008). Talent identification and development programmes in sport. *Sports Medicine*, 38: 703–714.

van Vuuren-Cassar, G., Swain, J., Rossato, C. & Chatziefstathiou, D. (2014). Karen. Striving to reach Olympic performance levels. In K. Armour (ed.) *Pedagogical Cases in Sport, Exercise and Physical Activity. Volume 1: Physical Education and Youth Sport*. London: Routledge.

Williams, A. & Reilly, T. (2000). Talent identification and development in soccer. *Journal of Sports Sciences*, 18: 657–667.

Willis, E. (1993). *The Sociological Quest: An Introduction to the Study of Social Life*. Sydney: Allen & Unwin.

Wiseman, A., Bracken, N., Horton, S. & Weir, P. (2014). The Difficulty of Talent Identification: Inconsistency Among Coaches Through Skill-Based Assessment of Youth Hockey Players. *International Journal of Sports Science and Coaching*, 9(3): 447–456.

## CHAPTER 11

# Understanding athletes' identities

## INTRODUCTION

Coaching is recognising situations, [it's] recognising and responding to the people that you work with (Steve Harrison in Jones *et al.* 2004: 18). This quotation is taken from an examination of the philosophies and practices of eight top-level coaches. In reflecting upon what made them successful (and sometimes less than successful), the coaches highlighted the importance of relating to their athletes as social beings and not just performing bodies. Considerable emphasis was placed 'on getting to know them [the athletes] and what makes them tick' in the quest to facilitate high-level sporting performances (Jones *et al.* 2004: 18).

While such early inquiry highlighted the importance of recognizing and appreciating athletes as unique beings, existing coach education continues to largely present sporting performers as homogenous groups (e.g. males, females, children and adults) (Jones 2000; Jones *et al.* 2011). Far from recognizing how an individual athlete is shaped and influenced by his or her gender, ethnicity, social class, and sexuality, such provision has largely adopted a dualistic representation. That is, athletes are seen to comprise of bodies and minds to be serviced by the coach (Jones 2000; Jones *et al.* 2011). In commenting upon the technical rationality that has underpinned much coach education provision, several authors (e.g. Denison & Avner 2011; Jones *et al.* 2011) have argued that coaches who are primarily driven by mechanistic considerations may have difficulty comprehending, and thus adapting to, the inherently social complexities of their work. This is not to say that coaches should solely focus on individual athlete's needs at the expense of all else. Doing so could easily lead to them being accused of inconsistency and even favouritism, and could be difficult to action in a team sport setting. Hence, a coach cannot afford to lavish too much attention (or to be seen to do so) on one athlete, even though that athlete may need such concern. Similarly, some athletes may prefer not to be highlighted in front of peers for a variety of reasons. The trick for coaches, then, is to often coach each athlete within the larger group.

The aim of this chapter is to explore how athletes' identities may come to bear on their experiences within sport. Following an introductory discussion of identity, we explore how notions of disability, sexuality, and ethnicity may influence how athletes come to view themselves, and the impact this may have on their self-understandings and sporting performances. The attention then shifts to providing some insights into how elite athletes negotiate and respond to the sporting cultures in which they participate. In particular, an examination of athletic identities and the problematic issues of over investment are undertaken (Carless & Douglas 2013; Jones *et al.* 2005). In keeping with the general ethos of this book, the aim here is not to provide prescriptions as to what coaches ought to do, but to sensitize readers to the critical influence of culture and context as they relate to an individual's identities, and his or her engagement in sport.

## WHAT IS IDENTITY?

The term identity is a highly complex phenomenon that remains the subject of much debate (Elliott 2014; Lawler 2008; Roberts 2009). Despite the existence of various perspectives (e.g. Elliott 2014), a generally accepted concept of identity is that of 'an individual's sense of self, and how [that] person is identified by others' (Roberts 2009: 127). This sense of self can be personal in terms of how an individual understands himself to be unique, as well as being social in terms of sharing particular roles, norms and beliefs with others (Elliott 2014; Lawler 2014). Additionally, an individual may possess several identities, which can sometimes be contradictory rather than contributing to a unified concept of the self (Alvesson 2010; Collinson 2003; Elliott 2014). Indeed, Roberts (2009: 128) described how life in modern societies has become so fragmented and fluid, 'that identities are subject to constant revision' and can, sometimes, 'be changed and chosen deliberately'.

Importantly, an individual's sense of identity can be understood to emanate from the meanings that he or she ascribes to himself or herself. These meanings are primarily based upon their understandings of how people behave in a particular role (e.g. as an athlete), as well as how they think others perceive and evaluate them in this role (Burke & Stets 2009). With regard to the latter, it has been argued that the identities and meanings we afford to ourselves are not entirely free of our interactions and (power) relationships with others. For example, social structures in the forms of localized networks such as neighbourhoods, organizations, and families cannot only constrain or facilitate an individual's entrance to particular groups or roles, but can also influence the subsequent social interactions and the identities that might evolve for that individual. That is, while individuals might develop their own self-definitions, they are not separate from the 'realities of the social structures in which they are embedded' (Stets & Serpe 2013: 34). In the following sections, we consider how individuals' identities potentially interconnect with their respective experiences of sport.

## DISABILITY

Sporting literature has increasingly explored how various inequalities and social divisions impact upon an individual's experiences of sport. It has highlighted how athletes with a disability have often been treated differently (or inferiorly) to their able bodied counterparts (e.g. DePauw & Gavron 2005; Fitzgerald 2005, 2009; Huang & Brittain 2006; Smith 2013). For example, it has been argued that celebrating the sporting achievements of disabled athletes, which often includes the portrayal of their achievements as 'heroic', contributes to reinforcing their minority status (Huang & Brittain 2006; Purdue & Howe 2012). This point has been well illustrated by disabled athletes, and the frustration felt when their achievements are viewed in such a fashion:

> We have done nothing heroic. All we have done is get out there and do what we are supposed to do ... I am just a normal person who does what he is interested in. I am an athlete, so I have just done what I am supposed to do.
>
> (Huang & Brittain 2006: 366)

> I like to think that I am just an elite athlete, but the circumstances we are in and the treatment we get in many ways makes me feel like I am just a disabled athlete. So how can I expect the public to regard me as an athlete? I think it is very difficult.
>
> (Huang & Brittain 2006: 366)

In addition to others' views of their achievements, disabled athletes and children have also described how their sense of self can be influenced by interactions with coaches and other able-bodied peers (Fitzgerald 2005). For example:

> The familiar hustle and bustle murmuring and giggling that follow the instruction 'Get into teams' are always accompanied by the predictable 'Aw Sir, do we have to?' or 'No way are we having him' as the games teacher allocates me to a random team, rather like a spare piece of baggage that no one can be bothered to carry.
>
> (Jackson 2002: 129)

> They don't want you to be there ... when we're with the rest of the group you can tell some of them, they don't want you there. It's not like I'm the worst. They think I am, and that is what it is like all the time.
>
> (Fitzgerald 2005: 51)

The experiences of disabled athletes in this respect may be understood in relation to the dominant medical discourse, which has generally portrayed such individuals in terms of their 'deficits' (De Pauw & Gavron 2005). Its widespread and deeply rooted place in social consciousness has, arguably, contributed to a situation where those who differ from mesomorphic and motoric ideals are subject to various forms of disenfranchisement, infantilization, and/or exclusion (Fitzgerald 2005). As such, it is important for coaches to critically interrogate their related beliefs and practices. This not only applies to coaches who engage exclusively with athletes with disability, but also to those who work where the mainstreaming of athletes with a disability is encouraged or, indeed, legally mandatory. Such reflection could focus on how their actions, as well as others within the coaching setting, challenge or reaffirm existing societal stereotypes. In order to do this, coaches could consider if they subscribe to inaccurate or oversimplified conceptualizations of athletes with disabilities, as well as the expectations they hold for them (Fitzgerald 2005).

## SEXUALITY

In broad terms, sexuality refers to the sexual behaviour and characteristics of human beings (Foucault 1978; Giddens 1997). People can have a wide variety of sexual tastes and inclinations. These include heterosexuals, lesbian women, gay men, bisexual men and women, transvestite men and women, and transsexual men and women. Before proceeding with an exploration of sexual identity as it relates to athletes, it is worth providing brief background information relating to homosexuality, as the literature has highlighted how athletes who do not conform to heterosexual norms can experience a variety of tensions and problems. While homosexuality has a long history in all cultures, the term 'homosexual person' is, by comparison, a relatively recent one (Foucault 1978; Giddens 1997). The historically negative reactions to homosexuals may be attributed to the process of heteronormativity (Carney & Chawansky 2014; Eng 2013; Hargreaves & Anderson 2014). This is defined as:

> the normalising processes which support heterosexuality as the elemental form of human association, as the very model of inter-gender relations, as the indivisible basis of all community, and as the means of reproduction with which society wouldn't exist.
>
> (Warner 1993: 21)

In the context of sport, Griffin's (1998) classic work highlighted many problematic myths surrounding lesbian athletes. This included them being considered sexual predators who prey on teammates in order to recruit them to their lifestyles. In more recent times, attitudes to homosexuality have in many Western nations changed, with such athletes being increasingly accepted by their heterosexual peers (Anderson & Bullingham 2013). However, their experiences are still far from being unproblematic. In this respect, research has highlighted how gay males have historically believed that their heterosexual colleagues might fear, mistrust, or stigmatize them based on their sexuality (Adams & Anderson 2012). The resulting anti-gay behaviour of the locker room has helped to reinforce a silence about sexuality, and a desire to avoid behaving in a way that could be identified (and could identify them) as 'gay' (Adams & Anderson 2012). Such practices arguably contributed to generate strong feelings of shame among men who have strong feelings towards other men; a sentiment well illustrated in the extract below:

> I could have been a very good major-league player if I was not so emotionally screwed up when I was playing. I was very hard on myself, and I think it all translates back to that feeling of, 'I'm not worthy'. I'm bad because I'm a gay man on the Dodger Stadium field. I don't belong out here. This is wrong. I hate myself. I remember walking in the clubhouse every day and feeling that people could see the kiss I gave my lover when I walked out the door ... Then you sit down and start talking about strip clubs.
>
> (Wine 2003)

As stated, in recent years, Western societies have experienced some positive social changes regarding the acceptance and inclusion of gay men in all aspects of social life (Adams & Anderson 2012; Bush *et al.* 2012; Hargreaves & Anderson 2014). In the context of professional football, for example, Magrath *et al.* (2013: 2) described the 'coming out' of Robbie Rogers, a gay professional footballer:

> In February 2013, a 25-year-old ex-Leeds United football player, Robbie Rogers, publicly revealed that he was gay. His coming out was met with overwhelmingly positive responses from the media, and support from his old teammates. In May, he signed with the Los Angeles Galaxy and took to the field as the world's only openly gay elite-level professional footballer – he received a standing ovation when introduced to the crowd.

Given the stigma that has surrounded homosexuality, it is not surprising that gay and lesbian athletes have often preferred not to reveal their sexual orientation to teammates and coaches (Anderson & Bullingham 2013). Indeed, the potential, and in some cases the actual, consequences of 'coming-out' include a sense of isolation, hostility, rejection, exclusion, and, for elite athletes, the loss of sponsorships and endorsements (Brackenridge *et al.* 2007; Fink *et al.* 2012; Griffin 1998). Although the attitudes of those involved in women's sport towards homosexuality are perceived to have become supportive, lesbian athletes' experiences remain somewhat characterized by less than full acceptance (Anderson & Bullingham 2013). This is well illustrated in the following vignette:

> The team became very discriminatory towards myself, both as a person and a player on the team ... I was basically excluded from any activities that were not a team function. I began to feel very isolated and when I talked to my coach about it, her advice was to try and not be with my girlfriend so much around them. She basically told us to separate ... I got to the point where I almost wanted to leave the team.
>
> (Anderson & Bullingham 2013: 10)

Similarly, despite decreasing homophobia, there are only a few openly gay males in elite-level team sport. Hence, it is important for coaches to continue to support gay and lesbian athletes in a positive and sensitive manner. Such actions may require personal courage on the part of the coach, and might prove to be a far from easy or unproblematic process (Adams, Anderson and McCormack 2010, Anderson 2012).

A further issue for coaches to consider is how the fear of being labelled lesbian or gay can impact upon athletes (Anderson & Bullingham 2013). It may influence not only the sports that athletes choose to participate in, but also the effort they expend and their willingness to engage in future programmes. For example, for women, this may be especially so if the results of training are bodies that differ from the prevailing images of femininity (Anderson & Bullingham 2013; Coakley 2001). While coaches are unable to totally eradicate the constraints placed on some women by existing discourses surrounding gender and sexuality, they could create a working environment that promotes the view that developing strength and muscle is a form of personal empowerment (Schempp & Oliver 2000). Indeed, coaches, through their professional practice, can help to challenge existing conceptions of femininity. This does not mean that coaches should advocate females adopting traditionally male behaviours, but rather they can encourage 'girls and women to explore and connect with the power of their bodies' (Coakley 2001: 237). Equally, in the context of male sport, coaches have an opportunity to challenge dominant forms of masculinity (i.e. what is it to be a man) that are not only homophobic, but also racist and patriarchal. Coaches could, in this respect, benefit from an in-depth understanding of males' interpretation and construction of masculinity in a particular sport, and use this to create sporting climates in which forms of masculinity that differ from traditional notions of independence, decisiveness, aggression, toughness and strength are accepted (Coakley & Pike 2009).

## ETHNICITY AND RELIGION

Unlike the concept of race, which has been used to classify people according to physical characteristics, ethnicity refers to 'categories of people who share a common cultural identity and heritage' (Coakley & Pike 2009; Nixon & Frey 1998: 227). In particular, ethnicity is determined by cultural characteristics, such as traditions, values, norms and ideas that constitute a particular way of life (Coakley & Pike 2009). In most Western societies, ethnic groups who do not identify with the majority group, which is often white, are frequently subject to inequality, discrimination and oppression (Coakley & Pike 2009). This particular state of affairs can be mirrored in sports coaching. Indeed, while coach education has sought to cater for athletes with different skill and performance levels, it has been slower to engage with issues relating to the needs and requirements of different ethnic and religious groups (Coakley & Pike 2009; Jones 2000, 2002). For example, Afro-Caribbean athletes are often believed to be physically powerful but lacking in leadership and decision-making skills, while Muslim males have been widely perceived to prefer academic pursuits to any involvement in sport (Coakley & Pike 2009). Similarly, Muslim girls have traditionally been considered to be problematic by educators because of their apparent resistance to partake in physical activity (Coakley & Pike 2009; Walseth 2006).

A further issue that athletes from minority groups may experience relates to their acceptance and treatment by others within sporting organizations. For example, Jones' (2002) examination of the everyday sporting experiences of Afro-Caribbean athletes in semi-professional football highlighted a variety of issues including racist insults, the racialized culture of the dressing room, to inequality of playing opportunity. Here, the players' responses included the following comments:

> The worst experience I had, although I find it funny now, was when we played in Surrey. It was the first game of the season and before the game I was tying my laces on the pitch when I heard this voice shout 'Get up you Black so-and-so!' Everyone started laughing, and there were about 2,000 people there and they started laughing, y'know, it wasn't good.
>
> (Jones 2002: 52)

> You get it in training, all the time, there's no getting away from it. If you're qualifying racism proper as insulting you based on your colour, we have people in the team here who do that. As an example, we have someone here who, although he says it in a humorous way, I think is quite genuine when he asks, 'Why do you go out with White girls? Why don't you stick to your own?'
>
> (Jones 2002: 55)

Similarly, the more recent work of Fletcher (2012), which addressed the experiences of British Asians in sport, highlighted how they sometimes considered themselves on the receiving end of prejudicial behaviours. In their own words:

> From my experience, there is definitely more racism in football. We're (British Asian team) regularly subjected to, 'Paki this and Paki that'; 'go home Paki' etcetera. And I think that's down to the type of people you get in football. Many are uneducated and not from good backgrounds.
>
> (Fletcher 2012: 235)

> I remember when I was seventeen, playing [cricket] for Yorkshire, it was horrendous. I got no support whatsoever. I made a fifty, and none of the white lads' parents even bothered to clap me...Yeah, I was playing for Yorkshire, but that was a sign I wasn't equal.
>
> (Fletcher 2012: 238)

Such findings highlight the need for coaches to critically consider how to positively support and work with athletes from different ethnic backgrounds, especially in terms of challenging behaviours and practices that are derogatory and which threaten athletes' rights and identities. Drawing upon the work of Schempp and Oliver (2000), we believe coaches should develop an understanding of, and sensitivity towards, the ethnic heritage of athletes if they are to generate widespread positive sporting experiences.

In much the same way, many coaches in Aotearoa/New Zealand could benefit from an appreciation of how being a Māori athlete may determine meanings and perceptions (Erueti & Palmer 2014; Salter 2000). In this respect, an appreciation of the cultural significance Māoridom attaches to *manaakitanga* (the showing of kindness, hospitality, and respect), *aroa-ki-te-tangata* (love of your fellow man or woman), *whanaungatanga* (familiness), *wairua* (spirituality) and *awhinatanga* (helping, assisting) could be useful (Bevan Brown in Salter 2000; Erueti & Palmer 2014). Furthermore, in terms of coach–athlete communication, coaches considering utilizing a question-based pedagogy with Māori athletes need to recognize that such an approach could conflict with the tradition of not engaging in debate with the *kamatua* (respected elders) (Thompson *et al.* 2000). Similarly, Wrathall (in Thompson *et al.* 2000) highlighted a number of issues related to cultural insensitivity, intolerance, and communication between top-level female Māori athletes and Pakeha coaches and sports administrators. Such issues provide the basis for reflection if such athletes' potentialities are to be realized. Consequently, 'it would make sense that coaches, managers, sport psychologists and agents be motivated to engage in sensitive behaviours that involve more than simply constructing athlete identity as a mono-dimensional "one size fits all" construct' (Eureti & Palmer 2014: 1072).

Similarly, we believe that coaches may benefit from an appreciation of how religious requirements may constrain an individual's sporting involvement. In particular, such understanding could help coaches deconstruct and dismiss stereotypical beliefs regarding the participation of various religious groups. This was well illustrated in the following quotation taken from Fleming's work with Muslim schoolboys in the United Kingdom:

> [i]t's quite difficult for me. I have to pray five times a day. If I have to pray at 12 o'clock and there's a match, I can't play … If it's a matter of 'life and death', you can pray afterwards. But sport doesn't count as a matter of 'life and death'.
>
> (Fleming 1991: 37)

Likewise, an understanding of Islamic religious practices and beliefs regarding modesty may help understand the issues that Muslim females face in relation to sport (Coakley & Pike 2009). For example, Muslim females may, if they expose their bodies and legs to non-Muslims and males, experience feelings of guilt and shame. In this case, rather than the Muslim females being 'problematic', it is the traditional sporting uniform that is the major barrier to participation (Coakley & Pike 2009; Hamzeh & Oliver 2012). Equally, coach education has largely ignored how family expectations about the roles of young Muslim women can affect their engagement (or non-engagement) with physical activity (Hamzeh & Oliver 2012; Kay 2006; Walseth 2006, 2015). Here, Hamzeh and Oliver (2012) provided insights into the visible (i.e. head scarf or long cloak), spatial (i.e. female Muslims' mobility in public spaces), and ethical obstacles that restrict female Muslims' engagement in sport and exercise (i.e. protecting Muslim girls from forbidden things such as meeting men without the presence of an immediate adult family member). For example, a Muslim female noted the following conflicts between their sporting interests and family expectations:

> I love swimming. I was starting to win competitions in this city but last year mom pulled me out. She thought Karate is good for me so I am not swimming anymore … She [her mother] tells me because I am Muslim [and] I cannot wear a swimsuit (Amy, 14 years old).
>
> (Hamzeh & Oliver 2012: 335)

Importantly, Hamzeh and Oliver's (2012) work highlighted how, through communicating directly with young Muslims and their parents, as well as thinking creatively about the structure and format of certain activities, young Muslim female participation in sport can be facilitated and supported. They also illustrated the potential benefits of coaches recognising that Muslims are a diverse religious group, and that the role of the 'hijab discourse' can be 'interpreted in multiple ways and is negotiable with them [young female Muslims] and with their parents' (Hamzeh & Oliver 2012: 337).

## ATHLETIC IDENTITY

In recent years, scholars have given increasing attention to the meanings that individuals attach to their identity as athletes (e.g. Jones *et al.* 2005; Carless & Douglas 2013). While a strong sense of athletic identity has many positives, including high levels of self-esteem and a clear sense of purpose and direction, it can also have negative implications (Lavallee *et al.* 1997). Hence, it has been suggested that those with a strong athletic identity may be prone to a variety of emotional and social adjustment difficulties when this identity is threatened through injury, deselection, retirement, and/or negative feedback from significant others (Brewer *et al.* 1993). In addition, those who principally understand themselves in terms of their athletic identity, may be prone to commit deviant acts of over conformity to the norms of sport. This includes dedicating themselves to the sport above all other things, relentlessly striving for improved performances, accepting risks and playing through pain, and not tolerating any obstacles in the pursuit of their athletic possibilities (Coakley & Pike 2009).

In illustrating some of the problematic issues associated with a largely one-dimensional athletic identity, Carless and Douglas (2013) provided insight into how elite hockey players understood their being athletes to necessitate personal sacrifice; a message reinforced by coaches. In the words of one:

> I have to say that relationships have suffered because of my hockey. So, if I hadn't been playing hockey, then I still think maybe I would have been with a certain person...you can be so blinded by the fact that it's so good to be an elite sportsperson that you'd sacrifice absolutely anything for it.
>
> (Carless & Douglas 2013: 703)

Interestingly, she outlined that, while athletes could make their own decisions regarding personal and family matters, coaches often emphasized the benefits of putting their sporting commitments first. In her own words:

> [Recently] a teammate's sister had a miscarriage ... and her sister really wanted her to go home. And the coach kind of suggested she shouldn't go home so she didn't ... And coaches can be blamed for that ... [They can] so emotionally bribe you about things.
>
> (Carless & Douglas 2013: 704)

In further examining the role of the coach–athlete relationship in relation to an individual's athletic identity, the following story details the case of Anne (a pseudonym), a former top-level swimmer whose career was interrupted and finally terminated by an eating disorder. The case highlights, first, how a strong swimming identity led to vulnerability in terms of an athlete's reaction to perceived body image within a conforming culture of slenderness (Jones *et al.* 2005; Tinning 1991); and second, the role the coach played in the process of athlete identity creation and disruption. The story starts in earnest when a new coach came to Anne's club. She took an instant liking to his innovations, energy and enthusiasm, which gave her burgeoning athletic identity a substantial boost. She wanted to do well for him as well as for herself. In her own words:

> [m]y new coach promised exciting things and had a lot of new ideas and philosophies. He showed a lot of enthusiasm about my potential, so I took a lot of effort to please him. It was expected that we would eat, live, and breathe swimming. Although I felt a bit under stress 'coz he kept putting pressure on us to lowering our [target] times and telling us what we should be eating and stuff, I still really wanted to do well, and was constantly encouraged by him as he seemed to have big plans for me.
>
> (Jones *et al.* 2005: 383)

Soon a strong link was established between Anne and her coach, as she 'bought in' to his ideas, knowledge and methods without question. Her swimming identity became even stronger, as her success became inextricably linked with the person she saw herself as being and becoming. In this respect, Anne's identity as a swimmer and her 'self-esteem within the athletic role became bound ever tighter to her coach's perception of her performance. What he thought and said really mattered' (Jones *et al.* 2005: 383). Then came what Anne termed 'the meeting', where her parents and the coach were brought together to discuss progress and future plans. In her own words:

> I remember it vividly because I respected him so much and I just wanted to be the best. He [the coach] told me that I was doing well, that I was showing progress with my swimming. But then he said 'it would probably be more beneficial if you were lighter and slimmer and could lose a bit of weight and maybe you should look at dieting a bit more'. It just shot me down completely ... That put doubts in my head about myself and the confidence I had in myself as a swimmer ... But I still wanted to be good [swimmer] ... I started by starving myself, so I could lose a bit of weight. You know, to me a diet was just not eating. But I had to eat though, so a way for me to control it was purging, to get rid of it. That's how I started binging and purging, and within a month of starting to diet, it [the cycle of binging and purging] had become a regular thing.
>
> (Jones *et al.* 2005: 384–385)

As illustrated in the passage above, the identity that Anne had painstakingly built had suddenly been devalued and disrupted by the person who had helped build it. Her coach had encouraged her to train harder and faster, had measured her improvements in terms of time and weight, and had promoted her ever-growing investment in a single identity at the expense of others. The process had made her vulnerable, because when such a heavily invested-in persona is disrupted, one that is so closely associated as an essential self, the fall can be great. Brewer *et al.* (1993) neatly refer to it as developing an Achilles' heel as opposed to Hercules' muscles, even though at first glance the opposite may be true. Linking Anne's story to the previous discussion highlights how the over-investment in her swimming identity exposed her to the potentialities of identity disruption, with the breakage occurring because the coach had judged her through a gendered lens; that is, what the coach thought female swimmers of her level should look like. Consequently, the value to coaches of considering athletes' identity construction, maintenance and possible disruption comes to the fore.

Of course, the issue of disordered eating or body image concerns is not just confined to elite sport or, indeed, women (Bratland-Sanda & Sundgot-Bergen 2013). Indeed, individuals in various sports settings may experience anxiety at the public display of the body (e.g. changing in the locker rooms, wearing a team uniform in competition), which is an integral feature of sporting participation. Equally, it is not just coaches' communication of their beliefs about physical appearance and the relationship between body fat and performance that might have an impact on how athletes thinks about their bodies. Comments and comparisons made by team members, administrators, and various significant others, as well as wider media representations of desirable body shapes, may also contribute towards this issue (Jones *et al.* 2005; Thompson & Sherman 2011, 2014). As such, in order to reduce the possibility of athletes developing negative feelings toward their bodies, coaches may wish to consider a number of strategies. These include, but are not limited to, avoiding group weigh-ins; publically displaying the weight of athletes; educating athletes with regard to nutrition and the relationship between body fat, muscle and sporting performance; discouraging team members, selectors, and administrators from making negative comments to, and about other athletes; and evaluating their own beliefs about body shape and the weight–performance relationship (Plateau *et al.* 2014a, 2014b; Thompson & Sherman 2011, 2014).

Finally, Hussain's tale somewhat parallels Anne's story above (Haleem 2005). He too was greatly influenced by a new, foreign coach who seemed to promise much. Taking on board the coach's advice and instructions, Hussain tied himself to the coach's methods and philosophies as his running gave him a previously undiscovered focus and purpose in life. As early success further increased his enthusiasm, Hussain's reverence for his coach took the form of zealous over conformity to tough training routines – an attitude that was encouraged and subsequently insisted upon by the coach. Following a better than expected performance at his first major championships, Hussain describes the scene immediately following the race:

> [m]y coach, my mentor, had tears in his eyes. I had never seen him so happy; nor have I since. He came over to me and lifted me off the ground in a bear hug as if I had won. He told me that I had done a great job – the best compliment I ever received from him. All day long he smiled constantly and patted me on the back. He gave me two tracksuits as a reward. He also told me I should train harder. 'Of course I will', I replied.
>
> (Haleem 2005: 144)

Soon, however, the relationship became dysfunctional as the coach ignored and increasingly ridiculed Hussain's Muslim faith and the practices he was obliged to undertake.

For him [the coach], the training load for each month should be similar, no exception for Ramadan [a month when Muslims fast during daylight hours]. For instance, on the first day of the Ramadan [usually the most tiring day of the month] a 5,000 metre time trial would be scheduled … We requested that the trials be moved to the following night. He refused to listen. I had limited energy and felt light headed, but still managed a decent time. I knew I had done well. Still, Coach was far from satisfied and demanded that we run the entire time trial again following a meagre 15-minute break. A few runners mumbled that they were starting to hate running. Despite feeling disgruntled, I couldn't, I still loved running, but I was starting to have my doubts.

(Haleem 2005: 194)

Hussain's identity as a Muslim man was increasingly ignored and derided, which, allied to the practices of his coach, led to a breakdown in their relationship. Emotionally tired, chronically injured and athletically unfulfilled, Hussain retired from running aged 24. He believes that had his coach taken time to get to know him as a person, to understand his cultural beliefs and practices, his potential as an athlete would have been better realized.

Although such stories paint coaches in a poor light, the point is not to ascribe sole blame. It could be argued that athletes not only willingly enter into the relationships they have with coaches when building their own athletic identities, but that they are also capable of resisting practices they consider problematic (Carless & Douglas 2013; Purdy *et al.* 2008). Indeed, such relationships and their lasting legacies are inevitably multi-causal and cannot be traced to a singular, linear issue or problem. However, as Jones *et al.* (2005) noted, such a conclusion ignores the 'developmental tunnels' entered into by young 'committing' athletes and the influence coaches, especially when they are revered, have over such charges. Indeed, narrow athlete social and self-perceptions are often the result when well-intentioned coaches insist on ever-greater commitment to sport. Coaches, then, would seem to have a responsibility in relation to protecting and nurturing athletes' various identities, especially their athletic one. Here, we believe that, in order to avoid the experiences outlined above, coaches should consider how they respect athletes' existing identities in addition to helping them develop new ones. This would ensure that self-worth is not solely dependent on successfully fulfilling the athlete role (Jones *et al.* 2005).

## CONCLUDING THOUGHTS

While the concepts of disability, ethnicity, sexuality, gender, religion, and athletic identity, and how they may influence an athlete's sense of self, have been discussed separately, they are, in reality, inextricably interlinked (Hamzeh & Oliver 2012; Melton & Cunningham 2012). For that reason, it is in their intersections that the key areas of understanding for coaches lie. Indeed, by recognizing that athletes are social beings rather than mechanistic bodies, coaches stand to gain an important insight into how the 'socio-cultural dynamics which shape identities in the wider society also impinge upon coaching and learning in sport, and ultimately the ability to perform well' (Jones 2000: 8). An awareness of social prejudices and concerns that may cause an athlete self-doubt or similar problems is essential if a coach is to understand the totality of an athlete's performances. Indeed, it is perhaps by understanding the social aspects of the coaching process in a thoroughly practical way that coaches can possibly mediate tensions and overcome difficulties (Jones *et al.* 2011).

## END-OF-CHAPTER TASKS

Having completed the readings, watch one of the following movies: *Bend it Like Beckham*, *Remember the Titans* or *The Perfect Body*. While watching the movie, make some notes related to the following questions:

1 What are the key issues that the athletes had to contend with both inside and outside of the sporting environment? (Identify specific problems, issues, and scenarios, and their respective impact on the athlete.)
2 How can the athletes' experiences be understood in relation to the concept of identity? (Make links from what you have seen and read regarding sexuality, disability, ethnicity, and religious and athletic identities.)
3 How did the coach or coaches address the issue of athlete identities within the movie? What did you think they did well? Why? What would you have done differently if you had been the coach? How? Why?

## REFERENCES

Adams, A., Anderson, E. & McCormack, M. (2010). Establishing and challenging masculinity: The influence of gendered discourses in organized sport. *Journal of Language and Social Psychology*, 29(3): 278–300.

Adams, A. & Anderson, E. (2012). Exploring the relationship between homosexuality and sport among the teammates of a small, Midwestern Catholic college soccer team. *Sport, Education and Society*, 17(3): 347–363.

Alvesson, M. (2010). Self-doubters, strugglers, storytellers, surfers and others: Images of self-identities in organization studies. *Human Relations*, 63(2): 193–217.

Anderson, E. (2012). The changing relationship between men's homosexuality and sport. In G. Cunningham (ed.) *Sexual orientation and gender identity in sport: Essays from activists, coaches, and scholars*. College Station, TX: Center for Sport Management Research and Education.

Anderson, E. & Bullingham, R. (2013). Openly lesbian team sport athletes in an era of decreasing homohysteria. *International Review for the Sociology of Sport* (ahead-of-print), 1–14.

Brackenridge, C., Rivers, I., Gough, B. & Llewellyn, K. (2007). Driving down participation: Homophobic bullying as a deterrent to doing sport. In C. Aitchison (ed.) *Sport and Gender Identities: Masculinities, Femininities and Sexualities*. London: Routledge.

Bratland-Sanda, S. & Sundgot-Borgen, J. (2013). Eating disorders in athletes: overview of prevalence, risk factors and recommendations for prevention and treatment. *European Journal of Sport Science*, 13(5): 499–508.

Brewer, B.W., van Raalte, J.L. & Linder, D.E. (1993). Athletic identity: Hercules' muscles or Achilles' heel? *International Journal of Sport Psychology*, 24(2): 237–254.

Burke, P.J. & Stets, J.E. (2009). *Identity Theory*. Oxford: Oxford University Press.

Bush, A., Anderson, E. & Carr, S. (2012). The declining existence of men's homophobia in British sport. *Journal for the Study of Sports and Athletes in Education*, 6(1): 107–120.

Carless, D. & Douglas, K. (2013). Living, resisting, and playing the part of athlete: Narrative tensions in elite sport. *Psychology of Sport and Exercise*, 14(5): 701–708.

Carney, A. & Chawansky, M. (2014). Taking sex off the sidelines: Challenging heteronormativity within sport in development research, *International Review for the Sociology of Sport* (ahead-of-print), 1–5.

Coakley, J. (2001). *Sport in Society: Issues and Controversies* (7th edition). New York, NY: McGraw-Hill.

Coakley, J. & Pike, E. (2009). *Sport in Society: Issues and Controversies*. New York, NY: McGraw-Hill.

Collinson, D.L. (2003). Identities and insecurities: Selves at work. *Organization*, 10(3): 527–547.

Cunningham, G. & Melton, N. (2012). Prejudice against lesbian, gay, and bisexual coaches: The influence of race, religious fundamentalism, modern sexism, and contact with sexual minorities. *Sociology of Sport Journal*, 29(3): 283–305.

Denison, J. & Avner, Z. (2011). Positive coaching: Ethical practices for athlete development. *Quest*, 63(2): 209–227.

DePauw, K. & Gavron, S.J. (2005). *Disability Sport*. Champaign, IL: Human Kinetics.

Elliott, A. (2014). *Concepts of the Self*. Cambridge: Polity Press.

Eng, H. (2013). Issues of gender and sexuality. In G. Pfister & M. Sisjord (eds.) *Gender and Sport: Changes and Challenges*. Germany: Waxman Verlag.

Erueti, B. & Palmer, F.R. (2014). Te Whariki Tuakiri (the identity mat): Māori elite athletes and the expression of ethno-cultural identity in global sport. *Sport in Society*, 17(8): 1061–1075.

Fink, J., Burton, L., Farrell, A. & Parker, H. (2012). Playing it out. *Journal for the Study of Sports and Athletes in Education*, 6(1): 83–106.

Fitzgerald, H. (2005). Still feeling like a spare piece of luggage? Embodied experiences of (dis)ability in physical education and school sport. *Physical Education and Sport Pedagogy*, 10(1): 41–59.

Fitzgerald, H. (2009). *Disability and Youth Sport*. London: Routledge.

Fleming, S. (1991). Sport, schooling and Asian male youth culture. In G. Jarvie (ed.) *Sport, racism and ethnicity*. London: The Falmer Press.

Fletcher, T. (2012). 'All Yorkshiremen are from Yorkshire, but some are more Yorkshire than others': British Asians and the myths of Yorkshire cricket. *Sport in Society*, 15(2): 227–245.

Foucault, M. (1978). *The History of Sexuality, Volume 1: An Introduction* (trans. R. Hurley). New York, NY: Pantheon.

Giddens, A. (1997). *Sociology*, 3rd edn. Cambridge: Polity Press.

Griffin, P. (1998). *Strong Women, Deep Closets: Lesbians and Homophobia in Sport*. Champaign, IL: Human Kinetics Publishers.

Griffin, P. (2012). LGBT equality in sports: Celebrating our successes and facing our challenges. In G. Cunningham (ed.) *Sexual Orientation and Gender Identity in Sport: Essays from Activists, Coaches, and Scholars*. Texas: Texas A & M University.

Haleem, H. (2005). Running in pain: An autoethnography of power, coercion, and injury in a coach–athlete relationship. Unpublished PhD thesis. University of Otago, Dunedin, New Zealand.

Hamzeh, M. & Oliver, K.L. (2012). 'Because I am Muslim, I cannot wear a swimsuit': Muslim girls negotiate participation opportunities for physical activity. *Research Quarterly for Exercise and Sport*, 83(2): 330–339.

Hargreaves, J. & Anderson, E. (2014). *Routledge Handbook of Sport, Gender and Sexuality*. London: Routledge.

Huang, C.J. & Brittain, I. (2006). Negotiating identities through disability sport. *Sociology of Sport Journal*, 23: 352–375.

Jackson, L. (2002). *Freaks, Geeks and Asperger Syndrome. A User Guide to Adolescence*. London: Jessica Kingsley Publishers.

Jones, R. (2000). Toward a sociology of coaching. In R. Jones and K. Armour (eds.) *The Sociology of Sport*. London: Addison-Wesley Longman.

Jones, R. (2002). The Black experience within English semi-professional soccer. *Journal of Sport and Social Issues*, 26(1): 47–65.

Jones, R., Armour, K. & Potrac, P. (2004). *Sports Coaching Cultures: From Practice to Theory*. London: Routledge.

Jones, R.L., Glintmeyer, N. & McKenzie, A. (2005). Slim bodies, eating disorders and the coach–athlete relationship: A tale of identity creation and disruption. *International Review for the Sociology of Sport*, 40(3): 377–391.

Jones, R., Potrac, P., Cushion, C. & Ronglan, L.T. (2011). *The Sociology of Sports Coaching*. London: Routledge.

Kay, T. (2006). Daughters of Islam: Family influences on Muslim young women's participation in sport. *International Review for the Sociology of Sport*, 41(3–4): 357–373.

Lavallee, D., Gordon, S. & Grove, J.R. (1997). Retirement from sport and the loss of athletic identity. *Journal of Personal and Interpersonal Loss*, 2(2): 129–147.

Lawler, S. (2014). *Identity: Sociological Perspectives*. London: John Wiley & Sons.

Magrath, R., Anderson, E. & Roberts, S. (2013). On the door-step of equality: Attitudes toward gay athletes among academy-level footballers. *International Review for the Sociology of Sport* (ahead-of-print), 1–18.

Melton, E. & Cunningham, G. (2012). When identities collide. *Journal for the Study of Sports and Athletes in Education*, 6(1): 45–66.

Nixon, H. & Frey, J. (1998). *A Sociology of Sport*. Boston: Wadsworth.

Plateau, C.R., Arcelus, J., McDermott, H.J. & Meyer, C. (2014a). Responses of track and field coaches to athletes with eating problems. *Scandinavian Journal of Medicine and Science in Sports* (ahead-of-print), 240–250.

Plateau, C., McDermott, H., Arcelus, J. & Meyer, C. (2014b). Identifying and preventing disordered eating among athletes: perceptions of track and field coaches. *Psychology of Sport and Exercise*, 15(6): 721–728.

Purdue, D. & Howe, P. (2012). See the sport, not the disability: Exploring the Paralympic paradox. *Qualitative Research in Sport, Exercise and Health*, 4(2): 189–205.

Purdy, L., Potrac, P. & Jones, R. (2008). Power, consent and resistance: An autoethnography of competitive rowing. *Sport, Education and Society*, 13(3): 319–336.

Roberts, K. (2009). *Key Concepts in Sociology*. London: Palgrave Macmillan.

Salter, G. (2000). Deciding between cultural identity or success in physical education: Describing attitudes and values. *Journal of Physical Education New Zealand*, 33(3): 67–83.

Schempp, P. & Oliver, K. (2000). Issues of equity and understanding in sport and physical education: A North American perspective. In R. Jones & K. Armour (eds.) *The Sociology of Sport: Theory and Practice*. London: Addison-Wesley Longman.

Smith, B. (2013). Disability, sport and men's narratives of health: A qualitative study. *Health Psychology*, 32(1): 110–119.

Stets, J. & Serpe, R. (2013). Identity theory. In J. Delamater & A. Ward (eds.) *Handbook of Social Psychology*. The Netherlands: Springer.

Thompson, R. & Sherman, R. (2011). *Eating Disorders in Sport*. London: Routledge.

Thompson, R. & Sherman, R. (2014). Reflections on athletes and eating disorders. *Psychology of Sport and Exercise*, 15(6): 729–734.

Thompson, S., Rewi, P. & Wrathall, D. (2000). Māori experiences in sport and physical activity. In C. Collins (ed.) *Sport in New Zealand Society*. Palmerston North: Dunmore Press.

Tinning, R. (1991). Physical education and the cult of slenderness. *ACHPER National Journal*, 107: 10–13.

Walseth, K. (2006). Young Muslim women and sport: The impact of identity work. *Leisure Studies*, 25(1): 75–94.

Walseth, K. (2015). Muslim girls' experiences in physical education in Norway: What role does religiosity play? *Sport, Education and Society*, 20(3): 304–322.

Warner, M. (1993). Introduction. In M. Warner (ed.) *Fear of a Queer Planet: Queer Politics and Social Theory*. Minneapolis: University of Minnesota Press.

Wine, S. (2003, 23 September). Billy Bean: I'm as out as could be. Queery.com. Available at http://www.queery.com/sybfusion.cgi?templ=q-item2.tpl&category=Q-indepth-feature&idx=69252.

# Section IV

# Knowledge

# Content knowledge

## INTRODUCTION

Researchers and coaches are increasingly expressing a desire for greater understanding of content knowledge. This ambition is not exclusive to those of us living and working in the English-speaking world. In this respect, content knowledge has been the focus of the *didactique* tradition of educational research in Europe (Amade-Escot 2006). According to Amade-Escot (2006: 348), the concept of *didactique* is related to '(i) the study of the content and its function in the teaching/learning process; [and] (ii) the way it [content] is embedded in instructional tasks and brought into play during the interactive teaching/learning process'. Two English language reviews of the *didactique* literature in physical education and sport provide a comprehensive insight into this body of research (see Amade-Escot 2000; David *et al.* 1999). In the UK, Abraham *et al.* (2006) observed that expert coaches have declarative knowledge of the specific sport; primarily, associated sport science and pedagogical knowledge, with the latter also being able to be expressed procedurally. In the US, McCullick *et al.* (2005: 129) reported that coaches value coach education programmes that adopt a broader concept of content knowledge. This was illustrated by the participants of the Ladies Professional Golf Association – National Education Program (LPGA-NEP) – that stated that the strength of the programme was that they 'learned pedagogical knowledge, that is, they learned about *how* to teach ... not just what to teach' (McCullick *et al.* 2005: 129). Despite the largely positive evaluation, the coaches recognized that the pedagogical content knowledge and subject-matter knowledge could not go unquestioned. The findings here, however, that coaches valued formal coach education, runs counter to other more critical research. This issue then remains a contested one.

The purpose of this chapter is to provide a framework that develops the notion of content knowledge by illustrating the (actual and potential) connection between pedagogical content knowledge and curriculum content knowledge. The chapter is organized in two sections: the first introduces a framework that was inspired by the work of Shulman (1986) and Metzler (2000). The second, meanwhile, reflects on the presented framework and associated coaching practices, thereby highlighting the complexities of content knowledge.

## THE SHULMAN-METZLER INSPIRED FRAMEWORK

Lee Shulman (1986) described content knowledge as comprising three subsets: subject-matter content knowledge (SMCK), pedagogical content knowledge (PCK), and curriculum content knowledge (CCK). When transferred to the coaching context, subject-matter content knowledge can be considered the knowledge a coach has, or has access to, that represents the extent of the activity being coached. For example, a coach needs to know the skills, tactics and strategies, as well as the rules of the game or event. Pedagogical content knowledge is the knowledge used by a coach to teach (or communicate) the subject-matter content knowledge to the athletes. McCaughtry (2004: 30) described PCK as a 'useful conceptual tool for explaining and analyzing the knowledge teachers use to transform subject matter for student learning'. For example, a coach needs to know when, why and how to act in response to contextual considerations. While debates surround what constitutes a curriculum, Shulman's definition of curriculum content knowledge is premised on a particular understanding of the term curriculum, i.e. as a set of materials. Consequently, CCK is considered the knowledge of resources available to the coach, which in turn can inform SMCK. For example, a basketball coach needs to be able to know how and where to access the most recent coaching manuals and/or DVDs that outline skills, techniques and tactics.

While Shulman's (1986) framework is a useful starting point for discussing content knowledge, Metzler (2000) suggested that, in order for teachers, and we would argue coaches, to become intimate with the content knowledge of their activity, it is useful to break each of Shulman's (1986) subsets into three further categories. These are identified and described by Metzler (2000) as:

- declarative knowledge (DK) – that which a coach can *express* verbally and/or in written form;
- procedural knowledge (PK) – that which a coach can *apply* before, during and after a coaching session;
- conditional knowledge (CK) – that which informs a coach's decisions in any particular moment or context, and enables him or her to *adapt* practice sessions to other settings with other groups.

According to Metzler (2000), a strong relationship exists between declarative, procedural and conditional types of knowledge. He contended that declarative knowledge was a 'prerequisite' for conditional and procedural knowledge. When adopting this view, a coach must have a basic knowledge of the sport or activity and be able to express this before she or he can attempt to run a practice session.

By drawing on the work of Shulman (1986) and Metzler (2000), it is possible to gain a more comprehensive and nuanced understanding of content knowledge. The basic developed framework can assist coaches to reflect on their content knowledge and to identify areas that they need to develop. The example provided below is deliberately designed with a generic rather than a sport-specific focus, hence, it can be applied to a diverse range of sports and activities.

---

SMCK:
DK – Knowledge of relevant information (e.g. knowledge of rules and biomechanics);
PK – Being able to model and adjudicate the rules of the game in any coaching session;
CK – Adapting tactics so they are suited to the specific opposition.

PCK:
DK – Knowledge of the different methods and strategies that can be adopted;
PK – Being able to apply those methods in a coaching session;
CK – Changing those methods to suit the learning preferences of the athletes.

CCK:
DK – Knowledge of what coaching resources are available;
PK – Being able to incorporate the ideas and activities into a coaching session;
CK – Adapting drills to suit the context and the type of athletes.

---

## REFLECTING ON THE SHULMAN-METZLER INSPIRED FRAMEWORK

While the above framework is a useful starting point for reflecting on coaches' knowledge, it is not without its limitations. Knowledge about our world is increasing exponentially. New so-called experts are being created on a regular basis, which makes it difficult to 'know who and what to believe' and what knowledge, if any, can be considered 'permanent' (Tinning 2002: 384). One consequence is that social practices, such as coaching, are constantly being assessed and revised in light of new information. This being the case, it should be acknowledged that the content knowledge of any activity or sport is not written in stone. Consequently, coaches can, and arguably should, question, 'why the subject matter is so, on whose authority it is so and under what conditions could this change … [and] why one topic is privileged over another' (Rossi & Cassidy 1999: 193).

If coaches view subject-matter content knowledge as only comprising knowledge directly related to the activity being coached, they can overlook the value of engaging with basic movement principles. By incorporating such principles as creating space in attack into practices, a coach can draw on many ideas found in other sports. To assist coaches to work with generic principles, games (read sports) have been classified into four forms: invasion (e.g. basketball, football and hockey); net/wall (e.g. tennis, volleyball and squash); striking/fielding (e.g. cricket and baseball); and target (e.g. golf, croquet and snooker) (Bunker & Thorpe 1982; Thorpe 1997). By utilizing the games classification system, a coach can make sessions more varied and interesting, for themselves and for those they are coaching. A coach can also utilize activities (within the same category) that are not specific to the sport being coached to develop tactics, rather than only focusing on sport-specific techniques (Werner *et al.* 1996). Examples already exist of how a focus on generic invasion principles, relating to scoring and preventing scoring, can improve soccer performance (see Mitchell 1996), whilst how adapting generic net/wall game tactics, such as setting up to attack, can improve volleyball playing (see Griffin 1996). (For an international perspective on Teaching Games for Understanding, see Light [2005]).

Not all agree with Metzler's (2000) premise that declarative knowledge is a 'prerequisite' for conditional and procedural knowledge. When Giddens (1984) explained the rationalization of action, which he also called 'knowledgeability', he claimed that actors can simply 'do' things while concentrating on activities that require conscious effort. Giddens (1984) argued that much of the knowledge required to 'go on' or simply 'do' things in everyday life, which includes coaching, is not consciously accessible to the actor, but is practical in character (Giddens 1984). He defined practical consciousness as 'tacit knowledge that is skilfully applied in the enactment of courses of conduct, but which the actor is not able to formulate discursively' (Giddens 1979: 57). In discussing the history of the professionalization of coaching, Taylor and Garratt (2013: 35) noted that tacit knowledge has played an important role in the 'craft-based histories and non-mediated learning' that has informed many coaching practices (see Chapter 5 for a fuller discussion of this).

A weakness in Shulman's (1986) conceptualization of PCK is that it supports a compartmentalized view of the pedagogical act by focusing on teaching at the expense of the learner and the context (Rossi & Cassidy 1999). This view is similar to Geddis and Wood's (1997) contention that the transformation of subject-matter content knowledge into PCK requires recognition of the learner, the context, the place and time. Another limitation of PCK is the lack of an emotional dimension. The empirical research in educational contexts has made it apparent that 'how teachers interpret and respond to student emotion also plays a key role in their pedagogical content knowledge' (McCaughtry 2004: 33). The importance of coaches having an emotional dimension to their knowledge was also recognized in Gilbert and Côté's (2013: 148) claim that 'interpersonal knowledge in a sport coaching context might best be framed as emotional intelligence'. Others have argued for the adoption of a broader understanding of emotion and 'exploration of the ambiguities, nuances, and emotional nature of coaching' (Potrac *et al.* 2013). To assist with this embryonic exploration, Potrac and colleagues introduced a selection of theoretical frameworks, which could stimulate such analysis.

Defining the curriculum is not as straightforward as Shulman's (1986) CCK category may suggest. Over the decades, in the educational literature, there have been intense debates about what is meant by the term curriculum (Marsh 1997). Yet in the coaching context, there has been little evidence of such discussion with the term commonly understood to mean 'sets of materials' often published by national sporting organizations (see for example, Fortanasce *et al.* 2001; Jobson 1998; Readhead 1997; http://www.sportnz. org.nz/get-into-sport/sport-makers-volunteers/become-a-coach/). These materials can be viewed as the 'overt curriculum', which Dodds (1985: 93) described as 'those publicly stated and shared items that teachers want students to acquire'. The overt curriculum materials are distributed to, or can be purchased by, coaches in attempts to increase knowledge and indirectly improve the skills of athletes. However, as a number of researchers have pointed out (see Dodds 1985; Kirk 1992; Marsh 1997), learners gain knowledge and values not only from the formal, overt or official curriculum, but also from covert, null and hidden sources (Dodds, 1985).

The Shulman-Metzler framework does little to illustrate the consequences of covert, null and hidden curricula. The covert curriculum incorporates the learning objectives, which although not officially stated in any coaching plans, is intentionally and explicitly communicated to athletes when implementing the plan. For example, a coach could talk to athletes about the value of perseverance and of obeying the referee. The null curriculum then, represents those ideas, concepts and values that are knowingly excluded from the formal coaching plan. For example, a junior-level athletics coach may choose not to coach javelin because he or she considers it too dangerous for junior athletes (Tinning *et al.* 1993).

The hidden curriculum can be thought of as the learnings of 'attitudes, norms, beliefs, values and assumptions often expressed as rules, rituals and regulations. They are rarely questioned and are just taken for granted' (Marsh 1997: 35). This can be illustrated in the ritual practices of a basketball coach, who focuses on offensive and defensive rebounds. The smaller players on the team may implicitly learn (from the hidden curriculum) that they are not very good at basketball. In contrast, the taller players may consider themselves good basketball players because, after successfully rebounding the ball, they receive positive feedback from the coach and their peers. However, another basketball coach may value players having agility, speed and ball dexterity. Here, the players with such attributes (who are likely to be the shorter players) learn that they are valued members of the team because of feedback they receive. Recently, Cushion and Jones (2012) used a Bourdieusian framework to explore the hidden curriculum within professional football. The above example and research highlights the complexities of the hidden curriculum, notably that the same coaching practice can be viewed positively or negatively depending on the individual's experience and perspective.

Giddens (1979) argued that many aspects of being able to 'go-on' and 'do things' are communicated through practical consciousness that has non-consciousness (as opposed to unconscious) and 'taken-for-granted' qualities. A coach's practical consciousness is influenced by social conventions, as well as by his or her unique personality and characteristics (Rossi & Cassidy 1999). For example, a beginner coach may choose to teach skills and drills with which they are very familiar, wear what they consider to be the 'right' clothes, and adopt practices, routines and regimes associated with being a 'good coach'. In addition, coaches who adopt 'taken for granted' practices often do so because they reduce the anxieties associated with coaching. Yet, there are hidden meanings associated with these practices that need to be acknowledged if the coach is going to progress.

Hidden messages are not only portrayed in what a coach chooses to say (declarative) and do (procedural), they are also communicated by the tone of voice or by non-verbal gestures. Consequently, all routines, including dress, body shape, as well as the coaching methods adopted all carry messages. While there will always be unintentionally imparted messages in any social practice, by reflecting on the possible covert, null and hidden curricula, coaches can gain insight into the way these practices can cause athletes to have pleasant and unpleasant experiences. What is more, by considering the various forms of content, coaches can develop practices that increase athletes' opportunities to learn. Some coaches may consider the individual incidents that make up the hidden curriculum to be trite or insignificant, since having one or two negative experiences never damaged anyone for life. We concur (to an extent), but also agree with Tinning *et al.* (1993: 108) that there is a powerful cumulative effect of the learning associated with the hidden curriculum, which can be compared to, 'the silt in a river bed which eventually hardens to form mudstone'.

## CONCLUDING THOUGHTS

The International Council for Coaching Excellence (2013) recognized the multifaceted nature of coaches' knowledge by acknowledging professional, interpersonal and intrapersonal knowledge. Similarly, in this chapter the work of Shulman (1986) and Metzler (2000) has been used to highlight the complexity of professional knowledge. Yet, it is imperative that our exploration of coaches' knowledge does not end here. Viewing coaches' knowledge as stable is driven by the modernist desire for certainty and for getting things 'right' (Cassidy & Tinning 2004). In this respect, it exists in contrast to the increasingly pervasive view that knowledge is socially constructed and is always dynamic and evolutionary in nature (Tinning 2002). The flux around what constitutes knowledge can provide an opportunity for coaches, and deliverers of coach education, to become more reflective, sceptical and modest, in what they claim they can do. It should also make them more willing to experiment and recognize that the coaching process cannot be completely controlled. The danger of not taking up the opportunity is evident in the questions posed by Taylor and Garratt (2013: 35):

> If, in the scramble to ring-fence what is and is not professional knowledge, do we exclude novel, contradictory and counter-hegemonic thought and prevent such notions from contesting the status quo? Moreover, do we risk the chance of stagnating the knowledge base, as vested interests serve to protect and preserve existing bodies of thought?

### END-OF-CHAPTER TASKS

1 Using a context with which you are familiar, and the generic framework described in the chapter, provide working examples of the specific types of content knowledge needed to coach your sport in order to provide athletes with maximum opportunities to learn.

2 Using a sporting context with which you are familiar, reflect on the 'hidden' messages that are portrayed by what the coach chooses to say (declarative) and do (procedural).

# REFERENCES

Abraham, A., Collins, D. & Martindale, R. (2006). The coaching schematic: Validation through expert coach consensus. *Journal of Sport Sciences*, 24(6): 549–564.

Amade-Escot, C. (2000). The contribution of two research programs on teaching content: PCK and didactics of physical education. *Journal of Teaching in Physical Education*, 20: 78–101.

Amade-Escot, C. (2006). Student learning within the *didactique* tradition. In D. Kirk, D. Macdonald & M. O'Sullivan (eds.) *The Handbook of Physical Education*. London: Sage.

Bunker, D. & Thorpe, R. (1982). A model for the teaching of games in secondary schools. *Bulletin of Physical Education*, 18(1): 5–8.

Cassidy, T. & Tinning, R. (2004). 'Slippage' is not a dirty word: Considering the usefulness of Giddens' notion of knowledgeability in understanding the possibilities for teacher education. *Journal of Teaching Education*, 15(2): 175–188.

Côté, J. & Gilbert, W. (2009). An integrative definition of coaching effectiveness and expertise. *International Journal of Sport Science and Coaching*, 4(3): 307–323.

Cushion, C. & Jones, R. (2012). A Bourdieusian analysis of cultural reproduction: Socialisation and the 'hidden curriculum' in professional football. *Sport, Education and Society*, 19(3): 276–298.

Cushion, C., Armour, K.M. & Jones, R.L. (2003). Coach education and continuing professional development: Experience and learning to coach. *Quest*, 55: 215–230.

David, B., Bouthier, D., Marsenach, J. & Durey, A. (1999). French research into the didactics and technology of physical activities and sports: An expanding new field. *Instructional Science*, 27: 147–163.

Dodds, P. (1985). Are hunters of the functional curriculum seeking quarks or snarks? *Journal of Teaching in Physical Education*, 4: 91–99.

Fortanasce, V., Robinson, L. & Ouellete, J. (2001). *The Official American Youth Soccer Organization Handbook: Rules, Regulations, Skills and Everything Else Kids, Parents and Coaches Need to Participate in Youth Soccer*, American Youth Soccer.

Geddis, A. & Wood, E. (1997). Transforming subject matter and managing dilemmas: A case study in teacher education. *Teaching and Teacher Education*, 13(6): 611–626.

Giddens, A. (1979). *Central Problems in Social Theory: Action Structure and Contradiction in Social Analysis*. London: Macmillan Press.

Giddens, A. (1984). *The Constitution of Society: Outline of a Theory of Structuration*. Cambridge: Polity Press.

Gilbert, W. & Côté, J. (2013). Defining coaching effectiveness: Focus on coaches' knowledge. In P. Potrac, W. Gilbert, & J. Denison (eds.) *Routledge Handbook of Sports Coaching*. London: Routledge.

Griffin, L. (1996). Tactical approaches to teaching games: Improving net/wall game performance. *JOPERD*, 67(2): 34–37.

International Council for Coaching Excellence (2013). *International Sport Coaching Framework*. Leeds Metropolitan University: Human Kinetics.

Jobson, G. (1998). *Sailing Fundamentals: The Official Learn-to-Sail Manual of the American Sailing Association and the United States Coast Guard Auxillary*. New York: Fireside.

Kirk, D. (1992). Physical education, discourse, and ideology: Bringing the hidden curriculum into view. *Quest*, 44: 35–56.

Light, R. (2005). Teaching games for understanding: An international perspective [Monograph]. *Physical Education and Sport Pedagogy*, 10.

Marsh, C. (1997). *Perspectives: Key Concepts for Understanding Curriculum 1*. London: Falmer Press.

McCaughtry, N. (2004). The emotional dimensions of a teacher's pedagogical content knowledge: Influences on content, curriculum, and pedagogy. *Journal of Teaching in Physical Education*, 23: 30–47.

McCullick, B., Belcher, D. & Schempp, P. (2005). What works in coaching and sport instructor certification programs? The participants view. *Physical Education and Sport Pedagogy*, 10(2): 121–137.

Metzler, M. (2000). *Instructional Models for Physical Education*. Needham Heights, MA: Allyn & Bacon.

Mitchell, S. (1996). Tactical approaches to teaching games: improving invasion game performance. *JOPERD*, 67(2): 30–33.

Potrac, P., Jones, R., Purdy, L., Nelson, L. & Marshall, P. (2013). Towards an emotional understanding of coaching: A suggested research agenda. In P. Potrac, W. Gilbert & J. Denison (eds.) *Routledge Handbook of Sports Coaching*. London: Routledge.

Readhead, L. (1997). *Men's Gymnastic Coaching Manual*. British Amateur Gymnastics Association.

Rossi, T. & Cassidy, T. (1999). Knowledgeable teachers in physical education: A view of teachers' knowledge. In C. Hardy & M. Mawer (eds.) *Learning and Teaching in Physical Education*. London: Falmer Press.

Shulman, L. (1986). Those who understand: Knowledge growth in teaching. *Educational Researcher*, 15(2): 4–14.

Taylor, W. & Garratt, D. (2013). Coaching and professionalization. In P. Potrac, W. Gilbert & J. Denison (eds.) *Routledge Handbook of Sports Coaching*. London: Routledge.

Thorpe, R. (1997). *Game Sense: Developing Thinking Players* (video recording). Belconnen, ACT: Australian Sports Commission.

Tinning, R. (2002). Engaging Siedentopian perspectives on content knowledge for physical education. *Quest*, 21: 378–391.

Tinning, R., Kirk, D. & Evans, J. (1993). *Learning to Teach Physical Education*. London: Prentice Hall.

Werner, P., Thorpe, R. & Bunker, D. (1996). Teaching games for understanding: evolution of a model. *JOPERD*, 67(1): 28–33.

## CHAPTER 13

# Discourse and the (re)production of coaching knowledge

## INTRODUCTION

This chapter examines the (re)production of coaching knowledge. This is particularly in relation to discourse; that is, the language used to describe and explain the activity. It considers how that language leads us to think about and perceive coaching, and those involved in it, in certain ways. The chapter is written from the premise that the creation of coaching knowledge doesn't take place in a political vacuum or exists as a science of transmission, but operates within a hierarchy of social power relations (Brown 1999). A principal way such relations are contested and reaffirmed is through text and talk, which subsequently legitimize certain ways of thinking and being (van Dijk 2014). Knowledge acquisition then, is largely discursive with discourses formed by, and reflective of, ideologies, and power arrangements (Cherryholmes 1988). In short, discourse (and the pedagogy that it engenders) is concerned with the process of knowledge (re)production, as well as the (re)production of values, beliefs and attitudes (Tinning 2010). Consequently, the study of discourse is an examination of how influence is achieved in and through talk; of what is said and the way it is said (Faulkener & Finlay 2002). It pays attention to the language-in-use and the power that such language has over perception and behaviour (McGannon & Mauws 2000). In investigating the representation and (re)production of knowledge through language as it relates to coaching, the chapter examines the discourse used both by coach educators and practising coaches, and the influence this has on athletes.

In doing so, it explores the apparent 'discourse of expertise', which feeds a dominant rationality-based coaching pedagogy. Within this current arrangement, coaches are viewed as knowledge givers and athletes as receivers who need this knowledge to improve their performances. As well as legitimizing the power-dominated means of preparing largely unquestioning and compliant athletes (Johns & Johns 2000), the discourse also situates other forms of thinking about coaching as marginalized. The chapter looks at how both coaches and athletes are situated within this dominant discourse, and how their respective locations 'afford and limit how they speak, feel and behave' (McGannon & Mauws 2000: 148). In this respect, it builds on the recent work of Cushion and Jones (2014) and Denison (2010) who illustrated how coaches' knowledge and related authoritarian discourse was enmeshed within given relations of influence. After a discussion on the nature of discourse and the value of studying it within the coaching context, we examine more particularly the discourse of 'coaching science' and its effect on athletes. Following this, a possible alternative coaching discourse and associated way of knowing is suggested (Johns & Johns 2000); one that is both sensitive and considered, and involves coaches and athletes in their mutual development.

## WHAT IS DISCOURSE AND HOW DOES IT CREATE KNOWLEDGE?

Traditional perspectives of examining language have been defined as representationalist (McGannon & Mauws 2000), where the words we speak are unproblematically considered to represent that to which they refer. Words are thought to be 'merely labels with which we refer to things in the world' (McGannon & Mauws 2000: 151). However, a differing interpretation of talking, which rejects this assumption as simplistic, comes from the discursive perspective. This focuses not on what words might refer to, but on what can be accomplished by using words in the ways we do, particularly in terms of knowledge production (Heritage 1984). Hence, where the primary consideration of the representative perspective is with verbal content, the discursive standpoint lies with the outcome of speaking. From the discursive perspective then, the task is to understand: (i) how talk is produced by, and for, its particular audiences; (ii) the beliefs and motives that create the talk: and (iii) the knowledge related consequences of such talk (Faulkener & Finlay 2002; Wilkinson 2000).

In delving deeper into its nature, we see that the discursive perspective is interested in the complex ways in which speakers construct and understand conversation, with all utterances being treated as 'meaningful social doings' (Wood & Kroger 2000: 12). Language is, therefore, considered not only as a tool for communication or description, but as a 'social practice … a way of doing things' (2000: 12). It is viewed as a 'domain in which our knowledge of the world is actively shaped' (Tonkiss 1998: 246) as it provides the means that allows us to make sense of our own identities and circumstances (McGannon & Mauws 2000). Consequently, any meanings we construct from information given are likely to be greatly affected by the choice of descriptors, metaphors and analogies used by the speaker, as they 'frame' the activity for us. Such 'framing' has been described as having the ability to 'paint pictures in our heads' with all the resultant implications (Sabo &

Jensen 1994). Language, thus, should never be viewed as neutral, but rather as a means of communication which is embedded and riddled with 'overt and covert social biases, stereotypes and inequities' (Messner *et al.* 1993: 110). We might say that discourse does ideological work (Kirk 1992), as it both embodies and rationalizes a value-laden structure, which allows for the promotion and perpetuation of some interests and practices over and above others (Penney 2000). Discourse, then, according to Ball (1990: 17), is essentially about power; it is about 'who can speak where, when and with what authority'. In this way, it endorses certain possibilities for thought while dismissing others. Hence, it becomes not only about what is said and heard but also about what is not, as what is left out in addition to what is included will influence participants' views of 'necessary' knowledge (Penney 2000).

## WHY STUDY DISCOURSE IN THE COACHING CONTEXT?

To answer this question we need only acknowledge the socially constructed nature of language. If we acknowledge that discourse is selective in terms of agenda, interests and values, we accept that it both privileges and legitimizes, and excludes and marginalizes. We need to study it therefore, primarily to acknowledge our roles in these processes of ideological (re)production, thus understanding how our ways of speaking influence our behaviour and the interactions we have with others (McGannon & Mauws 2000). In this respect, knowledge of a discourse's power can help us better manage and frame conversations towards preferred ends. The initial task here is to examine our everyday coaching language-in-use. This allows us to deconstruct the signifiers, behaviours and language of coaches in considering the 'logic' of their privileged positions, and why they come to define both themselves and their athletes in particular ways. It is an 'exercise in vigilance' in relation to 'imagined values' (Bromley 1995: 155), thus treating with considerable suspicion the seductive power of dominant discourses in simplifying, stereotyping and dulling individual experiences (McCarthy *et al.* 2003). Once we understand the micro workings of language and how these are linked to the cultural macro effect and the production of knowledge, we can then recognize our own positions and influence in relation to the discourses that we use. Doing so, allows a consideration of prospects and the potential for change. An examination of what we say and how we say it is also significant because our interactions are not characterized by infinite possibility, as 'both what can be said and how it is said are constrained by the characteristics of the discourse within which it occurs' (McGannon & Mauws 2000: 156). We thus need to identify the boundaries of the predominant discourse that we inhabit, as only then can we become aware of different sites within it (McGannon & Mauws 2000). Such awareness helps us to recognize that the current coaching discourse and the 'knowledge' which sustains it are reflective of vested interests, and of the need to treat it as such. In effect, we need to study discourse, so that we can, if desired, 'change our talk' and, because language is reflective of our realities, 'change our practice' (Wood & Kroger 2000).

However, we are very aware that the discourses within which we speak are enabling as well as limiting forces. Consequently, we have no intention of 'throwing the baby out with the bathwater'. Discourses are enabling in that they allow us to speak of things in particular ways, thus increasing our 'sense making' capabilities. In essence, they allow us 'to understand, to think and [to] make sense' (Kirk 1992: 48). On the other hand, they are limiting in that, as outlined above, they proscribe definite ways of thinking and speaking, hence, restricting 'conditions of possibility' (Foucault 1972). The point in highlighting the workings and influence of language is not to call for an 'objective' neutral substitute within which we can communicate, as such objectivity in a social world is not a credible option. Rather, acknowledging that we will always live within value-laden discourses, our interest here is in exploring the freedom to work creatively within the existing framework. In doing so, we can bring to the fore aspects of the current discourse that have previously remained in the background or at the periphery of our practice (Penney 2000). The value of critically examining coaching discourse then is multiple. First, through employing a deconstructive strategy to confront the current validity of coaching 'expertise', we can challenge conventional understandings of coaching theories and that which they purport to represent. Hence, we can examine and understand the status quo for what it is, and why it is as it is, before reflecting on other ways to possibly improve it. The least we can do here according to Kirk (1992) is to question definitions, purposes and current relevance. Secondly, studying talk allows us to beg the question of what are coaches doing with their words? That is, what is being transmitted and accomplished by their speaking as they do? (McGannon & Mauws 2000). This would enable us to credibly examine the legitimacy of such experts and the knowledges they espouse. Finally, through giving us the ability to uncover what determines actions and thoughts, analyzing discourse also gives us the freedom to explore other discursive coaching options, opening the search for ways to 'do it better'. Getting coaches to critically examine their discourse then leads to a better understanding of self and behaviour, whilst encouraging them to 'think outside the box' to creatively solve problems. It consequently offers the potential for coaches to be central to, and proactive in, shaping the future of coaching and coach education in particular ways.

## THE DOMINANT DISCOURSE OF 'COACHING SCIENCE': PERFORMANCE, RATIONALITY AND A HIERARCHICAL COACH–ATHLETE RELATIONSHIP

According to Johns and Johns (2000) among others, the discourse of modern sport is embedded in a performance pedagogy that is based on scientific functionalism. Here, the body is viewed as a 'machine' which can be developed and improved through appropriate exercises and training regimes (Prain & Hickey 1995). Similarly, much of the current coaching discourse is also biomedical in nature, which arguably has emanated from coaches and officials whose positions of power depend on its promotion (Cherryholmes 1988; Johns & Johns 2000; Schön 1983; Tinning 1991). It is a discourse that favours technical description and procedure, with value placed on the specialist 'factual' knowledge of coaches to provide direction and sequence (Prain & Hickey 1995). It is also a discourse which views the athlete's body as a 'biological object to be studied, manipulated and its movements minutely measured' (Wright 2000: 35). For example, witness the topics covered at a recent conference sponsored by the UK Sports Institute (2002) entitled 'Leadership: World Class Coaching'. They included the biological and rationality dominated 'Optimising trunk muscle recruitment', 'Athens – Heat, humidity and pollution', 'The pose method running' and 'The performance enhancement team' among others, leaving delegates in no doubt as to what sort of knowledge 'expert' coaches should have.

Such an approach views coaching as unproblematic, thus assuming the establishment of a clear set of achievable, sequential goals. As a consequence, coaches have been encouraged to 'take charge' and control the coaching process, which includes their athletes, as much as possible (Seaborn *et al.* 1998). Indeed, the current coach–athlete relationship is characterized by rank and power, with one party perceived as having knowledge, and the other as needing it. This situation has, in turn, reaffirmed the hierarchical discourse often employed in coaching as it takes for granted the structures of power that exist within the traditional coach–athlete relationship (Slack 2000). In this way, the discourse used tends to bolster the status quo, inclusive of the 'common sense' assumption that coaches should 'lead from the front'. Athletes, on the other hand, should subordinate themselves to those who can 'help' them achieve their objectives (Slack 2000). It is a presumed top-down structure of leadership, with strategy and expertise necessarily and legitimately viewed as being the domain of the coach. In addition to a subject-specific vocabulary, the discourse has also resulted in what can be described as a coach-initiation, athlete-response, coach-evaluation pattern of interaction (Prain & Hickey 1995). Such a structure can easily degenerate into being automatic 'recitations' (Cazden 1988) rather than opportunities for athletes to genuinely interact with their coaches to develop new understandings (Prain & Hickey 1995). Within such conversations, coaches inevitably control the turn-taking contributions, thus ensuring that a 'desired' agenda is maintained. A basic problem here, which is reflective of the rationality approach in general, is the frequent failure of coaches to account for individual athlete diversity, leaving the latter, to various degrees, unfulfilled and demotivated. As Alvesson and Willmott (1996) pointed out, in such orthodox manifestations of the coaching role, athletes only really have 'relevance' when the implementation of plans directly depends upon their conscious compliance. The issue for coaches then becomes how can the support of athletes be effectively 'engineered', rather than how best to appreciate and address athletes' underlying concerns (Slack 2000). Alvesson and Willmott (1996) refer to such a situation as the use of 'strategy talk'. This works to restrain the involvement of certain groups (like athletes) in decision-making processes, in that the discourse used by those in positions of power 'frame issues in a way that privileges [their] reason', thus giving them the initiative in any interactions that take place (Alvesson & Willmott 1996: 136). Through using the dominant discourse and identifying with its practices, coaches are able to legitimize their positions and gain influence and credibility, thereby demonstrating the relevance of their role. Additionally, as a consequence of adhering to the dominant discourse which, more often than not, is heavily supported by formal coach education and related policy initiatives, coaches are well placed to receive both assistance from governing bodies and compliance from athletes to whom they act as unquestioning authorities in setting workloads and establishing ways of behaving (Johns & Johns 2000).

Not surprisingly, the prevailing rationalistic-performance coaching discourse has led to the development of language within the profession which is infused with the driving concepts of productivity, efficiency, prediction and accountability. This has led to binary thinking among coaches, which has not only profoundly influenced the nature of the coach–athlete relationship, but also the subsequent preparation of athletes (Johns & Johns 2000). Consequently, although one can easily assume that athletes are empowered by their own goal orientation and the self-chosen means to achieve it (Johns & Johns 2000), a more critical interrogation of coaches' discourse reveals a power-dominated control mechanism which results in the 'production of docile bodies that monitor, guard and discipline themselves' (Eskes *et al.* 1998: 319). In this way, through continuing to speak and coach in rationalistic terms, coaches can be seen to influence the behaviour of their athletes as well as their own. This was the case recently made by Cushion and Jones (2014) in their examination of coaching's 'hidden curriculum' as manifest in professional football. Here, 'taken-for-granted' practice was uncovered as far from being a socially 'neutral' act. Rather, selected messages related to the 'objectification' of the players were constantly reinforced by coaches and passed to players to the extent that they became accepted as legitimate; as 'the way things were'.

## THE EFFECT OF A POWER-DOMINATED DISCOURSE ON ATHLETES

A clear example of the current power-dominated coaching discourse in action lies in the increasing emphasis placed on athlete conformity and compliance. Here, any 'conflict' in the coach–athlete relationship is considered as dysfunctional; a concept clearly at odds with the messy reality of coaching. It is also a stance that implies that individuality cannot be a force for positive change and progression. The result of the situation is that both coaches and athletes are encouraged to see the 'proper' coaching environment as one that is characterized by cooperation, consensus and conformity (Kirk 1992). It is a view that can lead to social oppression, physically and cognitively: physically in terms of reproducing an acceptably formed athletic body, and cognitively in relation to inhibiting individual creativity (Apple 1979).

Before examining scenarios of both instances, it is worth noting that the success of this drive for conformity, although instigated by the coach and his/her discourse, is largely achieved through athlete self-regulation. Here, athletes are often seen to rigorously comply with, and strictly adhere to, coach-produced training regimes that include carefully controlled lifestyle and weight management programmes (Johns & Johns 2000). Such apparent voluntary actions have been referred to as the 'technologies of the self' (Foucault 1977), where athletes adopt the means by which they police their own preparation and appearance in line with coaches' expectations. This compliance is often ensured as athletes have limited discourses upon which to draw. Consequently, they 'take their cues' from their coaches in terms of how to think and speak of their preparation, performances and of themselves as athletes. Indeed, the crucial point here, is that coaches 'frame' the sporting experience for their athletes. They talk in terms of efficiency, productivity and time, hence athletes similarly come to think of themselves in mechanistic terms. In this way, discourse given from positions of power can be considered akin to the 'hidden curriculum' in education (Kirk 1992), which refers to the often subconscious learning of knowledge, attitudes and assumptions as a result of participation in an activity. These learned values become unwritten rules, etched in the mind, and come to significantly influence our behaviours, strategies and the people we become (Kirk 1992). Such readily adopted practices provide clear examples of how power is woven into the fabric of culture (Williams 1977).

The drive for physical conformity and its potential negative consequences has been particularly evident with regard to the female body image, in terms of what it visually means to be an athlete. It appears that the sporting body, as viewed in 'subjective' women's sports such as gymnastics, synchronized swimming, figure skating and diving among others, has increasingly come to rely on the way in which it conforms to social trends and styles, in addition to how it athletically performs (Johns 1998). This has brought the visuality of the body and its preparation within sport, as a site for critical examination, to the fore. Not surprisingly, investigations have revealed paradoxes between the desired body 'look' and weight, and its optimum performance condition (Franklin 1996). They have also revealed a complex set of power and domination structures, which normalizes many practices in sport that might be considered harmful outside it (Birrell & Cole 1994; Chapman 1997).

In many ways, such a situation promotes an ethic of excess (Johns 1998) and is often played out along the thin edge of the body's natural limits (Franklin 1996). It is sustained by the politics of athlete self-surveillance, which, in turn, is made up of a sense of personal responsibility, obligation to constant practice, and continual self-regulation, and is often manifest through the keeping of training diaries. Such diaries ensure that training workloads become accepted by athletes as 'regimes of truth' (Chapman 1997) over which they have 'control'. Here, athletes are subject to what Foucault (1977: 184–185) has termed a 'normalizing gaze' from coaches (and other athletes) to see if the training has been adhered to. It is a gaze that makes it 'possible to classify and to punish', and thus further encourages athletes to engage in disciplinary practices. Not surprisingly, such practices can have negative consequences for athletes, as witnessed by two participants from Johns and Johns' (2000) study who recalled how their self-esteem was eroded by similar technologies of power:

> One [gymnastic] coach would weigh us four times a day: that was ridiculous. We had to weigh in before each practice and that made us really self conscious. And then she would say "You're fat, why do you weigh more than you weighed this morning? What did you eat this afternoon?" It was an interrogation and it was terrible.
>
> (Johns & Johns 2000: 228)

> Coaches in rhythmic gymnastics just love to control their athletes. They said I may as well quit 'coz I wasn't mentally ready to lose weight. It gave me insecurities about my body image and I remember thinking I looked like a whale. I came to realize that it was a question of respect. I don't think a lot of gymnasts are treated with respect, so you end up hating the sport [and] feeling bitter.
>
> (Johns & Johns 2000: 227)

To give another example of how the drive for productivity and conformity can result in negative experiences for athletes, consider a football player who has a tendency and ability to execute creative, individual tasks very well. Hence, she brings an imaginative dimension to team play. On the occasion when, in possession of the ball, she takes the riskier option to penetrate opposing defences, which she is fully capable of doing, she feels a sense of fulfilment, adventure and actualization. If, however, possession is lost as a consequence of the move, she receives criticisms from the coach, and possibly, from the other players for losing the ball they worked so hard to gain. Despite some moves working, her colleagues become loath to support her play as they believe more-than-often the ball will be lost (i.e. her play lacks an 'end product'). Even if the move works, she is often isolated, as her colleagues do not support in enough numbers, as they are not confident that possession will be retained. With less support, this becomes a self-fulfilling prophecy as, indeed, the ball is increasingly lost, which, in turn, leads to more castigation from both colleagues and coach. Subsequently, even when opportunities to be creative present themselves, she begins to experience fear, both of losing the ball and of her teammates' and coach's reactions if she does. As a result, she ceases to try the difficult and innovative, preferring to adopt a safer, less imaginative passing option, thus sacrificing her talent and the unique contribution she brings to the team. In effect, she conforms to the norm.

This example illustrates the influence that a dominant 'product' orientated discourse, can have over a young athlete's development. The starting point of analysis is the player's position within the discourse; how she is seen by others and how she sees herself as a player (McGannon & Mauws 2000). Here, the individual athlete is constantly positioned as a 'team player', a cog in a larger wheel. Hence, she has similar functions to other cogs who must contribute equally to a collective outcome, within an encompassing coach-dominated context. Furthermore, with respect to the socially constructed role of player, the 'good' player is thought of as one who listens to the coach and subsequently carries out instructions without question, trains hard, considers the efforts of teammates, and puts the team's needs ahead of her own: a concept recently brought to life by Cushion and Jones' (2006) examination of the culture apparent in English professional football. To reinforce such values, players are constantly bombarded with such dressing-room signs and sentiments relating to sacrificing the self for the good of the team (e.g. 'there is no I in team' and 'teamwork works'). Consequently, there are a range of expectations, expressed through a particular discourse associated with the term 'player', or more accurately 'good player', that structures how players make sense of their situation and behaviours. The carrying out of these expectations dictates whether the player is regarded as 'good' or not, by others (particularly coaches), and themselves (McGannon & Mauws 2000).

In our example, the contextual discourse established by the coach becomes too strong for our creative player to resist. To keep her place in the team, she will have to conform, thus inhibiting her creative talent and enjoyment of the sport. Indeed, it appears that athletes in general aim for the achievement of an ideal representation of an unwritten subjective standard as set by the coach (Johns & Johns 2000). Furthermore, successful athletes are seen to apply a rigid technology of the self to comply with this 'coaches' view of the world', which is strengthened by the perceived constant gaze of coaches, peers and self.

# AN ALTERNATIVE COACHING DISCOURSE AND WAY OF KNOWING

The critical analysis embarked upon in this chapter has highlighted the problematic nature of the coach–athlete relationship, particularly within high-performance sport. It is a relationship characterized by one side having knowledge and influence, while the other is defined by a 'need to know', a desire to conform and an inability to risk (Johns & Johns 2000). Realistically, we are very aware that coach and athlete require much self-sacrifice and commitment to be successful in sport. Consequently, compliance and productivity are needed. Indeed, there is no need to reject all notions associated with the current discourse. Alternatively, the point here is to become aware of the relativity of what we hold true and how we express it, and to promote questioning about the consequences of these truths and practices before progressing to examine ways of improving (Wright 2000). It is to make coaches increasingly aware of the social construction of knowledge, which grounds its pillars on power relations. Indeed, if we take any curriculum to be made by 'flesh-and-blood people acting in coalitions motivated by particular beliefs and values', then the possibility exists to develop strategies 'to make more incisive interventions in change processes' (Kirk *et al.* 1997: 274). In the words of Cushion and Jones (2014: 295), such 'critical reflection by coaches can help engender cultural dislocation and provides the momentum and materials of self understanding to build a new consciousness around coaching'. However, echoing the earlier call by Johns and Johns (2000), we are not suggesting a total change in the ways of competition preparation and talking about it but, rather, that the power arrangements upon which the highly rationalized sport discourse is based be amended somewhat, thus being subject to greater balance.

Johns and Johns (2000) provide an interesting possible reformulation of the current sport performance-pedagogy discourse. They reject the current binary coach–athlete structure, and alternatively emphasize a greater respect for athletes through the establishment of more equitable relationships. This would include a discourse that is more 'symmetrical and non-dominated' and not 'distorted by power and ideology' (Cherryholmes 1988: 89). It thus reflects an altered performance pedagogy based on a structured freedom, which emphasizes the importance of the individual within the collective, and the social responsibilities of athletes and coaches within the relationship both to themselves and to each other.

A concrete starting point for developing such a discourse could be to attach greater importance, as a coaching resource, to the personal knowledge of athletes, which, in turn, is based on individual experiences and practices. Undoubtedly, athletes possess a wealth of knowledge about achievement and, in particular, what 'works' for them, which is not currently being effectively drawn upon in their preparation. The challenge here is to elevate and integrate this knowledge into good practice, as opposed to ignoring or downplaying it. Respecting and building on athletes' knowledge would also alter the lop-sided power dynamic in traditional coach–athlete relationships to a more equitable one. Such a change in thinking could then lead to a change in speaking; that is, to an altered coaching discourse characterized less by binary 'us' and 'them' thinking to one more defined by a collective 'we', within which the individual's unique and creative talents are valued. The altered relationships would be nondidactic in nature, with athletes actively contributing to their development through a deeper reflection of their own performances (Cazden 1988). Through such a process, they could experience greater success, pleasure and understanding of their sporting experience. Alternatively, coaches would be forced to develop flexible discursive practices to continually challenge their athletes at many levels, whilst allowing more time to better observe, analyze and creatively assess development (Prain & Hickey 1995). This would afford the coach further resources and experiences to develop athletes in more holistic ways, whilst allowing both coach and athlete new and different means to construct and understand their situations. This type of relationship is needed if athletes are to experience the true value of their commitment. We, therefore, need to educate coaches to 'gamble' less on the compliance of athletes through claims to expertise, and alternatively to engage in a joint process of knowledge generation involving both parties which could tap into and develop deeper levels of potential.

Such a development, however, should not exclusively be seen as being (so-called) athlete centred. In this respect, Ellsworth's (1989) cautionary question is very much heeded: 'which diversities or voices are silenced when using a "liberatory" pedagogy and discourse?' Rather, our call here also involves pro-active actions by coaches, in two principal, albeit related, ways. First, the call for a less didactic relationship with athletes does not mean an abdication of coaching responsibility. In this instance, we still believe that a coach should be considered a 'first among equals' or 'a more capable other' (Vygotsky 1978), with a coaching role being akin to leading or guiding the athlete to improved levels of performance as opposed to merely supporting the athlete's (self) stated 'needs'. Second, and in order to somewhat facilitate this development, coaches should be encouraged to explore personal life experiences. Establishing such individual narratives holds the power to develop increased empathy with athletes' (and relevant others') experiences, particularly in relations to how identities become both emboldened and marginalized. Such a process holds the potential to forge previously unconsidered connectivities and new ways of knowing. In this way, coaches can become more sensitive and imaginative active agents in their own development, and in the development of others.

Discourse and language reflect our beliefs and values and, as such, attempts to amend them are often met with some resistance. This is because our utterances serve others, as well as ourselves, in understanding the differing roles each of us plays within the discourse. Consequently, changing our ways of speaking and knowing could encounter resistance from others, as, 'in addition to repositioning ourselves, [such changes] also serve to reposition those with whom we speak' (McGannon & Mauws 2000: 158). As both coaches and athletes have become socialized into accepting their complementary roles, they are bound to feel uncomfortable and uncertain when the boundaries shift. Thus, a coach could experience resistance from athletes if he or she attempts to change the discourse to one that is unfamiliar (further substantiation, if it were needed, that such language is anything but benign). Indeed, evidence suggests this is the case. Consequently, unless care and sensitivity are exercised, athletes may be unwilling to accept radical new strategies, which are alien to them (Jones 2001). Similarly, an athlete who wants to reposition him- or herself within an empowerment discourse may encounter resistance from a coach, who is reluctant to view the athlete's behaviours in anything other than the traditional coach-dominated way. Changing the way we talk then takes patience, perseverance, effort and understanding. To make a lasting alteration we must be aware of how the conversations we have with others and ourselves affect how we feel, think and behave. This note of caution should not dampen the drive for improved change, however, as to coach is to occupy a very privileged position, one that is accompanied by many social responsibilities (Penney 2000). Therefore, we have a duty to choose our words and our talk carefully, to be aware of their legacies, and to search constantly for ways to improve.

## CONCLUDING THOUGHTS

In line with previous thinking (e.g. Bernstein 1990), this chapter was written from the perspective that pedagogic and, hence, coaching discourse, is socially constructed. In this way, knowledge is produced and re-produced, while the subjective and political nature of the process remains hidden (Cushion & Jones 2014). The discourse that currently dominates sports coaching can be seen as providing boundaries that define the nature of the coach–athlete relationship and the roles each party plays within it. It is a knowledge based on, and driven by, a scientific, performance pedagogy, emanating from a power-dominated relationship where the coach is seen as knowledgeable and the athlete not. Although athletes willingly enter the activity, it is a pathway founded on deeply established practice (Johns & Johns 2000). Consequently, athletes generally accept and internalize the discourse present, which is espoused as 'truth' by hierarchically positioned coaches who possess certain contextual 'legitimations' (Cushion & Jones 2014). Although some have argued for a radical overhaul of power arrangements in sport to counter the existing discourse (Shogan 1999), a more realistic goal would be to reposition coaching within it. By doing so, we could establish an amended coach–athlete relationship based on a more equitable power balance relationship. Indeed, athletes in Johns and Johns' (2000) study declared that they were willing to settle for such an amended power structure as long as they understood the reasons for it and their precise place within it. This relates not only to when they could have an increased say in their own development, but also when they could expect guidance and help from coaches. This is not to say that such an amended discourse does not itself require close future scrutiny in the quest for optimal athlete improvement and self-actualization.

In concluding this chapter, we would like to echo the words of Penney (2000). She stated that one of the key things to realize in considering issues such as discourse is that 'we are not all going to agree upon what the focus of attention should be, what aims our energies should be directed to, and how these can be best achieved' (Penney 2000: 62). However, there is a need to be aware of the variety of discourses than can potentially, and perhaps should, find expression in coaching, whilst recognizing that these will have different implications for the interests of different groups. Indeed, this is perhaps where our energies in relation to coaching knowledge and its (re)production should lie; in introducing and further evaluating critical perspectives so that hegemonic reproductive knowledge cycles become increasingly visible (Brown 1999). Doing so can help rework coaches' habitus, discourse and knowledge, thus facilitating an expansion of alternative ways of thinking and doing. At the very least, it gives coaches the opportunity to resist or change (Cushion & Jones 2014). Before we decide on alternative discourses then, issues of whom and what coach education and coaches ought to promote and exclude, merit consideration (Penney 2000). Whatever the outcome of such a process, it is worth remembering that the dominance of certain discourses can and should always be contested, and that perhaps the time is now right for such a challenge in coaching.

## END-OF-CHAPTER TASKS

1 Consider how discourse (i.e. the language in use) contributes to the production and (re)production of knowledge.
2 What kind of discourse is evident in your sporting context (be it as an athlete or coach)?
3 What knowledge does such discourse privilege? What do you think are its effects?
4 What could be alternative forms of coaching discourses? What sort of new knowledge(s) would they create?

## REFERENCES

Alvesson, M. & Willmott, H. (1996). *Making Sense of Management: A Critical Analysis.* London: Sage.

Apple, M.W. (1979). *Ideology and Curriculum.* London: Routledge and Kegan Paul.

Ball, S.J. (1990). *Politics and Policy-Making in Education: Explorations in Policy Sociology.* London: Routledge.

Bernstein, B. (1990). *The Structuring of Pedagogic Discourse: Volume IV, Class, Codes and Control.* London: Routledge.

Birrell, S. & Cole, C. (1994). *Women, Sport and Culture.* Champaign, IL: Human Kinetics.

Bromley, R. (1995). Richard Hoggart: The real world of people: Illustrations from popular art – Peg's paper. In J. Munns and G. Rajan (eds.) *A Cultural Studies Reader: History, Theory and Practice.* London: Longman.

Brown, D. (1999). Complicity and reproduction in teaching physical education. *Sport, Education and Society,* 4(2): 143–159.

Cazden, C. (1988). *Classroom Discourse: The Language of Teaching and Learning.* Portsmouth, NH: Heinemann.

Chapman, G.E. (1997). Making weight: Lightweight rowing, technologies of power and technologies of the self. *Sociology of Sport Journal,* 14: 205–223.

Cherryholmes, C. (1988). *Power and Criticism: Post-structural Investigations in Education.* New York: Teachers' College.

Cushion, C. & Jones, R.L. (2006). Power, discourse and symbolic violence in professional youth soccer: The case of Albion F.C. *Sociology of Sport Journal,* 23(2): 142–161.

Cushion, C. & Jones, R.L. (2014). A Bourdieusian analysis of cultural reproduction: Socialisation and the hidden curriculum in professional football. *Sport, Education and Society,* 19(3): 276–298.

Denison, J. (2010). Planning, practice and performance: The discursive formation of coaches' knowledge. *Sport, Education and Society*, 15(4): 461–478.

Ellsworth, E. (1989). Why doesn't this feel empowering? Working through the representative myths of critical pedagogy. *Harvard Educational Review*, 59(3): 297–324.

Eskes, T.B., Duncan, C.M. & Miller, M.M. (1998). The discourse of empowerment: Foucault, Marcuse and the women's fitness texts. *Journal of Sport and Social Issues*, 18: 48–55.

Faulkener, G. & Finlay, S.J. (2002). It's not what you say, it's the way you say it! Conversation analysis: A discursive methodology for sport, exercise and physical education. *Quest*, 54: 49–66.

Foucault, M. (1972). *The Archeology of Knowledge*. New York: Random House.

Foucault, M. (1977). *Discipline and Punish: The Birth of the Prison*. New York: Pantheon Books.

Franklin, S. (1996). Postmodern body techniques: Some anthropological considerations in natural and post-natural bodies. *Journal of Sport and Exercise Psychology*, 18: 95–106.

Heritage, J. (1984). *Garfinkel and Ethnomethodology*. Cambridge, MA: Polity Press.

Johns, D.P. (1998). Fasting and feasting: Paradoxes of the sport ethic. *Sociology of Sport Journal*, 15: 41–63.

Johns, D.P. and Johns, J. (2000). Surveillance, subjectivism and technologies of power: An analysis of the discursive practice of high-performance sport. *International Review for the Sociology of Sport*, 35: 219–234.

Jones, R.L. (2001). Applying empowerment in coaching: Some thoughts and considerations. In L. Kidman (ed.) *Innovative Coaching: Empowering your Athletes*. Christchurch, NZ: Innovative Communications.

Kirk, D. (1992). Physical education, discourse, and ideology: Bringing the hidden curriculum into view. *Quest*, 44: 35–56.

Kirk, D., Macdonald, D. & Tinning, R. (1997). The social construction of pedagogic discourse in physical education teacher education in Australia. *The Curriculum Journal*, 8(2): 271–298.

McCarthy, D., Jones, R.L. & Potrac, P. (2003). Constructing images and interpreting realities: The representation of black footballers in top-level English football. *International Review for the Sociology of Sport*, 38(2): 217–238.

McGannon, K.R. & Mauws, M.K. (2000). Discursive psychology: An alternative approach for studying adherence to exercise and physical activity. *Quest*, 52: 148–165.

Messner, M.A., Duncan, M.C. & Jensen, K. (1993). Separating the men from the girls: The gendered language of televised sports. *Gender and Society*, 7: 121–137.

Penney, D. (2000). Physical education...in what and whose interests? In R.L. Jones and K.M. Armour (eds.) *Sociology of Sport: Theory and Practice*, London: Longman.

Prain, V. & Hickey, C. (1995). Using discourse analysis to change physical education. *Quest*, 47: 76–90.

Sabo, D. & Jensen, S.C. (1994). Seen but not heard: Images of Black men in sports media. In M.A. Messner and D.F. Sabo (eds.) *Sex, Violence and Power in Sports: Rethinking Masculinity*. Freedom, CA: The Crossing Press.

Schön, D. (1983). *The Reflective Practitioner: How Professionals Think in Action*. New York: Basic Books.

Seaborn, P., Trudel, P. & Gilbert, W. (1998). Instructional content provided to female ice hockey players during games. *Applied Research in Coaching and Athletics Annual*, 13: 119–141.

Shogan, D. (1999). *The Making of High Performance Athletes: Discipline, Diversity and Ethics*. Toronto: University of Toronto Press.

Slack, T. (2000). Managing voluntary sports organizations: A critique of popular trends. In R.L. Jones & K.M. Armour (eds.) *Sociology of Sport: Theory and Practice*. London: Longman.

Tinning, R. (1991). Teacher education pedagogy: Dominant discourses and the process of problem setting. *Journal of Teaching in Physical Education*, 11: 1–20.

Tinning, R. (2010). *Pedagogy and Human Movement: Theory, Practice and Research*. New York: Routledge.

Tonkiss, F. (1998). Analysing discourse. In C. Seale (ed.) *Researching Society and Culture*. London: Sage.

UK Sports Institute (2002). 'Leadership', paper presented at the World Class Coaching Conference, The Belfry, Birmingham, November 25–27.

van Dijk, T.A. (2014). *Discourse and Knowledge: A Socio-Cognitive Approach*. Cambridge: University Press.

Vygotsky, L. (1978). *Mind in Society: The Development of Higher Psychological Processes*. Cambridge MA: Harvard University Press.

Wilkinson, S. (2000). Women with breast cancer talking causes: Comparing content, biographical and discursive analyses. *Feminism and Psychology*, 10: 431–460.

Williams, R. (1977). *Marxism and Literature*. New York: Oxford University Press.

Wood, L.A. & Kroger, R.O. (2000). *Doing Discourse Analysis: Methods for Studying Action in Talk and Text*. Thousand Oaks, CA: Sage.

Wright, J. (2000). Bodies, meanings and movement: A comparison of the language of a physical education lesson and a Feldenkrais movement class. *Sport, Education and Society*, 5: 35–49.

## CHAPTER 14

# Assessing knowledge and ability

## INTRODUCTION

In earlier editions of this text, we made the claim that assessment in sports coaching had not been a 'hot topic'. The evidence lay in an annotated bibliography (Gilbert 2002), which showed that up until that point, only four per cent of articles focused on assessment. Over a decade later, the situation seems to have changed little, as witnessed by the absence of any related discussion in the *Routledge Handbook of Sports Coaching* (Potrac *et al.* 2013). This lack of engagement by the research community is surprising given the interest in 'sport analytics' (see *International Journal of Performance Analysis in Sport*) and the use of more authentic and comprehensive measures to assess players. In an attempt to address what they considered a 'significant oversight that both fails to recognize key aspects of pedagogy and learning, and overlooks opportunities for optimizing coach and athlete development', Hay *et al.* (2012) explored the potential of assessment efficacy in sports coaching. This became a focus for debate (for details see *International Journal of Sports Science and Coaching*, 7[2], 2012). The aim of this chapter is to use a sociocultural perspective to highlight the complexities associated with assessment, and to discuss what this could mean for coaches' practice. The chapter begins with an introduction to a sociocultural perspective on assessment, discussing its principal aspects, before making links between assessment and ability.

# A SOCIOCULTURAL PERSPECTIVE ON ASSESSMENT

Our discussion here is informed by the work of Hay and colleagues, particularly that of Hay and Penney (2013), who draw on theorists such as Bernstein (1971) and Bourdieu (1986) to frame an analysis and discussion of assessment. According to Hay and Penney (2013), adopting a sociocultural perspective does not foreground the technicalities and/or practicalities of assessment. Rather, it focuses on the complexities related to its diverse origins, and is interested in the consequences that assessment practices have on learners. They go on to say that adopting a sociocultural perspective explicitly highlights that 'assessment is fundamentally a *social activity*. Assessments are required by people, developed by people, implemented by people, and performed by people and have implications for people' (2013: 3). When viewed as such, three principal assumptions of assessment exist: (i) it is 'socially, culturally, historically and politically situated', and has a 'dynamic relation with the educational and social contexts in which it is set' (Hay and Penney 2013: 15); (ii) it is 'imbued with the values, beliefs and expectations of those designing the tasks, and impacts upon the views, values and understandings of those who are being assessed' (2013: 127); and (iii) it is part of 'a whole message system that is influenced by and influencing the other two education message systems of curriculum and pedagogy' (2013: 127). Assessment, therefore, is seen as having a role in '*communicating value*' (2013: 6). Drawing on Bernstein, Hay and Penney (2013: 5) stated that 'the selection, classification, transmission and assessment of educational knowledge could be viewed as occurring through the three interrelated message systems of pedagogy, curriculum and evaluation (or in our current vernacular, assessment)'. The curriculum message system works to outline '*what* should be taught and learnt', e.g. skills, tactics and rules, which are often communicated via texts such as coaching manuals and websites (Hay *et al.* 2012: 189). The pedagogy message system requires a relationship to exist between those who deliver the knowledge, e.g. a coach, and the 'acquirer' of the knowledge, e.g. the athlete. In addition, the pedagogy message system foregrounds the 'processes or techniques through which the delivery and/or acquisition of content might occur' (2012: 189). Finally, assessment as a message system defines, communicates and ascribes value to practices. As Hay *et al.* (2012:189) pointed out when 'some facets of a learning field are assessed and others are not, by implication a distinction is made between relative values of those facets'.

According to Hay *et al.* (2012: 190), the effective realization of learning outcomes '*depends* on the alignment and coherence of the three message systems'. One consequence of the coaching science research community not discussing assessment is that it potentially limits the opportunities for coaches to better understand what they do and why they do it. This is because they may not acknowledge the potential negative consequences of assessment, or realize the 'intended learning or performance outcomes' (2012: 190).

In a further effort to promote 'critical research dialogue and widen the possibilities of assessment practices' through the integration of pedagogy, curriculum and assessment, Hay *et al.* (2015: 33) introduced the concepts of pedagogical work (Tinning 2008, 2010) and assessment efficacy. The basis for doing so lay in the belief that pedagogical work, as conceptualized, provides insight into particular perspectives of assessment. Specifically, that 'assessment does pedagogical work through its *formative* potential', whilst pedagogical work, in turn, represents 'the pursuit of "assessment efficacy"' (Hay *et al.* 2015: 36).

In an effort to reduce definitional confusion relating to 'assessment', we take a lead from Hay and Penney (2013). They argued the merits of a pragmatic stance, and proposed a definition of assessment related to its theoretical and conceptual underpinnings. Hence, they defined assessment to 'include *any action of information collection within education settings that is initiated for the purpose of making some interpretive judgements about students*' (2013: 6). While the definition is explicitly located within education, it is easily transferable to sports coaching with the focus on the judgement being about athletes.

The central features of the definition rely on certain assumptions. First, that if information is purposefully collected, you will know what and why you are assessing. Second, if information is systematically collected, then 'decisions have been made about when and how assessment will be implemented' (Glasby 2006: 219). Third, if the collection of information is ongoing, then 'assessment will occur throughout the learning process, and the cumulative evidence of student achievement over time will be the basis of your judgments about the quality of student learning' (2006: 219). Finally, that the information collected is relevant for the purposes of the assessment (Hay 2006).

Several scholars (see Broadfoot & Black 2004; Hay 2006; Penney *et al.* 2005; Tinning *et al.* 2001) have suggested that one way an assessor can be clear on the purpose of the assessment is to ask him- or herself the following questions:

- Who is to be assessed?
- What is to be assessed?
- How is the assessment to occur?
- When is the assessment going to occur?

Once the purpose of assessment is clear, the next step is to decide upon what type of assessment will be 'appropriate and effective' (Penney *et al.* 2005: 58). The purposes of assessment can be classified into two broad groups: assessment for learning, and assessment for accountability (Hay 2006). With the development and acceptance of constructivist learning theories, the purpose of assessment has come to be viewed as related to student learning. Hence, it has been variously described, amongst other things, as formative and educative (Hay & Penney 2013). Constructivist theorists view learning as a consequence of contextualized interactions between teachers and learners, with the latter *actively* appropriating and adapting 'new knowledge in relation to former understandings and cognitive structures' (2013: 9). When making the connection between assessment and pedagogical work, Hay *et al.* (2015) suggest that learning can take place 'through participating in assessment tasks' (2015: 38), which is 'as valuable as the information that is collected' on learners' capacities at the completion of an assessment task (2015: 38). Therefore, when the purpose of assessment is to promote learning, the assessment tasks require learners 'to demonstrate a *range* of knowledges and processes in a manner beyond the passive recall of content' (Hay & Penney 2013: 9).

# ASSESSMENT FOR LEARNING

An assessment for learning paradigm, which is informed by constructivist perspectives on learning, emerged in response to the perceived limitations of behavioural learning theories and traditional assessment techniques (Hay 2006). As noted above, formative assessment is one descriptor used for assessment practices that aim to support the learning process. Formative assessment has been defined as 'encompassing all those activities undertaken by teachers [read coaches] and/or their students [athletes], which provide information to be used as feedback to modify the teaching and learning activities in which they are engaged' (Black & Wiliam in Hay 2006: 316). When assessing formatively, the information must be collected throughout the learning process rather than at the end of it. Since the assessment task is viewed as a learning opportunity that challenges learners' 'existing knowledge structures and beliefs' (Hay 2006: 313), its timing is crucial. The feedback generated is considered an important apparatus for monitoring and reflecting upon learning. Drawing on the work of Sadler, Hay (2006: 316) concluded that while feedback is 'an essential aspect of meaningful and useful formative assessment', it only has meaning if the person receiving it knows what to do with the information. It has been suggested that learners could make better use of information received if the learning outcomes were explicitly stated[1], and if the information and strategies provided were directly related to those outcomes (Hay 2006). Echoing such beliefs, Alton-Lee's (2003: 86) *Best Evidence Synthesis* highlighted that 'when assessment takes the form of effective and formative feedback, it is one of the most influential elements of quality teaching'. This requires teachers [read coaches] to have a range of knowledges including:

- content knowledge;
- general and specific pedagogical knowledge;
- curriculum knowledge;
- knowledge of the learner;
- knowledge of contexts; and
- a knowledge of educational aims (including desired outcomes).

A more detailed discussion of some of these knowledges occurs in Chapter 12.

Constructivist learning theories are increasingly informing initiatives in coaching and coach education. This being the case, formative assessment can assist the learning process in the ways outlined as well as motivating learners to achieve (Siedentop & Tannehill 2000). Yet, formative assessment will only do this if the practices are integrated into high-quality teaching, and do not become the focus of the teaching (Alton-Lee 2003). One example of a sports coaching practice that reflects assessment for learning is the collection of statistics throughout the season. For example, at the start of the season, a basketball coach and athlete may set the following outcome: 'The athlete will successfully complete 20 defensive rebounds in a competitive game situation'. Over the course of the season, related statistics are gathered. After each game, the athlete's progress against the learning outcome is assessed, which assists in the design of means to further the likelihood of the set outcome being realized. Here, the three message systems, pedagogy, curriculum and assessment, are woven together to achieve or better approximate the outcome.

# ASSESSMENT EFFICACY AND AUTHENTIC ASSESSMENT

Pursuing assessment efficacy is similar to seeking assessment validity (Hay *et al.* 2012). An appreciation of such efficacy is central to any discussion of assessment. This is because assessment efficacy is considered a 'foundational principle of all assessment practices' (Hay & Penney 2013: 56). Informed by a sociocultural perspective, Hay *et al.* (2012) suggested that for assessment to be efficacious, certain conditions had to be met. These included that the assessment had to be 'learning orientated, authentic, valid and socially just' (2012: 191). Efficacious assessment practices can assist coaches to produce sound interpretations enabling them to collect relevant evidence of athlete learning. (For a detailed discussion on a sociocultural view of assessment validity see Chapter 5 in Hay & Penney [2013] and for assessment efficacy see Hay *et al.* [2015]).

When coaches assess for learning they need to be mindful to adopt assessment practices that support the learning process. One way of doing this is to implement practices that are authentic and meaningful to the learner. According to Hay (2006: 313), authentic assessment is 'contextually relevant' whilst developing students' 'higher-order knowledge and skills that can be transferred beyond the classroom' (2006: 313). Drawing on the work of Wiggins, Hay suggested that authentic assessment 'should be realistic, replicating the manner in which the knowledge and processes being assessed are utilized in real-life contexts' (2006: 316). For the assessment tasks to be authentic, they should also be structured, so that learners are provided with opportunities to demonstrate knowledges and skills beyond those they have been taught. The assessment tasks can then 'contribute to an improvement in students' learning and teachers' practice' (Hay 2006: 316). For it to be authentic in a sports coaching context, the assessment task should be 'based in movement and capture the cognitive and psychomotor processes involved in the competent performance of physical activities' (Hay 2006: 317). The notion of authenticity is 'closely linked to a need for greater *individualisation* of learning and assessment' (Penney *et al.* 2005: 59). What this means for sport coaches is that they shift from the historical practice of mass assessment (e.g. pre-season team-wide fitness tests) and move towards designing practices that support the achievement of learning goals (e.g. individual and position specific fitness tests).

If coaches are to design authentic and meaningful assessment, then they should be aware of what they and athletes want to achieve. The assessment would then be designed around the co-constructed learning outcomes. Some questions that the coach and athletes could ask to stimulate this process are:

- What are the important outcomes? (Remembering that the learning outcomes have to be meaningful and authentic, otherwise why will the athletes bother trying to attain them?)
- What must athletes be able to demonstrate to show that they understand the content?
- What opportunities do athletes have to demonstrate skills and knowledge in a way that is unique to them? (Siedentop & Tannehill 2000)

Furthermore, a coach may wish to consider some of the principles identified below to increase the involvement of learners in the assessment process:

- outline the rationale and assessment tasks within the unit of work 'in "real world terms", making the "real life" relevance explicit' to learners' (Penney *et al.* 2005: 60);
- make connections between what is being learned in one context with the learner's general life experience(s);
- 'set assessment tasks that are realistic, inter-linked and cumulative in effect' (2005: 65);
- highlight the connections between the various aspects of the unit that will 'produce the desired learning outcomes' (2005: 66).

## ASSESSMENT AND ABILITY

What we consider the purpose of assessment and how we adopt related practices are 'largely mitigated by our understanding of ability' (Hay 2005:42). What is more, making judgments as to who has ability 'contributes to differentiating effects for young people in relation to gender, race and social class' (Wright & Burrows 2006: 287). As Hay and Penney (2013) noted, 'the experience of being assessed and the outcomes of that assessment are significant contributors to students' understanding of what is valued in a subject' (2013: 45). Every time a coach assesses an athlete, or makes a comment about the athlete's ability, a judgement is made. The degree to which the judgement is socially just depends on the level of transparency. Ideally, if a coach is assessing an athlete, the latter is aware of the criteria against which judgement is made. The level of awareness is akin to a level of transparency. However, as Hay (2005: 42) pointed out, our considerations are often 'based upon far less visible judgments and [hence] are much less open to challenge' and scrutiny. He goes on to say that this is potentially problematic, because perceptions of ability may shape the judgements that occur during assessment. Consequently, Wright and Burrows (2006: 287) argued that it is 'imperative to conceptualise "ability" as embedded in social and cultural relations'. The following vignette demonstrates how such relations inform 'common sense' assumptions about ability. At its conclusion, we briefly introduce work that has critically examined the notion of ability, and discuss possible implications this has for assessment practices in the sports coaching community.

### Vignette 14:1 Interpreting ability on the court

Maurice played for the Tall Blacks[2] in his twenties before taking up a career in coaching 25 years ago, the last 10 of which he spent in Europe. Recently, he returned to New Zealand to coach a team playing in the Australian National Basketball League (ANBL). He considered himself ready for the challenge, basing the judgement on prior experience. The players in the squad came from a range of ethnic backgrounds, including Māori, Samoan, and Pākehā as well as two African-American players.

Half way through the season, Maurice confided in his assistant that he couldn't work out why some of the players weren't practising the drills and skills he had set them. This is not what he had experienced in Europe. He wanted to be confident that during mid-game pressure, he could call a particular drill and that it would be executed as intended. While Maurice thought the players in New Zealand had more natural ability than those he had coached in Europe, the ANBL players frustrated him because they often wanted to make up fancy 'plays' and, even though he would tell them not to, they were quite prepared to throw the '50:50' pass on the chance that it would work.

What Maurice didn't know was that some of the players had also confided in the assistant coach. The players wanted more input into the running of the practices. They also wanted Maurice to acknowledge that because some of the squad had started playing together when they were at school, they enjoyed playing 'pick up', even during team practices. The players knew Maurice saw this as 'fooling around', but they wanted him to recognize that this was them being creative and that it was OK to have fun.

Historically, ability has been viewed as relatively stable, although it can be changed somewhat through training regimes. This view is informed by what is known as a 'positive eugenic' perspective (Hay 2005: 44). When assessment is considered thus, any poor achievement is considered to reflect the learner's abilities or engagement (Hay 2005). Rarely is the assessment instrument considered to be the one that is limited.

In exploring ability as a 'dynamic, sociocultural construct and process', Evans (2004: 99) drew on Bourdieu's concepts of field and habitus (for an explanation of these concepts see Chapter 8 on Athlete Learning). In doing so, he re-conceptualized the notion of ability, and problematized the relationship between assessment and ability. The rationale for doing such work lay in the recognition that '[w]e cannot "read" or interpret "ability" … without reference to a person's gender, age, ethnicity, "disability" and the values prevailing within and across particular fields' (2004: 101). Evans's work encourages us to question the basis on which coaches, administrators and selectors make judgments on athletes' abilities. He proposed that ability could be viewed as the value a person's habitus has to a specific field. This is reflected in the example of a child growing up in a family who loves basketball. Such an environment is likely to influence the child's thoughts, social practices, competencies and dispositions associated with basketball. If/when that child plays competitive basketball, it is likely that his or her habitus will be valued by the coaches, selectors and administrators, because there exists some symmetry between the child's habitus and that particular field. According to Hay (2005), the greater the symmetry between an athlete's habitus and field, the more likely it will be that he or she is judged as having ability.

With reference to the earlier vignette, Maurice perceived the players he coached in Europe to be more able than his ANBL franchise players. We would suggest that this was because the attributes and dispositions of the European players, such as being prepared to practice drills for hours on end, had symmetry with Maurice's expectation of what a professional basketball player should do. Yet, it is not only the athletes' habitus that is implicated in the judgments about ability. Maurice's expectations and perceptions are part of his habitus, which then influence his judgments on what constitutes ability. For example, when the expected and desirable characteristics and dispositions are not forthcoming, athletes 'who work to challenge what is deemed legitimate may be relegated to labels such as "behavioral problems", "lacking effort" or "unable"' (Hay & lisahunter 2006: 309). This was highlighted in the vignette when Maurice described the ANBL players as not having 'dedication', and bemoaning the fact that the players ignored his request not to throw risky passes. Even the players noticed Maurice's perceptions by saying that they knew he saw their behaviour as 'fooling around'.

Others have also challenged the eugenic perspective of ability. For example, Wright and Burrows (2006) utilised Bourdieu's notion of capital to do so. While Bourdieu usually analyzed embodied capital under the heading of cultural capital, Shilling (1991: 654) argued that '"the physical" is too important to be seen merely as a component of cultural capital'. Shilling went on to refer to the production of physical capital as 'the *social formation* of bodies through sporting leisure and other activities in ways that express a class location and which are accorded symbolic value' (2001: 654). Like other forms of capital, physical capital can be converted into economic, cultural or social capital (Bourdieu 1984). Wright and Burrows (2006: 283) pointed out that 'ability as a form of physical capital is profoundly classed'. They argued it is classed because of the 'unequal opportunities to develop ability both through differential physical and human resources available; and the ways particular cultural and social capital are associated with particular abilities and capacities.' (2006: 283). In developing this position, they drew on the work of Hokowhitu (2003, 2004) to demonstrate the way physical ability has been used to differentiate between ethnicities.

In mapping ways in which Māori have historically, and continue to be, regarded as achievers in the physical realm, yet limited in the academic field, Hokowhitu (2003) gave the example, in the nineteenth century, of Māori being constructed as 'physical, unintelligent and savage' by missionaries and European settlers (2003: 193). At the turn of the twenty-first century, this construction is still apparent through comments about Māori athletes having a 'warrior instinct' or that their athleticism 'is in the blood' or Māori have 'natural rhythm'. Using Hokowhitu's work, Wright and Burrows (2006) observed that: Māori and Polynesian boys are over-represented in school sport 'academies'; professional rugby is actively promoted as a lifestyle choice for Māori and Pacific Islanders; and, that young people of Māori and Pacific descent (with sporting prowess) are deliberately targeted for recruitment into elite state and private schools. They noted that these practices are implicitly based on the assumption that Māori and Pacific Islanders have 'physical capital', which has been 'inherited' by virtue of race.

Hokowhitu (2003: 193) pointed out that 'such "normal" depictions of Māori are undoubtedly tied to a bio-racist history contrived by colonizer privilege'. He went on to say that while some may argue that the above descriptions and situations could be viewed as complimentary, he pointed out that they 'reinforced prevailing stereotypes that Māori lacked the psychology of a white person' and that it is 'implicitly linked' to the Cartesian mind/body dualism (2003: 212) (see Chapter 10 for a description of the Cartesian dualism). The Cartesian dualism is reflected in the view that 'natural physical ability is paralleled by an inherent lack of mental resolve' (2003: 212).

In the above vignette, Maurice's view of the ability of some of the players in the ANBL team also reflects a Cartesian dualism. Unfortunately, this view is not only held by fictitious coaches, but has also been apparent in the discourse of some leading sporting commentators in Aotearoa/New Zealand. For example, Murray Deaker, a well-known sports analyst said:

> I think it is fantastic that we have this wonderfully athletic group of people [Māori and Pacific Islanders] that can help us develop our sport ... But I also want the hard, tough white farmer to be part of my All Black[s] side ... [The type of player who is] there for 80 minutes in a ruthless uncompromising way.
>
> (Matheson in Hokowhitu 2003: 212–213)

Similarly, ex-All Black turned commentator Grant Fox stated:

> Polynesian players were naturally superior to us [Pākehās] in talent, but a lot of them aren't there now because they didn't have the discipline for physical conditioning. They lacked the right kind of mental attitude. They'd just turn up and play.
>
> (Hyde in Hokowhitu 2003: 213)

Some years after the above comments, Hippolite (2010) highlighted the personal, cultural and institutional racism that still exists in New Zealand sport. When portraying the experiences of 10 Māori sport participants, coaches and administrators, Hippolite highlighted 'the power differentials in society', and how this impacted 'on the ability of Māori to practice important cultural values in Pakeha-dominated contexts' (2010: ii).

Māori are not the only ones whose depictions are linked to a 'bio-racist history' (Hokowhitu 2003: 193). Players and coaches of Pacific decent are also stereotyped in similar ways to Māori as evidenced by the response to the underperformance of the Auckland based Super 15 rugby union franchise known as the 'Blues'. In an article entitled 'Pat Lam [the coach] breaks down over racist taunts', it was noted that 'Lam has faced some vitriol from fans over the Blues' performance so far this season but said comments that the Blues were losing because he was a Pacific Islander were just offensive' (Gray 2012).

The comments above construct Māori and Pacific Islanders as only having ability in the physical realm. One potential consequence is that Māori and Pacific Islanders are disenfranchised from 'resources, both economic and social, that are derived from involvement in the "academic" or "intellectual" world' (Wright & Burrows 2006: 287). Athletes, too, make links between physical ability and ethnicity. Shane Battier (of NBL Houston Rockets and Miami Heat fame) is the son of a black father and a white mother who grew up in the suburbs of an American city. He said '[e]verything I have done since then [8th grade] is because of what I went through with this'. He said the '[s]uburban kids ... treated him like a visitor from the planet where they kept black people', while the '[i]nner city kids ... treated him like a suburban kid with a white game' (Lewis 2009). This insight highlights the usefulness of habitus to understand ability and encourages us to continue asking questions about how we judge ability. For example '[i]s it a coincidence that many of the things a player does in [so-called] 'white basketball' to prove his [sic] character – take a charge, scramble for a loose ball – are all more pleasantly done on a polished wooden floor than they are on inner-city asphalt?' (Lewis 2009).

## CONCLUDING THOUGHTS

While assessment may still not be a hot topic amongst coaches or the associated research community, it is nonetheless an important topic in the coaching process. This is because assessment is a tool to measure whether or not learning is occurring or has occurred. By neglecting to consider the complexities associated with assessment, coaches are unable to gain an accurate picture of what athletes are learning, nor are they able to recognize how 'common sense' assumptions of ability influence assessment practices. The work of Evans (2004), Hay (2005, 2006) Hay and Penney (2013) and Wright and Burrows (2006) demonstrate alternative ways to look at ability other than those informed by the traditional eugenic perspectives. By not considering these alternative perspectives, we potentially limit what is possible (Hay 2005). In a coaching context, this means potentially constraining athletes' learning possibilities as well as those of a coach to make a difference. Therefore, when involved in assessment it is important to recognize the habitus of all involved, and to subsequently adopt meaningful and authentic practices. Similarly, it is crucial to ask '[q]uestions about what "abilities" count, why, how and with what effects' realizing that the answers 'cannot be considered outside of "culture"' (Wright & Burrows 2006: 287–288). Echoing Hay and Penney's (2013) lament to the physical education community, we believe that assessment in sports coaching needs and deserves far greater conceptual and empirical attention.

### END-OF-CHAPTER TASKS

1 Watch the movie *Moneyball* (2011) and discuss the following:
   a In one scene, the baseball scouts/recruiters discussed potential recruits to Oakland Athletics. Discuss the merits, or not, of using such criteria for selecting players.
   b Peter Brandt (the analyst) identified an 'epic failure' in baseball, in other words he identified a problem. What was the problem and what was his solution? Use Lawson's (1993) article on problem setting to discuss the issues associated with problem setting and problem solving.
2 Observe the athletes with whom you work or train. Rank them in terms of ability, then reflect on, and describe, ways in which your ranking could be informed by assumptions based on gender, ethnicity or social class.

## NOTES

1   According to the New Zealand Ministry of Education (1999: 55) a learning outcome is the 'expected learning that occurs as a result of a particular learning activity'.
2   The name of the New Zealand national men's basketball team.

# REFERENCES

Alton-Lee, A. (2003). *Quality Teaching for Diverse Students in Schooling: Best Evidence Synthesis*. Wellington: Ministry of Education.

Bernstein, B. (1971). *Class Codes and Control*. London: Routledge.

Bourdieu, P. (1984). *Distinction: A Social Critique of the Judgement of Taste*. London: Routledge.

Bourdieu, P. (1986). The forms of capital. In J. Richardson (ed.) *Handbook of Theory and Research of the Sociology of Education*. Westport, CT: Greenwood.

Broadfoot, P. & Black, P. (2004). Redefining assessment? The first 10 years of assessment in education. *Assessment in Education*, 11(1): 7–27.

Evans, J. (2004). Making a difference? Education and 'ability' in physical education. *European Journal of Physical Education*, 10(1): 95–108.

Gilbert, W. (2002). An annotated bibliography and analysis of coaching science. Unpublished report sponsored by the Research Consortium of the American Alliance for Health, Physical Education, Recreation and Dance.

Glasby, T. (2006). Assessment and reporting of learning outcomes in PE. In R. Tinning, L. McCuaig & lisahunter (eds.) *Teaching Health and Physical Education in Australian Schools*. Frenchs Forest, NSW, Australia: Prentice Hall.

Gray, W. (2012). Rugby: Pat Lam Breaks Down Over Racist Taunts. Available at http://www.nzherald.co.nz/sport/news/article.cfm?c_id=4&objectid=10798136. [Accessed on 30 April 2015].

Hay, P. (2005). Making judgements – student ability and assessment in physical education. *Journal of Physical Education New Zealand*, 38(1): 41–50.

Hay, P. (2006). Assessment for learning in physical education. In D. Kirk, D. Macdonald & M. O'Sullivan (eds.) *The Handbook of Physical Education*. London: Sage.

Hay, P. & lisahunter. (2006). Please Mr Hay, what are my poss(abilities)?: Legitimation of ability through physical education practices. *Sport, Education and Society*, 11(3): 293–310.

Hay, P. & Penney, D. (2013). *Assessment in Physical Education: A Sociocultural Perspective*. London: Routledge.

Hay, P., Dickens, S., Crudgington, B. & Engstrom, C. (2012). Exploring the potential of assessment efficacy in sports coaching. *International Journal of Sports Science and Coaching*, 7(2): 187–198.

Hay, P., Tinning, R. & Engstrom, C. (2015). Assessment as pedagogy: A consideration of pedagogical work and the preparation of kinesiology professionals. *Physical Education and Sport Pedagogy*, 20(1): 31–44.

Hippolite, H. (2010). Speaking the unspoken: Māori, experiences of racism in New Zealand sport. Unpublished Masters thesis, University of Waikato.

Hokowhitu, B. (2003). 'Physical beings': Stereotypes, sport and 'physical education' of New Zealand Māori. *Culture, Sport and Society*, 6(2/3): 192–218.

Hokowhitu, B. (2004). Challenges to state physical education: Tikanga Māori, physical education curricula, historical deconstruction, inclusivism and decolonization. *Waikato Journal of Education*, 10: 71–83.

Lawson, H. (1993). Dominant discourses, problem setting, and teacher education pedagogies: A critique. *Journal of Teaching in Physical Education*, 12: 149–160.

Lewis, M. (2009). The No-Stats All-Star. Available at http://www.nytimes.com/2009/02/15/magazine/15Battier-t.html?pagewanted=all. [Accessed on 30 April 2015].

Penney, D., Clarke, G., Quill, M. & Kinchin, G. (2005). *Sport Education in Physical Education*. London: Routledge.

Potrac, P., Gilbert, W. & Denison, J. (eds.) (2013). *Routledge Handbook of Sports Coaching*. London: Routledge.

Shilling, C. (1991). Educating the body: Physical capital and the production of social inequalities. *Sociology*, 25(4): 653–672.

Siedentop, D. & Tannehill, D. (2000). *Developing Teaching Skills in Physical Education*, 4th edn. Mountain View, CA: Mayfield.

Tinning, R. (2008). Pedagogy, sport pedagogy, and the field of kinesiology. *Quest*, 60(3): 405–424.

Tinning, R. (2010). *Pedagogy and Human Movement: Theory, Practice, Research*. London: Routledge.

Tinning, R., Macdonald, D., Wright, J. & Hickey, C. (2001). *Becoming a Physical Education Teacher: Contemporary and Enduring Issues*. Frenchs Forest, NSW, Australia: Prentice Hall.

Wright, J. & Burrows, L. (2006). Re-conceiving ability in physical education: A social analysis. *Sport, Education and Society*, 11(3): 275–291.

# Index